An Introduction to.....

Cashflow Analysis

Robert J. Donohue CCIM

THE REGENT SCHOOL PRESS

INTRODUCTION TO CASHFLOW ANALYSIS
FOURTH EDITION

PUBLISHED BY

THE REGENT SCHOOL PRESS
26453 VERDUGO
MISSION VIEJO, CA 92692

ISBN 1-886654-02-6
LIBRARY OF CONGRESS CATALOG CARD NUMBER 94-74922

DEDICATED TO MY MOTHER, ILA

Table of Contents

Table of Contents

Chapter 2: Working With Uneven Cashflows

Chapter 3: The Internal & Modified Rates of Return

Chapter 4: Valuing Cashflows from Stocks & Bonds

Chapter 5: Cashflows from Notes & Mortgages

Table of Contents

Chapter 6: Valuing Cashflows from Real Estate

Chapter 7: Sell, Hold, Trade or Refinance?

Table of Contents

Introduction

The old axiom ,"A Bird in the Hand is Worth Two in the Bush," is evidence that all of us have some appreciation of the fact that there is a difference between something of value which can be realized today vs. the receipt of the something more down the road.

All investment is a matter of exchanging something of value today for what we hope may become something of more value tomorrow. When we express these exchanges in terms of money, we create *cashflow* situations.

This text attempts to uncover and illustrate, for those whose primary professional concern is *not* finance, the basic financial concepts and principles involved in cashflow problems and decisions. Examples are drawn from a wide variety of financial investments: stocks, bonds, real estate, promissory notes, leases, mortgages, all set in the practical circumstances of everyday business.

The text makes ample use of the financial calculator, but assumes the reader initially has only the most basic skills in using the machine. It uses the machine as a convenience-tool rather than as an end in itself. It is a text aimed at *understanding,* and not another book on how to operate a financial calculator. This seems to me to be an important goal since the skills required to solve financial cashflow problems depend more on a basic understanding of the underlying concepts rather than the ability to push keys by rote.

Although there are many excellent hand-held financial calculators, it is impractical to write a text such as this for every different machine. That's probably why the Hewlett-Packard–12C has remained the choice of most professionals for over 20 years: it does all things reasonably well, and what it doesn't do well is cause to move to a computer. If you have a calculator other than the HP–12C, you should take a few minutes to learn how its financial registers can be accessed. After that, following the methodology here is not at all difficult since all financial calculators use the same symbols.

Regardless of the calculator used, the text focuses on understanding the underlying financial concepts and their application in everyday business situations. One benefit of such an understanding is the ability to transfer acquired skills to the computer and its spreadsheet. Every skill learned with a hand-held calculator can be readily transferred to a computer's financial spreadsheet. Both Excel® and Lotus 1-2-3,® perhaps the two most popular spreadsheet programs, incorporate financial functions which parallel all the functions of the hand-held machine. The computer offers the great advantage of being able to solve truly complex and inter-related problems whose elements can be linked and solved in a fraction of the time required to program a hand-held machine.

The key to mastery of these concepts is in the solution of problems. Therefore the text makes ample use of problems and their solutions, step by step, to help the reader extract the financial principle involved. I have also included a chapter with over 60 word problems and their solutions because the process of mastering these techniques is a process of abstracting principles from specific, relevant examples. Financial principles becomes evident only through the working of many problems.

In depicting the calculator keystrokes we have often omitted drawing a box around the key. In those instances where the omission was deemed likely to be especially confusing, or where the key is used for the first time, we have boxed the key to help identify it. Also, we have used a shorthand to identify key locations on the HP–12C: a location (1,3), for example, denotes the key located on the the first (top) row, third key (from the left). $\boxed{\text{PV}}$

Lastly, I wish to thank the students at the University of California, Irvine, for their excellent suggestions and for their invaluable assistance in ferreting out errors and miscalculations. I am also grateful to Dr. Charles Cuney of the University's Graduate School of Business who was especially helpful in developing the section on Bond Duration.

I hope *An Introduction to Cashflow Analysis* will be a significant learning experience for you.

Robert J. Donohue CCIM

Irvine, California
1997

to solve truly complex and inter-related problems whose elements can be linked and solved in a fraction of the time required to program a hand-held machine.

The key to mastery of these concepts is in the solution of problems. Therefore the text makes ample use of problems and their solutions, step by step, to help the reader extract the financial principle involved. I have also included a chapter with over 60 word problems and their solutions because the process of mastering these techniques is a process of abstracting principles from specific, relevant examples. Financial principles becomes evident only through the working of many problems.

In depicting the calculator keystrokes we have often omitted drawing a box around the key. In those instances where the omission was deemed likely to be especially confusing, or where the key is used for the first time, we have boxed the key to help identify it. Also, we have used a shorthand to identify key locations on the HP–12C: a location (1,3), for example, denotes the key located on the the first (top) row, third key (from the left). $\boxed{\text{PV}}$

Lastly, I wish to thank the students at the University of California, Irvine, for their excellent suggestions and for their invaluable assistance in ferreting out errors and miscalculations. I am also grateful to Dr. Charles Cuney of the University's Graduate School of Business who was especially helpful in developing the section on Bond Duration.

I hope *An Introduction to Cashflow Analysis* will be a significant learning experience for you.

Robert J. Donohue CCIM

Irvine, California
1997

Chapter 1
Present Values
Future Values

This text is about the passage of money through time. For, as we shall see, money takes on different values in relation to the time over which it is paid or received.

The Time Value of Money is an important financial concept, since many investments in business (and in our personal lives, as well) involve the payment or receipt of money over a period of time. And, as most experienced business people know, financial value is a combination of cash paid today, and the terms for the balance of the payment tomorrow.

Most often affected are our major business investments: the purchase or sale of a major income property; a direct investment in a business venture; an investment in a partnership which, in turn, invests in a business or real estate venture; the lease of both personal and real property; business and personal loans; investments in stocks and bonds; and a host of transactions which create cashflows over time.

We are concerned with our ability to measure and compare the value of cash to be paid tomorrow with an equivalent amount paid today, or with tomorrow's value of an amount invested today. These concepts involve Future Value cashflows and Present Value cashflows. But first, let's define our terms and establish a few basic concepts.

What is a Cashflow?

Cashflows[1] are not profits, though some use the terms interchangeably.

A **Cashflow**, in the context in which we will be working, simply means the flow of money from one set of hands into another. The party providing the cash experiences a **negative** out-of-pocket **cashflow**; the party receiving the cash experiences a **positive** into-the-pocket **cashflow**. Every financial transaction involves both a positive cashflow and a negative cashflow.

Present Value and Future Value

Both these terms, Present Value and Future Value, rely for their meaning on the fact that money has a *time-value*. By *time-value*. we mean that money can be worth more or worth less than its apparent face value, depending on when it is to be paid out or when it is to be received.

For example, a tax which can be deferred has a lower Present Value than its face amount because a sum smaller than the tax can be invested to grow to the amount necessary to pay the full tax in the future. Similarly, a sum can be invested now to grow to a Future Value greater than its original value. Cashflow analysis concerns itself with the Present and Future Values of money paid or received over time, often comparing these value to some predetermined investment yardstick.

Nominal vs. Real Profits and Losses

If we invest today's $1 in an investment which will add to our wealth, the $1 will grow into some Future Value. If the $1 is invested in such a way that it just keeps pace with inflation, we will have preserved the purchasing power, or "constant value," of the dollar. We will have a nominal profit, but in actuality the future dollar received will have no more purchasing power than the original dollar invested. If we invest $1 in such a way that the amount realized at the end of one year will buy more than $1's worth of goods or services, we will have made a real profit. If our investment of $1 today increases in value, but does not keep pace with inflation, we will have suffered a real loss in purchasing power, even though we may have a nominal profit. The concept of nominal and real profits and losses is important to us all, but especially important to those whose responsibility it is to plan for real profits, or to plan to meet future expenses.

---

1   Technically, cashflow refers to net earnings after taxes, plus depreciation and amortization.

The Sign Convention

Since every financial transaction involves at least one positive and one negative cashflow, the description of the transaction must observe positive and negative signs. Whenever you enter a cashflow problem into a financial calculator or computer spreadsheet, the PV and FV value must be opposite in sign. (The PMT may either be positive or negative.) This rule is so inviolable that if you enter a cashflow problem into the (HP–12C) machine without designating a giver (-) and a receiver (+), the HP calculator will flash an **"Error 5"** message. You will know that you did not observe the proper **sign convention** which requires that in every cashflow sequence someone gives (–) and someone gets (+) the cash.

Positive or Negative Cashflow is a Relative Concept

Cashflows may be either positive or negative, depending on the vantage point from which you view the transaction.

If you are a banker, the loan of $100,000 would be a negative (out-of-pocket) cashflow event for your bank. Later, re-payments to your bank would be positive cashflow events. If you are the borrower, the initial receipt of $100,000 would be a positive cashflow; later, the same re-payments you make would be negative (out-of-pocket) cashflows.

Importance of Maintaining Single Vantage Point

In analyzing cashflows, you must discipline yourself to adopt a single vantage point from which to describe the cashflow scenario – and then stick to it. You must be either the lender or the borrower, the lessor or the lessee, the mortgagor or the mortgagee. Viewing a loan transaction from the lender's point of view one moment, and then from the borrower's point of view the next, is a sure-fire way to introduce fatal signing errors into the structure of your cashflow analysis. Any analysis based on this error will itself be incorrect. Be consistent. Be either the lender or the borrower; either the lessor or the lessee; either the mortgagor or the mortgagee. In sticking to one point of view, you will avoid signing errors. Or, to put it another way, you will avoid crediting (+) a party to the transaction when you should be debiting the same party (–).

Failure to follow this rule is one of the most common errors in analyzing cashflows.

Depicting Cashflows

It helps a great deal if you can depict the cashflow situation with which you are attempting to work. A very useful graphic device to accomplish this is a **T–Bar** which will enable you to portray the negative and positive movements of cash through the transaction. If you learn to use this device to depict the flow of the cash you are attempting to evaluate, *it is difficult to imagine any financial problem that will not yield to a proper analysis..*

The T-Bar graphic is superior to the horizontal graphic devices pictured in the handbook of most financial calculators because the T-Bar can be expanded to the right and left whereas the horizontal graphic cannot be so easily modified. The ability to expand the T-Bar laterally means that other cashflows which are concurrent in time can be added to, or subtracted from, the principal cashflow. This ability to add and subtract T-Bars graphically to yield *net* T-Bars is a great aid in visualizing, simplifying and understanding the *net* cashflow transaction.

Fortunately the T–Bar which we will use contains a "place setting" for all financial components which correspond to the keys of the (horizontal) financial register of your HP–12C. These are the keys which extend from positions (1,1) to (1,5) on the keyboard. They are the keys which are common to all financial calculators. They are also the symbols used by computer spreadsheets in financial formulas:

$$\textbf{n} \quad \textbf{i} \quad \textbf{PV} \quad \textbf{PMT} \quad \textbf{FV}$$

Therefore if you can depict the problem graphically with the aid of the T–Bar, you can transfer the elements of the graphic to the calculator for a rapid solution.

Consider, for example, a T–Bar constructed to represent a loan by a banker for $1,000 to be repaid *monthly* over a five-month period, including interest at an *annual* rate of 10%.

THE BASIC T-BAR WILL LOOK LIKE THIS

```
                      | (PV)
                   n  |
                   1  | PMT
                   2  | PMT
         i =       3  | PMT
           .10/12  4  | PMT
                   5  | PMT + FV
```

This loan will be depicted from the point of view of the banker-lender. The amount of –$1,000 will be entered in the T-Bar in the position occupied by (Present Value), at the top of the T–Bar. It is entered as a negative number because it represents a negative (out-of-pocket) cashflow for the banker-lender. **Payments** made by the borrower will be represented by positive numbers because these are positive (into the pocket) cashflows .

Next, the number of **periods** is entered under the letter **n**(umber). Here we shall enter the numbers 1,2,3,4 and 5 representing the 5 separate periods over which a cashflow will be received as a periodic payment. A "period" can be any measure of time as you wish to define it: it may be a day, month, year, quarter, half-year – or any other period of time you choose. In this example it represents monthly periods.

The position indicated by Future Value will be represented by a zero (**0**) because, in this case, the loan is meant to be fully repaid at the end of the fifth month (period) and (**0**) will remain as the future balance. The position **FV** in loan situations always represents the remaining balance of the loan. In other situations it represents a value present at the end of a sequence of cashflows. For example, if you rent equipment to others, **FV** would be the *reversionary value* , or worth, of your property at the end of the lease. If you are leasing an automobile, dealers call the Future Value of the auto at the end of the lease the *residual value.*

The interest rate **i** is annotated to the left of the T–Bar as a mnemonic to indicate that (in this example) the interest rate is 10%. We have divided the interest rate (.10 ÷ 12) to convert it to a monthly rate. Note that in order to enter a 10% interest rate into **i** you should *not* enter into the calculator the decimal **.10**. **Any number entered into i is automatically divided by 100.** Therefore to enter an interest rate of 10%, you should simply **key-in** the number 10, and press the i button (1,2). The calculator will do the rest.

Time Consistency Among Variables

Another common error made in dealing with cashflows is that the interest rate **i** per period does not conform with the period, **n,** for which payments are to be made or received. If payments are to be considered monthly payments, the interest rate in **i** should be a monthly interest rate (e.g. 0.10 ÷ 12); if the payments are to be considered quarterly payments, the number in **i** should represent the quarterly interest rate (e.g. 0.10 ÷ 4); if the payments are to be annual payments, the number in **i** should represent the annual interest rate (e.g. 0.10 ÷ 1). The interest rate **i** should always be time-consistent with the period **n.**

The last position is the **PMT** position. If we **solve** this particular loan problem for the amount of the payment necessary to repay the principal and monthly interest due, the solution will be transferred to the **PMT** position to represent the completed cashflow event.

Our T–Bar will now look like this:

		-1,000.00 **(PV)**
EOM[2]	1	205.03 **(PMT)**
	2	205.03
i = .10/12	3	205.03
	4	205.03
	5	205.03 + 0 **(FV)**

---

2   **End of Month. EOY** = End of Year; **EOQ** = End of Quarter, etc.

Let's now transfer the problem of determining the **PMT** in this T-Bar to the financial registers of the HP-12C.

n	i	PV	PMT	FV
5	0.83	-1,000.00	?	0

Here are the keystrokes and what should appear in the display window after each entry:

Key-In	Display Shows
5 n	5.00[3]
10 g i	0.83
1000 CHS PV	-1,000.00
0 FV	0.00
solving (push) PMT	205.03

TIP

The second entry, **10 g i** , is a convenient way of dividing the interest rate by 12. Whenever you precede the entry of a number into **i** by first pressing the blue key **g** (4,3), the number entered into **i** is automatically divided by 12. If you need to express the interest rate for any period other than monthly, do it using the keypad; e.g. if **n** were a quarterly period, then you would handle the interest rate as follows: (**10 Enter** 4, **÷** , delivers **2.5**) which is then directly entered into **i**. The **CHS** key (1,6) **CH**anges the Sign to the opposite sign. In this case it changes a positive 1,000 to a negative -1,000.

Suppose, on the other hand, that you elect to depict the cashflow from the viewpoint of the borrower. Everything is the same except that the signs are reversed:

		+1,000.00 **(PV)**
EOM	1	-205.03 **(PMT)**
	2	-205.03
i = .10/12	3	-205.03
	4	-205.03
	5	-205.03 + 0 **(FV)**

---

3   If your calculator does not show two decimal places, set it to two places by pressing $\boxed{f}$ **2** .

If you enter these data into the calculator, the result will be:

	Key In	Display Shows
	5 [n]	5.00
	10 [g] [i]	0.83
	1000 [PV]	1,000.00
	0 [FV]	0.00
solving	[PMT]	−205.03

or,

n	i	PV	PMT	FV
5	0.83	1,000	?	0
solving			:	
			−205.03	

In solving certain problems you will provide the values for **PV** and **PMT** and **FV**, and attempt to solve for **n or i**. If you fail to make either **PV** or **FV** a negative number, your calculator will rebel with the **"ERROR 5"** message. Rethink your T–Bar and decide which cash flows are positive and which negative, remembering always to be consistent in viewing the transaction from the vantage point of a single observer.

Present Value, Future Value

The Present Value, **PV**, of one dollar held today is one dollar because it can buy one dollar's worth of goods or services.

The **FV** of one dollar invested today, however, cannot be determined until you decide how many **periods,** [n], will elapse until you receive it, and the rate of growth, the rate [i], which the cash will earn for the number of periods over which it is invested.

If we are trying to determine the future value of a dollar, held for **n** periods and earning interest at the rate **i** per period, then **i** is called an **interest rate.**[4] If, on the other hand, we want to determine the present value of a sum to be received **n** periods in the future, **i** is called a **discount rate.**

---

[4]   In some cases the letter **r** will be used to indicate rate.

In other words, **i** can represent either an interest rate or a discount rate, depending on the **direction in time** we want to go. Going forward in time **i** is an interest rate; but going backward in time, **i** is a discount rate. They are different sides of the very same coin. That's why these kinds of calculations are often referred to as calculations involving the **"present worth of money"** or the **"time value of money."** These phrases suggest, as we have already noted, that cash has a value today, and a different value tomorrow.

The Underlying Basic

There is a mathematical relationship between the Future Value (**FV**) of a dollar and its Present Value (**PV**), a relationship which is very helpful to understand. It is described by this simple expression:

$$PV = \frac{FV}{(1+i)^n}$$

where,

> **PV** is the value of an amount of cash today – its **Present Value**
> **FV** is the **Future Value** of the cash to be received in the future
> **i** is the interest (or discount) rate to be applied
> **n** is the number of periods (time) between the **PV** and the **FV**

Mathematically, the relationship tells us that the **PV** of a single sum, **FV**, to be received in the future, is equal to the **FV** divided by the *expression* (1 + the discount rate **i**) raised to the power **n.** Let's clarify what we mean by "raised to the power **n.**"

When we raise a number to a power **n**, we simply multiply a number <u>times itself</u> for as many times as is indicated by the number **n.** Therefore:

$$10^1 \quad = \quad 10$$
$$10^2 \quad = \quad 10 \times 10 = 100$$
$$(1+.10)^4 \quad = \quad 1.10 \times 1.10 \times 1.10 \times 1.10 = \quad 1.46$$
$$3^6 \quad = \quad 3 \times 3 \times 3 \times 3 \times 3 \times 3 \ = 729$$
$$(1 + .10)^3 \quad = \quad 1.10 \quad \times \ 1.10 \times 1.10 = 1.33$$

Any number or expression raised to the zero power (n = 0) equals one.

Knowing these simple facts enables you to convert the future receipt of a single sum of money into a **Present Value** (today) provided you specify a **discount rate** (because we are moving backward in time), and further specify the number of periods, **n,** between **PV** and **FV.**

Solve This Problem

> You agree to take part of your consulting fee in the form of a note which calls for you to receive $5,000 at the end of 3 years. The notes carries no interest rate and no intermediate payments.
>
> What is the present value (or present worth) of this note?

It is easy to see that:

$$\mathbf{PV} = \text{?}$$
$$\mathbf{FV} = 5,000$$
$$\mathbf{n} = 3$$

But what is **i** ?

You determine that if you had a comparable sum in your hand today, you could invest it (in another investment of <u>similar</u> risk[5]) at an annual interest rate of 10%. Therefore, you assign **i** a value of 10% or 0.10.

Now you can substitute into the formula above all the values you have at hand:

$$\mathbf{PV} = \frac{F\ V}{(1+i)^{\mathbf{n}}}$$

$$\mathbf{PV} = \frac{\mathbf{5000}}{(1+.10)^{3}}$$

$$\mathbf{PV} = \frac{\mathbf{5000}}{(1+.10)(1+.10)(1+.10)}$$

$$\mathbf{PV} = \frac{\mathbf{5000}}{1.33}$$

$$\mathbf{PV} = \mathbf{3,756.57}$$

Therefore your promissory note has a **Present Value** to you, under the terms and conditions stipulated, of not $5,000, but $3,756.57 *today*. To someone else who has a

---

5   The rate which could be earned on the next best investment of similar risk is known as the "Hurdle Rate" or the "Opportunity Cost" of money. In this case you are estimating that if you were paid your fee at closing you could invest it to earn 10% per year. Therefore your Opportunity Cost is 10%.

different Opportunity Cost, this note will have a different Present Value. Therefore the value of this note is, in the last analysis, fairly subjective.

Using the Calculator's Financial Register

Now that you understand how **PVs** are determined, you could process one with a discount-store calculator. But financial calculators, such as the HP–12C, make the entire exercise very easy. Simply enter the data into the appropriate financial registers:

	n	i	PV	PMT	FV
solving	3	10.00	? :	0	5,000.00
			–3,756.57		

The keystrokes are:

Key-In	Display Shows
3 [n]	3.00
10 [i]	10.00
0 [PMT]	0.00
5000 [FV]	5,000.00
solving	
[PV]	– 3,756.57

Determining the Future Value of a Single Sum Over Time

It is frequently required to estimate the value to which a single sum invested today (a **PV**) will grow if invested at **i** rate of interest for **n** periods.

For example:

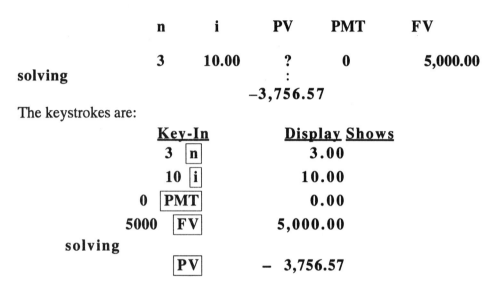

Smith invests $300,000 in a parcel of vacant land in the path of progress. He estimates that land values will grow at an annually compounded rate of 8% over the next 5 years.

What is the likely value of Smith's land at the end of 5 years?

This problem can also be solved on the same calculator you purchased at the discount store to solve the Present Value problem. We need only to rearrange the **PV-FV** formula:

$$PV = \frac{FV}{(1+i)^n}$$

$FV = PV * (1+i)^n$ (This is the formula for compound interest)

Therefore –   FV = 300,000 x $(1 + .08)^5$
                FV = 300,000 x 1.08 x 1.08 x 1.08 x 1.08 x 1.08
                FV = 440,798.42

Using the calculator, the problem is very easily (and quickly) solved:

	n	i	PV	PMT	FV
	5	8.00[6]	-300,000.00	0	?
solving					:
					440,798.42

The key strokes are:

<u>Key In</u>	<u>Display Shows</u>
5 $\boxed{n}$	5.00
8 $\boxed{i}$	8.00
300000 $\boxed{CHS}$ $\boxed{PV}$	–300,000.00
0 $\boxed{PMT}$	0.00
solving	
$\boxed{FV}$	440,798.42

When i Is a Negative Number

Notice the different result when **i** is a negative rate:

> Suppose Smith were absolutely wrong in his prognostications, and the value of the land *declined* at the rate of 8% per year for 5 years.
>
> What would Smith's lot then be worth?

---

6   The digit 8 was placed directly into **i** because the interest rate is 8% <u>annually,</u> which conforms with **n.**

$$FV = 300,000 \times (1 - .08)^5$$
$$FV = 300,000 \times 0.92 \times 0.92 \times 0.92 \times 0.92 \times 0.92$$
$$FV = 197,724.46$$

On the calculator –

	n	i	PV	PMT	FV
	5	-8.00	-300,000.00	0	?
solving					:
					197,724.46

The keystrokes are virtually identical except that the interest rate, **i**, is entered as a negative number:

Key In	Display Shows
5 n	5.00
8 CHS i	– 8.00
300000 CHS PV	–300,000.00
0 PMT	0.00
solving	
FV	197,724.46

Try another:

> You deposit $10,000 in a bank which compounds interest at the end of every month at the annual rate of 4.5% per year.
>
> What will be your bank balance at the end of 5 years?

The quirk in this problem is that the interest rate is expressed annually but applied every month. Therefore **i** per period is not 4.5% but (4.5% ÷ 12). Since the annual interest rate is to be expressed and applied monthly, you must also convert the periods **n** to months.

In 5 years there are 12 x 5 = 60 months. Therefore **n** = 60.

Now solve the problem using your non-financial calculator.

$$FV = PV \times (1+ i)^n$$
$$FV = 10{,}000 \times (1 + (0.045 \div 12))^{60} \quad \text{see footnote}[7]$$
$$FV = 10{,}000 \times (1 + .00375)^{60}$$
$$FV = 10{,}000 \times 1.25180$$
$$FV = 12{,}517.96$$

It's much easier on the financial calculator:

n	i	PV	PMT	FV
60	$\frac{4.5}{12}$	-10,000.00	0	?

solving

12,517.96

The keystrokes are:

Key In	Display Shows	
5 g n	60.00	
4.5 g i	0.38	(0.375, actually[8])
10000 CHS PV	−10,000.00	
0 PMT	0.00	
solving		
FV	12,517.96	

---

7 There is an alternate way to calculate the value of $(1+ (0.045 \div 12))^{60}$. Follow these steps:

Key-In	Display
f 6	0.000000
.045 Enter	0.045000
12 ÷	0.003750
1 +	1.003750
60 y^x (2,1)	1.251796
10000 x	12,517.9582
f 2	12,517.96

8 Press f 3 to view the number with the decimal point set to three places

The results would be exactly the same if you had entered **n** as follows:

<u>Key In</u>	<u>Display Shows</u>
5 Enter	5.00
12 x n	60.00
4.5 g i	0.38
10000 CHS PV	−10,000.00
0 PMT	0.00
solving	
FV	12,517.96

PV and FV Derived from Periodic Payments

So far we have determined **PV**s and **FV**s without any regard to **PMT**s. But the financial world is simply not that simple. Most financial cashflows involve periodic payments or periodic receipts of cash. To complicate matters slightly, these periodic **PMT**s can be either negative cashflows or positive cashflows. The difference between a **FV** and a **PMT** is that a **FV** occurs only once, while **PMT**s may occur at the beginning or at the end of a period. **Any value you enter into FV is always regarded by the calculator as occurring at the end of period n, and occurs only once.**

This is as good a time as any to tell you that this *horizontal* financial register –

$$n \quad i \quad PV \quad PMT \quad FV$$

can *only* be used, in problems where there are no **PMT**s or where the **PMT**s are *equal*. By "equal" we mean equal in amount *and* equal in sign (+,–). If the payments are of different amounts, or if, though equal in amount, they change signs during the cashflow series, this register cannot be used. There is a separate register which will solve these problems, and we will get to that shortly. [9]

The value of the number entered into the **PMT** register is a payment either *made* **or** *received* in each period, **n.** For example, suppose you expect to receive $100 per month for the next 2 months. If you enter the number 100 into **PMT** and the number 2 into **n,**

---

9 If the cashflow series has a period when no payment is received or made, this period must be represented by a zero. Cashflows containing zero payments combined with either positive or negative payments are uneven cashflows and the horizontal register cannot be used.

you are informing the calculator that the cashflow will be *positive* (into your pocket), will be *equal to 100,* and will occur *2 times.*

n	i	PV	PMT	FV
2			100	

Now let us inform the calculator that the rate **i** is 10% *annually.* You may not enter 10 directly into **i** because 10 is the *annual* rate and you have already defined that **n** will be expressed in *months.* Therefore you must convert the annual rate into a monthly rate.

<u>Key In</u>	<u>Display Shows</u>
10 [g] [i]	0.83

The registers now contain:

n	i	PV	PMT	FV
2	0.83		100	

You must now decide whether to move forward in time to solve for **FV**, or move backward in time to solve for **PV**. If we move forward in time to solve for the Future Value of these payments, we ask the calculator to determine the interest on the payments received, and to add the interest to the payment amounts and to display the results in the **FV** register.

Payments at the Beginning or End of Period

But before we can go on, we need to discuss *when* these **PMTs** are to be received. We know that they are to be received at monthly intervals, but the question is: "At the beginning or at the end of the month?" It makes a financial difference.

The difference between **PMTs** received from a lease and those from a mortgage, for example, will serve to illustrate this important point. Lease **PMTs** are customarily made at the beginning of the month (**BEG**). Therefore if you were to receive two lease payments of $100 per month, you could earn interest on the first payment of $100 for two months; you could also earn interest on the second month's **PMT** of $100 for one month.

If these **PMTs** flowed from a mortgage, however, the payment of $100 would be made at the end of the month (**END**). In this case you could earn interest on the first payment for only one month, and you would earn no interest on the second payment of $100 because it occurs at the end of the second month, which is also the end of the cashflow period under consideration. Therefore you need to inform the calculator *when* the **PMT**s will occur: at the **BEG**inning or at the **END** of the month.

On the lower face of keys (1,7) and (1,8) you will see – printed in blue – the letters **BEG** on (1,7) and **END** on (1,8). You can access these functions by first pressing the blue key, $\boxed{\text{g}}$ (4,3) and then pressing either **BEG** or **END**. Depending on which you choose, you inform the calculator that the **PMT** will occur either at the **beg**inning or **end** of the period **n**. When **BEG** is selected the word "BEGIN" will appear in the display window. When **END** is selected, the word "BEGIN" will *not* appear (the same position in the window will be blank).

Let's assume that in our example the **PMT** of 100 will flow from a lease and will occur at the beginning of the period. We need, then, to set the calculator to "BEGIN." Once that is done we can solve the problem.[10] Here are the keystrokes:

<u>Key In</u>	<u>Display Shows</u>	
$\boxed{\text{g}}$ $\boxed{\text{BEG}}$ (1,7)	**0.00**	(window reads "BEGIN")
2 $\boxed{\text{n}}$	**2.00**	
10 $\boxed{\text{g}}$ $\boxed{\text{i}}$	**0.83**	
100 $\boxed{\text{PMT}}$	**100.00**	
solve		
$\boxed{\text{FV}}$	**–202.51**	(notice sign convention)

Now consider that the **PMT**s derive from a mortgage or bond you hold. Since mortgage and bond payments are made at the end of the period, you need to inform the calculator to treat the **PMT**s as end-of-the-period **PMT**s. There is no need to key in all the values again. Simply change to **END** and re-solve by pressing **FV**:

<u>Key In</u>	<u>Display Shows</u>	
$\boxed{\text{g}}$ $\boxed{\text{END}}$ (1,8)	**-202.51**	("BEGIN" disappears)
solve		
$\boxed{\text{FV}}$	**-200.83**	

---

10 On computer spreadsheets this choice is available in relevant financial function commands by the insertion of either 0 or 1 at the "TYPE" position in the formula; e.g =PMT(rate, nper, PV, FV,TYPE). When TYPE = 1, PMTS are at the beginning of the period. When TYPE = 0, PMTs are at the end of the period. Default = 0

As you can see, the value of a series of **PMTs** depends not only on the interest rate you apply but also *when* you will receive the **PMT**. In this example, the promise of **PMT** of $100 to be received at the beginning of the month has a value of $202.51 whereas the same **PMT** received at the end of the month has a value of only $200.83. This difference is small because we are dealing with a small number. But when the **PMT** is large, the difference can be very significant. Adding a few zeros usually commands attention.

Combining PVs & FVs with Positive & Negative PMTs

A savings account is an excellent example of a combination of an initial **PV** and subsequent **PMTs**.

> Suppose that you deposit (a negative cashflow to you) $10,000 in a savings account which pays interest **i** at the rate of 5% per year. You also plan to deposit an additional $2,309.75 to this account at the end of each year (again, a negative cashflow to you). Interest is credited to your account annually.
>
> What would be your account's balance be at the end of year 1?

	n	i	PV	PMT	FV
	1	5.00	-10,000.00	-2309.75	?
Solving					:
					12,809.75

Take careful notice that **PMT** is a negative number because it represents an out-of-pocket cashflow to you.

At the end of the first year (period) your balance would consist of a recent **PMT** of $2,309.75 plus the original $10,000 deposit plus the interest earned on the original $10,000 deposit for one year ($500). This explains the total (10,000 + 500 + 2309.75 = 12,809.75). You earned no interest on the $2,309.75 you deposited because it was deposited at the end of the period. Suppose now, that after entering the original sum of 10,000 in your account, you *withdraw* the amount of $2,309.75 each year. What would be your balance after the first year's withdrawal?

Let's change the sign of the **PMT** to reflect an into-your- pocket cash flow:

Key In	Display Shows
RCL (4,5) PMT	-2,309.75
CHS (1,6) PMT	2,309.75
re-solving	
FV	8,190.25

During the year, your original deposit earned interest at the rate of 5% annually and therefore the total in the account was $10,500. But after your year-end withdrawal of $2,309.75, your balance fell to $8,190.25 (10,500 - 2,309.75).

What would be your balance at the end of 5 years?

n	i	PV	PMT	FV
5	5.00	-10000.00	2309.75	?

solve

?

(Did you make yourself a fully-amortizing loan payable $2,309.75 annually for 5 years, including interest at the rate of 5% per annum? Think about this.)

Discounting Amounts To Be Received in the Future

So far we have dealt with converting **PVs**, either alone or combined with positive and negative **PMTs**, into **FVs**. An equally important skill involves converting **PMTs** into Present Value amounts, single sums (**FVs**) into Present Values, and the combination of **FVs** and **PMTs** into **PVs**.

Let's take simple future **PMTs** first.

> Suppose that you grant your neighbor, Jones, a 5-year easement over your property in return for his promissory note which specifies monthly payments of $125 for the next five years. You visit three banks to determine how much you can borrow against this note. You are well known to each banker and have the financial ability to guarantee the payments on the note.

> Banker <u>A</u> tells you that he will lend 50% of the value of the (note)
> PMTs, discounted at 10% annually.
> Banker <u>B</u> tells you that he will lend 55% of the value of the (note)
> PMTs, discounted at 11% annually.
> Banker <u>C</u> tells you that he will lend 60% of the value of the (note)
> PMTs, discounted at 12% annually
>
> Which is the best offer?

There is a priority involved in solving this problem: first, you must determine the **PV** of the note in the hands of each banker; then you must determine what percentage of the **PV** he will lend.

Let's quickly determine the **PV** of this note to each banker:

Banker A:

	n	i	PV	PMT	FV
solving	60	10÷12	? : -5,883.17	125.00	0

To solve for Banker B it is not necessary to clear the entire register. Simply "write over" the discount rate:

	Key In	**Display Shows**
solving	11 [g] [i]	0.92
	[PV]	-5,749.13

To solve for Banker <u>C</u>, again "write over" the discount rate **i:**

	Key In	**Display Shows**
solving	12 [g] [i]	1.00
	[PV]	-5,619.38

Therefore Banker A estimates the **PV** of this note at $5,883.17; Banker B values it at $5,749.13, while Banker C holds for a value of $5,619.38. Notice that as the discount rate increases, the **PV** of the future **PMTs** decreases. You should make permanent mental storage of the fact that in discounting cashflows, the **higher the discount rate applied, the lower the Present Value** of the cashflow.[11]

To determine the amount each banker will lend on this note we need only multiply the **PV** value times the percentage listed above:

Banker	PV	% of Value	Loan Amt.
A	5,883.17	50	2,941.59
B	5,749.13	55	3,162.02
C	5,619.38	60	3,371.63

Obviously, Banker C will advance a greater amount on the collateral of your note.

The problem above involves the discounting of future **PMT**s only. No **FV** was involved. Frequently, however, cashflows to be received in the future come in the form of periodic **PMT**s together with a lump sum at the end of the period. Many **Promissory Notes** are a good example of periodic PMTs combined with a FV (the loan payoff).

Discounting a Promissory (Trust Deed) Note

"Discounting" a promissory note is an exercise in determining the **Present Value** of future cashflows, given a desired yield or discount rate.

Consider, for example, the following common situation:

A client has negotiated the sale of her residence. The price is very satisfactory but the buyer's offer requires the client/seller to carry back a promissory note in the amount of $25,000, payable monthly, interest only, at the rate of 10% per year, with the remaining balance and interest all due and payable three years "from date" (the date of the note).

Your client/seller agrees to accept the price only if you can liquidate the note at the close of escrow. A physician whom you know invests in discounted promissory notes for his 401K plan. He agrees to buy the note provided it furnishes him with a 12% annual yield.

At what price must the note be sold to the physician's retirement account and what will be the percent discount of the note from its face value?

---

11 Bonds behave this way also. As the interest rates rise, bond values fall. See-saw Majorie Daw.

Let's enter the cashflow represented by the note into the T-Bar:

```
                        ─────┬──── −25,000 (PV)
            EOM   1     │    208.33 (PMT)
                  2     │    208.33
                  :     │      :
      i = .10/12  :     │      :
                  :     │      :
                  36    │    208.33 + 25,000  (FV)
```

Note that the principal payoff (**FV**) occurs at the **End Of Month** 36 and <u>not in the following month.</u> It is a common mistake to set up a problem such as this indicating 36 monthly payments and then to place the payoff (**FV**) one period later. This mistake converts the term of the note, **n**, to 37 months, not 36 months as it should be.

The T-Bar now depicts the way this note will perform. But the problem to be solved is to determine the **Present Value** of this cash flow discounted at 12%, the minimum rate the physician requires. In other words:

```
                        ─────┬──── ?      (PV)
            EOM   1     │    208.33 (PMT)
                  2     │    208.33
                  :     │      :
      i = .12/12  :     │      :
                  :     │      :
                  36    │    208.33 + 25,000 (FV)
```

We can now transfer these values to the calculator and solve for **PV**.

	n	i	PV	PMT	FV
	36	1.00	?	208.33	25,000.00
solving			:		
			-23,745.22		

Therefore the physician can buy this note for $23,745.22 and earn exactly 12% per annum on his invested cash for 3 years. His **PMT**s will be $208.33 per month for <u>35</u> months with a final payment of $208.33 plus the remaining balance of $25,000.

The keystrokes for this problem are as follows:

Key In	Display Shows
36 [n]	36.00
12 [g] [i]	1.00
208.33 [PMT]	208.33
25000 [FV]	25,000.00
solving [PV]	-23,745.22

> Suppose, for a moment, that the physician requires not a 12% return on his cash invested, but a 15% return.
>
> What would the PV of this note become?

Again, it is not necessary to re-enter all the values. Simply "write over" the discount rate **i** as follows:

Key In	Display Shows
15 [g] [i]	1.25
solving [PV]	−21,994.98[1][2]

As you can see, the <u>higher the discount rate</u>, the <u>lower the PV</u> of the cashflow.

The percentage of discount <u>from face value</u> is also easily expressed. In the first case:

Key In	Display Shows
25000 [Enter]	25,000.00
23745.22 [Δ%] (2,4)	-5.02

Therefore the seller would be required to discount the $25,000 note 5.02% to deliver a 12% yield to the physician.

---

[12] This number is negative as a convention of the calculator and does not imply negative worth.

In the second case:

Key In	Display Shows
25000 Enter	25,000.00
21,994.98 Δ% (2,4)	-12.02[13]

If a 15% yield were required, the note would be discounted 12.02% from face value.

The first two sets of examples and problems involved the discounting of **PMT**s only and then the discounting of **PMT**s combined with a lump sum, **FV**, to be received at the end of the periods. If you are required to determine the **PV** of a single future sum, **FV**, you have the easiest problem of all.

For example, here's a dramatization of the **PV** of a **FV**, discounted at a certain rate:

> Suppose your home has a current market value of $250,000. Would you sell it for $50,000? "Of course not," you say. But what if you were offered $1,000,000 for your property? Most individuals would jump at the chance.
> But you haven't yet been told **when** you would receive the cash. If you were told that the cash would be paid in 50 years (a bit hyperbolic, but play along), would you still accept the offer?

The situation really poses the financial question: "What is the **PV** (today) of $1,000,000 to be received 50 years in the future?

In order to answer the question, you must again choose a discount rate **i,** which will enable you to move the value of money backward in time. Let's assume that if you had a large sum of money in hand, you could safely invest the cash to earn 8% per year. This, then, is the *opportunity cost* of money to you. It is also the discount rate you would use to value the offer, and to convert the promise of a future receipt of cash into its equivalent value today:

	n	i	PV	PMT	FV
	50	8.00	?	0	1,000,000.00
solving					
			-21,321.23		

Now that you know you would not accept the $1,000,000 offer because it has an equivalent **PV** of only $21,321.23, what *is* the longest period of time until you could receive the money without losing the present value of your $250,000 home?

---

13 Notice how easy it is to measure the percent difference between two numbers using the Δ% key, which is in position (2,4) on the keyboard.

We can solve this problem by entering –250,000 into the **PV** register and solving for **n**, the number of periods required for $250,000 to grow to $1,000,000 if the **PV** grows at the rate of 8% annually for 50 years.

Uncovering an Idiosyncrasy of the HP–12C

We can also restate this problem to ask "Over how many periods must we discount the receipt of $1,000,000 to create a Present Value of $250,000, if we discount at the rate of 8% per period?"

	n	i	PV	PMT	FV
solving	? : 19.00	8.00	-250,000.00	0	1,000,000.00

Caveat

When solving for **n,** the HP–12C rounds **up** the answer[14] and delivers the value of **n** only in whole numbers (integers). In this example, the answer for **n** *appears* to be 19 years. But the calculator has rounded it up. If you re-solve this problem for **FV** using **n** = 19 you will find a different value for **FV**...

	n	i	PV	PMT	FV
solving	19.00	8.00	-250,000.00	0	? : 1,078,975.27

The fact that the **FV** exceeds $1,000,000 means that **n** should be slightly less than 19.00 years. Unfortunately, there is no way, using the *financial* registers of this calculator,[15] to determine exactly what **n** should be. This problem surfaces again in dealing with amortizing promissory notes, and we will amplify on its significance in that chapter.

---

14 **n** rounds UP to the next higher integer whenever the decimal portion of the answer exceeds .005

15 There is a way to do this on the HP 12-C using the natural logarithm LN (2,3) function: $(1.08)^n =$ FV/PV = 1,000,000/250,000 = 4. $(1.08)^n = 4$. Therefore n = LN(4) ÷ LN(1.08) = 18.012937 (years). (Use key (2,3) to determine values of LN.) Substituting 18.012937 in n will deliver FV = 1,000,000.

Determining a Yield (i) From Even Payments

> Suppose the physician in the previous example
> desires to know what rate of return he could achieve if he could
> buy the seller's carry-back note of $25,000 at a 20%
> discount from face value?

Remember that the note is scheduled to pay interest-only **PMTs** of $208.33 each month for 35 months and then a final payoff of the last interest **PMT** and the **FV** (balance) of $25,000. This variation is a problem in determining the yield, or discount rate, on the investment of $20,000. A T-Bar constructed to depict this cashflow would look like this:

```
                        _____-20,000 (PV)__
            EOM     1  |   208.33 (PMT)
                    2  |   208.33
                    :  |     :
  i = ?/12          :  |     :
                   36  |   208.33  +  25,000 (FV)
```

Transferring these values to the calculator:

	n	i	PV	PMT	FV
	36.00	?	-20,000	208.33	25,000.00
solving		:			
		1.56			

The answer obtained, 1.56%, is the *monthly* interest rate, because we expressed both the period **n** and the **PMT** in months. We need only to multiply this answer by 12 to express the annual rate of 18.77%. The keystrokes are:

	Key In	Display Shows
	36 [n]	36.00
20000	[CHS] [PV]	-20,000.00
208.33	[PMT]	208.33
25000	[FV]	25,000.00
solving		
	[i]	1.56
12	[x]	18.77

Distinguishing Between PMTs and FV

If you are dealing with only one **PMT** to be received <u>at the end of the period</u>, or one **FV** at the end of the period, it doesn't matter whether you treat the sum as a **PMT** or as a **FV**.

For example:

> Determine the **PV** of a sum, $5,000, to be received one year in the future and discounted at 10%.

As a <u>**PMT**</u>:

	n	i	PV	Pmt	FV
	1	.10	?	5,000	0
solving			-4,545,45		

As a <u>**FV**</u>:

	n	i	PV	Pmt	FV
	1	.10	?	0	5,000
solving			-4,545,45		

If **n** is something other than 1, however, it does make a difference. Here's why...

If **n** = 2, and $5,000 is entered as a **PMT**, the calculator considers the sum of $5,000 to be received twice, once at the end of period 1 and again at the end of period 2. If **n** = 2, and the $5,000 is entered as a **FV**, the calculator considers that the sum of $5,000 is to be received only <u>once</u>, at the end of the second period.

If **n** = 2, and the $5,000 is entered both as a **PMT** <u>and</u> as a **FV**, the calculator considers that the **PMT** of $5,000 is to be received twice and the **FV** to be received only once, at the end of period 2.

If you instruct the calculator to consider the receipt of the **PMT** as occurring at the beginning of each period, such instruction will not alter the fact that the calculator <u>always treats the receipt of a **FV** to be a one-time event occurring at the end of period **n**.</u>

Present Value of Annuities in Perpetuity

Financial texts refer to a regularly occurring sum of cash, either paid or received, as an *annuity*. "Annuity" once meant sums paid on an *annual* schedule,[16] but the term is now more loosely applied to any sum paid *regularly* .[17]

When a **PMT** is received over a limited time, we can say that it is a *finite* annuity to be received for **n** periods, and we can discount or compound this annuity easily. But if the annuity were to be received forever, we would describe it as an *infinite* annuity, or as an *annuity in perpetuity*.

For example, consider the following situation:

> A philanthropist wishes to endow a library with a lump sum
> in order to provide annual operating funds of $100,000 per
> year forever. He determines that his capital endowment could earn
> 8% each year. What must be the amount of his endowment if
> payments will begin one year from the date of the endowment.?

This situation represents a minor problem for us in that the **PMT** of $100,000 is expected to be received "forever." Therefore **n** would have to be set to infinity – a challenge neither the calculator nor the computer's spreadsheet is quite equal to. You can see that the amount of the endowment must be equal to the sum of the **PVs** of all future **PMTs**, discounted at 8% per year. Or,

$$\mathbf{PV} = \frac{100000}{(1+.08)^1} + \frac{100000}{(1+.08)^2} + \frac{100000}{(1+.08)^3} + \frac{100000}{(1+.08)^4} \ \cdots\cdots \ \infty$$

There is a simple way to calculate the **PV** of an infinite series of equal **PMTs**. This calculation is based on the formula[18] for the sum of an infinite series:

$$\mathbf{PV} = \frac{C}{i} \quad \text{(where } \mathbf{C} \text{ is the regularly occurring equal } \mathbf{PMT})$$

Therefore the philanthropist must set aside:

$$\mathbf{PV} = \frac{\$100000}{.08} \quad = \$1,250,000$$

---

16 From L. annus, year.

17 *Ordinary* annuities are those paid at the end of a period; *Annuities-due* are paid at the beginning.

18 The derivations of this formula, and other cashflow formulas, are presented in the Appendix.
    They are recommended reading for the interested analyst.

This kind of valuation of an infinite series of future **PMT**s forms the basis for the **Capitalization Method** of valuing a level stream of income from real estate or stocks. We will discuss the "cap method" of establishing the value of income-producing property by "capitalizing" income in Chapter 6, and the valuation of stocks by "capitalizing" dividends in Chapter 4.

Present Value of Annuities for A Definite Period of Time

A more common need in financial planning, is the need to fund a trust or an account to meet future cash requirements such as an education fund, a retirement plan or any special needs account. These kinds of accounts can be funded in one lump sum, but are more commonly provided by investing periodic payments which will grow to meet the future need.

The Present Value of a series of equal cashflows for a finite period, **n**, is really the difference between the Present Values of two infinite series of cashflows, one of which begins today and the other at the end of period **n:**

```
<---------------------- This Infinite series ----------------------------> ∞
                        <---minus this Infinite series ---> ∞
<-- Leaves this Finite series---->
```

or,

$$\frac{C}{i} \quad \text{minus} \quad \frac{C}{i*(1+i)^n}$$

Therefore the Present Value of a finite series of equal cashflows **n** long, discounted at rate **i** becomes:

$$PV = \frac{C}{i} - \frac{C}{i*(1+i)^n} = \frac{C}{i}\left(1 - \frac{1}{(1+i)^n}\right)$$

The derivations of the formulas for finite annuities are presented in the Appendix as formula #5 (PMT at end of period), and #6 (PMT at beginning of period).

Fortunately, the determination of the Present Value of a finite series of equal cashflows is a problem easily handled by either the calculator or the computer's spreadsheet. When a Future Value is involved, its Present Value can be added to (or subtracted from) the Present Value of the cashflows:

$$PV = \frac{C}{i}\left(1 - \frac{1}{(1+i)^n}\right) + \frac{FV}{(1+i)^n}$$

Note that the FV occurs at the end of period **n.**

Perpetual Annuities Adjusted for Growth Factors

It is often necessary to determine the **Present Value** of an annuity which grows by a constant factor each period. Here's an example:

> The philanthropist who wishes to endow the library realizes that a constant sum of $100,000 each year will be subject to inflation, so that each dollar in later years will have less and less purchasing power. In order to allow for inflation, he must set aside a sufficiently large sum which will allow for an estimated 4% annual inflation rate.
>
> With what amount must he now endow the fund?

Once again, the future annual amounts will have a Present Value of:

$$\textbf{PV} = \frac{100000}{(1+.08)^1} + \frac{100000(1+g)^1}{(1+.08)^2} + \frac{100000(1+g)^2}{(1+.08)^3} + \frac{100000(1+g)^3}{(1+.08)^4} \dots \dots \infty$$

where **g** = growth (inflation) factor. The formula (# 7 in Appendix) for an infinite series of cash payments (**C**), growing at a constant rate, **g,** per period is:

$$\textbf{PV} = \frac{C}{(i\text{-}g)}$$

Therefore, if the philanthropist anticipates future inflation to be 4% per year, he must contribute:

$$\textbf{PV} = \frac{\$100000}{(.08 - .04)} = \$2,500,000$$

Notice that the **PV** of this **growing annuity in perpetuity** increases in value with any combination of decreasing rates of return (**i**) and increasing rates of inflation rate (**g**). If the endowment could be managed for a greater annual return (e.g., **i** = 10%), the amount of the required endowment could be reduced substantially, e.g.:

$$\textbf{PV} = \frac{\$100000}{(.10 - .04)} = \$1,666,667$$

PV of Finite Annuities Subject to a Growth Factor

> If we continue with the endowment problem, we can postulate that our flagging philanthropist has decided to limit his generosity to 20 years. In order to provide $100,000 in constant dollars annually, we can ask what amount must now be set aside to allow for inflation of 4% per year over the next 20 years? Cash in the fund will still earn 8% per year, and the first payment will still be made one year following the establishment of the fund (an important factor).

We need the formula for the Present Value of a finite cashflow series, growing at rate **g** per period, which returns a yield of **i** per period, whose payments are limited to 20 years (**n**), and whose first payment begins <u>at the end of the year</u> in which the fund is established (EOP). The first payment, though occurring at the end of the first period, is unadjusted for inflation.

This is formula #8 in the Appendix:

$$\mathbf{PV} = \frac{C}{(i\text{-}g)}\left(1\text{-}\frac{(1+g)^n}{(1+i)^n}\right)$$

$$\mathbf{PV} = \frac{C}{(.08-.04)}\left(1\text{-}\frac{(1+.04)^{20}}{(1+.08)^{20}}\right)$$

$$\mathbf{PV} = \frac{\$100000}{.04}(1\text{-}0.47010)$$

$$\mathbf{PV} = \$2,500,000 * 0.52990$$

$$\mathbf{PV} = \$1,324,746.14$$

Although this formula seems to be complicated, it can be very useful, and quite convenient, when the task turns to determining the Present Value of a long series of end-of-period **PMT**s which grow at a steady rate.[19]

If the first payment is to be disbursed at the time the fund is established, then we seek the formula for a finite series of cashflows, growing at **g** rate per year and discounted at **i** rate per year, and whose first payment occurs at the BOP. The first payment would be adjusted neither for inflation nor for a yield.

---

19 Particularly when the number of separate cashflows exceeds the storage capacity (20) of the HP–12C.

This is formula #10 in the Appendix:

$$PV = \frac{C(1+i)}{(i-g)}\left(1 - \frac{(1+g)^n}{(1+i)^n}\right)$$

$$PV = \frac{\$100000*(1.08)}{(.08-.04)}\left(1 - \frac{(1+g)^n}{(1+i)^n}\right)$$

$$PV = \frac{\$108000}{.04}\left(1 - \frac{(1+.04)^{20}}{(1+.08)^{20}}\right)$$

$$PV = \$1,430,725.84$$

> To complicate matters still, a member of the staff points out
> to the philanthropist that if funds are not to be disbursed until the
> end of the first period, then the $100,000 annuity would already
> have lost 4% of its purchasing power. Therefore, the initially
> planned annuity must be increased by 4% to allow for inflation.
> With what amount must the endowment now be funded?

Now we need a formula to reflect the Present Value of an annuity which will be paid at the end of the first period, but which will be adjusted for inflation. This formula is # 9 in the Appendix:

$$PV = \frac{C(1+g)}{(i-g)}\left(1 - \frac{(1+g)^n}{(1+i)^n}\right)$$

$$PV = \$1,377,735.99$$

It is evident that when a trust fund or endowment is to be funded, care should be taken to determine when the first payment is to be made. If it to be made at the end of the first period, – say one year later – it is important to determine whether this first payment will be adjusted for inflation or not.

If the first payment is to be made at the time of creation of the fund, then the first payment is neither inflated nor discounted.

Isn't there an easier way? Yes, there is – for two of the three situations above.

Adjusting Rates To Compensate for Inflation

There is a more convenient method to adjust PMTs for inflation, and it holds true in almost all cases. Consider the following rationale:

If $1 is invested to yield an 8% return in one year, the FV of the investment will be:

$$FV = PV *(1+.08)$$

If, however, inflation has advanced during this period at a 4% annual rate, then in order to achieve a true (constant dollar) 8% yield, the investor must receive a return which includes an allowance for inflation:

$$FV = PV *(1+.08) * (1+.04) = 1.12320. \textbf{ Rate = 12.32\%}$$

If no allowance is made for inflation, the real or effective[20] return will be:

$$FV = PV * \frac{(1+ \text{nominal rate})}{(1+ \text{inflation rate})} = \frac{1.08}{1.04} = PV * 1.03846$$

The inflation-adjusted effective **rate**[21] will be: **1.03846 − 1** = .03846 * 100 = 3.846%.

This inflation-adjusted rate is handy in a number of situations. For example:

> What sum most be invested today to provide for constant dollar annuities of $100,000 for 20 years if cash in the investment earns 8% p.a. and inflation averages 4% p.a.? Payments are BOP.

This problem could be solved by applying formula # 10, as above.

It can be more conveniently handled by use of the **inflation-adjusted rate** of 3.846% which we calculated above:

Set calculator to BEG

	n	i	PV	PMT	FV
	20	3.846	?	100,000	0
solving			−1,430,725.84		

---

[20] Measured in constant dollars
[21] If the rate were monthly the nominal rate would be 1 + (.08/12), **not** (1+.08)/12

In solving for a PMT occurring at the beginning of the period, the calculator sets aside the first payment and neither inflates it nor discounts it. But when the first payment occurs at the end of the period, the use of the inflation-adjusted rate will lead to an error whether the first payment is or is not to be adjusted for inflation.[22] Let's re-visit the philanthropist seeking to endow his library in order to illustrate this point.

The original version of the problem called for a payment of $100,000 <u>at the end of the first year</u> of the establishment of the endowment, and a like amount, adjusted for inflation, in each succeeding year for 20 years. The inflation factor (**g**) is 4%, and the yield on funds (**i**) is 8%.

In this case, the inflation-adjusted rate is 3.846%, as calculated above. If we use the inflation-adjusted rate we produce the following result:

	n	**i**	**PV**	**PMT**	**FV**
	20	3.846	0	-100,000	0
solving			−1,377,754.88		

You will recall that the answer furnished by application of formula #8 (p.30) is $1,324,746.14. The difference is exactly 4%, the amount of the inflation factor. This discrepancy occurs because the use of the inflation-adjusted rate *always* inflates *every* PMT for inflation. Even though the first payment occurring at the EOP 1 is not to be inflated, the inflation-adjusted rate applies such an inflation factor – in this case 4%. Therefore the answer $1,377,754.88 is exactly 4% too high. If we divided this answer by 1.04, the correct answer results: $1,324,746.14.

The following matrix may be helpful as a mnemonic in choosing the correct method:

	Annuity Due (BOP)	Ordinary Annuity (EOP)
Solving for PV	I.A.R.	Long Formula (#8)
Solving for FV	I.A.R.	I.A.R.

where I.A.R. = Inflation–Adjusted Rate

---

[22] If the first PMT is not to be adjusted, use of the inflation-adjusted rate will inflate it. If it is already adjusted for inflation, the inflation-adjusted rate will compound the adjustment.

Nominal vs. Effective Rates

The difference between nominal rates of interest and effective rates of interest is created by the effect of compounding. For example, if $1 is invested for 1 year at a 10% nominal rate of interest applied annually, the FV of the investment is easy to calculate:

$$\textbf{FV} = \textbf{PV} (1+i)^n$$
$$\textbf{FV} = \$1(1+.10)^1 = \$1.10$$

The effective interest rate $\quad (\textbf{i}) = \textbf{FV}-1, = \$1.10 - 1, = .10 = 10\%$

But when the interest rate is compounded over a number of periods, the result is different. Suppose the annual interest rate of 10% is broken up into a monthly rate and compounded 12 times during the year:

$$\textbf{FV} = \textbf{PV}(1+ \tfrac{.10}{12})^{12} = 1.1047$$

$$\textbf{Effective Rate} = 1.1047 - 1 = .1047, \text{ or } \textbf{10.47\%}$$

As the compounding period becomes more and more frequent, the effective rate of interest increases. If the annual 10% rate is divided into daily rates and compounded daily then,

$$\textbf{FV} = \textbf{PV}(1+ \tfrac{.10}{360})^{360} = 1.10\textbf{516}$$

The effective rate has risen to 10.516%. This trend toward higher and higher effective rates continues as **n** approaches infinity.

To determine an effective rate, simply determine the future value of 1, compounded over **n** periods at rate **i** per period.

For example,

What is the effective annual rate when a 9% interest rate is compounded monthly?				
n	**i**	**PV**	**PMT**	**FV**
12	.09÷12	-1	0	?
				1.09381

solving

The effective rate is (1.09381 − 1) = .09381, or **9.381%**

If the effective rate is given and the nominal rate sought, reverse the process and put one plus the effective rate into FV, (−1) into PV, and then solve for i.

Continuously Compounded Rates

If we begin with an interest rate equal to 100% payable over **n** periods, the interest rate per period **n** will be $\frac{100\%}{n}$.

The Future Value of 1 compounded for **n** periods becomes $1 * \left(1 + \frac{100\%}{n}\right)^n$.

As **n** grows, the value of this expression converges to a limit:

$$FV = 1 * (1 + \frac{1}{100})^{100} = 2.7048$$

$$FV = 1 * (1 + \frac{1}{1000})^{1000} = 2.71692$$

$$FV = 1 * (1 + \frac{1}{10000})^{10000} = 2.71815$$

$$FV = 1 * (1 + \frac{1}{1000000000})^{1000000000} = 2.71828$$

This "magic" number, 2.71828, is known as **episilon**, represented as **e**.[23]

Epsilon represents the absolute limit to which 1 can grow when the rate of growth (100%) is divided into infinitely small parts and compounded over an equally infinite number of periods. The result is:

$$FV = PV(e)$$

When the rate (**i**) is other than 1, and **n** is other 1, the formula becomes:

$$FV = PV(e)^{i*n}$$

where **i** is the rate and **n** is the corresponding number of periods over which **i** applies. For example, $1 continuously compounded over 1 year at an annual interest rate (i) of 10% would have a maximum future value of:

$$FV = \$1(e)^{i*n}$$
$$FV = \$1(e)^{.10*1}$$
$$FV = \$1.10517$$

The effective rate = FV -1 = 1.10517 - 1 = .10517 = 10.517%.

---

23 Epsilon forms the base for Napier's natural logarithm system, which is available on the HP–12C.

$1 continuously compounded over 2 years at an annual interest rate (i) of 10% would have a maximum future value of:

$$FV = \$1(e)^{i*n}$$
$$FV = \$1(e)^{.10*2}$$
$$FV = \$1(e)^{.20}$$
$$FV = \$1.2214$$

Making Use of e(psilon)

We have seen that the present value of a cashflow can be calculated when the cash is available either at the beginning or at the end of a period. But that doesn't help the CFO who must set aside money for equipment to be purchased over the course of the coming year.

If he sets aside all the cash needed at the beginning of the year, he may overestimate the amount required since cash not used for early purchases can be invested until needed. If he calculates the required cash to be needed at the end of the period, he may fall short since any expenditures made during the period will deprive his account of interest to be earned on his reserves.

This problem can be mitigated, though not entirely overcome, by budgeting the cash required as though it were to be supplied continuously over the specified time frame. This is where epsilon proves useful.

The value $(e)^{i*n}$ or $(e)^{g*n}$ can be inserted in any of the formulae we have discussed in place of $(1+i)^n$ or $(1+g)^n$, and is particularly useful when we wish to express the Present Value of **PMT**s distributed evenly (continuously) over time. While the PMTs cannot actually be spread out continuously, the use of epsilon is very handy in compiling capital budgets where PV estimates based on PMTs required at the beginning of the year or at the end of the year do not reflect the actual timing of the required amounts.

For example:

> The philanthropist who originally had intentions of making an endowment to the library to provide operating cash in perpetuity has now decided he wishes to limit his endowment to 20 years, but also wishes to recognize that the cash will be made available *continuously* throughout the year.
>
> What amount will be required?

Recall the formula for an **Annuity For a Limited (finite)Time**:

$$PV = \frac{C}{i} * \left(1 - \frac{1}{(1+i)^n}\right)$$

We can insert e^{i*n} into the formula in place of $(1+i)^n$

$$PV = \frac{C}{i} * \left(1 - \frac{1}{(e)^{i*n}}\right)$$

$$PV = \frac{\$100000}{.08} * \left(1 - \frac{\$1}{(e)^{.08*20}}\right)$$

$$PV = \$1,250,000 * 0.798103 = \$997,629$$

This result, $997,629, is slightly more than the Present Value obtained by discounting $100 000, to be received at the **end** of the period ($981,814) and slightly less than the same cashflow discounted at the same rate but to be received at the **beginning** of the period ($1,060,360). It is also different from the average of the two ($1,021,087).

Discounting cashflows which are to be received or to be paid continuously over a definite time period is a very useful tool in capital budgeting.

Chapter Summary

In this section, you have learned how to determine the Future and Present Values of cashflows involving single sums and *even* payments.

You also know how to determine the rate, or **yield**, on a cashflow (such as a trust deed note) and to determine the number of periods required to establish certain cashflows. You also now know how to value perpetual annuities, including those whose payments are adjusted for regular, periodic increases or inflation. And you understand the methods for valuation of a single sum annuity for a definite, or finite, length of time.

A number of points are worth re-emphasizing:

1. Cashflows represent financial <u>transactions</u>. There is a flow of money from one pocket to another. Therefore every cashflow situation must be represented by a positive cashflow sign and a negative cashflow sign. When this convention is not observed, the calculator will flash an "Error 5" message.

2. The application of *interest rates* permits us to express the worth of a single sum, or a series of periodic, equal payments, or the combination of a single sum

In solving for a PMT occurring at the beginning of the period, the calculator sets aside the first payment and neither inflates it nor discounts it. But when the first payment occurs at the end of the period, the use of the inflation-adjusted rate will lead to an error whether the first payment is or is not to be adjusted for inflation.[22] Let's re-visit the philanthropist seeking to endow his library in order to illustrate this point.

The original version of the problem called for a payment of $100,000 <u>at the end of the first year</u> of the establishment of the endowment, and a like amount, adjusted for inflation, in each succeeding year for 20 years. The inflation factor (**g**) is 4%, and the yield on funds (**i**) is 8%.

In this case, the inflation-adjusted rate is 3.846%, as calculated above. If we use the inflation-adjusted rate we produce the following result:

	n	i	PV	PMT	FV
solving	20	3.846	0	-100,000	0
			−1,377,754.88		

You will recall that the answer furnished by application of formula #8 (p.30) is $1,324,746.14. The difference is exactly 4%, the amount of the inflation factor. This discrepancy occurs because the use of the inflation-adjusted rate *always* inflates *every* PMT for inflation. Even though the first payment occurring at the EOP 1 is not to be inflated, the inflation-adjusted rate applies such an inflation factor – in this case 4%. Therefore the answer $1,377,754.88 is exactly 4% too high. If we divided this answer by 1.04, the correct answer results: $1,324,746.14.

The following matrix may be helpful as a mnemonic in choosing the correct method:

	Annuity Due (BOP)	Ordinary Annuity (EOP)
Solving for PV	I.A.R.	Long Formula (#8)
Solving for FV	I.A.R.	I.A.R.

where I.A.R. = Inflation–Adjusted Rate

---

[22] If the first PMT is not to be adjusted, use of the inflation-adjusted rate will inflate it. If it is already adjusted for inflation, the inflation-adjusted rate will compound the adjustment.

Chapter 2
Working With Uneven Cashflows

In Chapter 1, we worked with cashflows which either did not contain **PMT**s or, if they did, the **PMT**s were equal. These situations occur with fixed-rate mortgages, payments under most promissory notes, the conversion of a single sum **annuity** to a Present Value, or the extension of a series of equal annuity **PMT**s into a Future Value or Present Value. But many financial situations involve payments which change from period to period, either in amount or from a positive to a negative sign. Many income-producing investments involve uneven cashflows, and some even involve negative cashflows.

Whenever you need to deal with uneven **PMT**s, the "horizontal" financial register which has been used,

n	i	PV	PMT	FV

is no longer applicable. You need to learn a different method.

Consider a situation in which you are scheduled to receive the following cashflows:

		?
End of Period	1	100
	2	200
i = .10	3	300

What is the **PV** of this series of **PMT**s?

The alternate financial register we must use in dealing with uneven cashflows is composed of keys (1,3), (1,4) and (1,5); specifically the functions printed *in blue* on the lower facet of these keys. These functions are, respectively:

CFo, CFj and **Nj.**

You already know that in order to access these functions in blue you must first press the blue key **g**,(4,3). You can consider that **CFo** stands for CashFlow**o**riginal, or that certain amount of cash invested at the very beginning of an investment; when it represents the initially invested cash, it will be entered as a negative number.

CFj stands for the separate *and different*, individual payments, **PMT**s, which you will enter per period **n**. **Nj** stands for the number of times a particular cashflow, **CFj**, will occur. We will continue to use the **i** register as before, but we will now use the expression **CFj** to indicate a payment.

The first rule to observe is that when you begin a *new* cashflow series involving uneven payments, you should always enter a value into **CFo**. By doing so you automatically reset the **n** register to zero and alert the calculator to get ready to count the number of *different* **CFj**s you are about to enter. You should do this even though (as in the problem above) there is no **CFo** - no original investment. Once done, the calculator will keep track of the number of *different* cashflows entered, increasing **n** by 1 each time you enter a *different* cashflow into **CFj**. Let's try it:

<u>Key In</u>	<u>Display Shows</u>	<u>Comment</u>
f CLX	0.00	clears memory (except PRGM)
0 g CFo	0.00	sets the n register to 0 and installs 0 in memory cell 0
100 g CFj	100.00	installs 100 in memory cell 1
200 g CFj	200.00	installs 200 in memory cell 2
300 g CFj	300.00	installs 300 in memory cell 3

Now that you have these uneven cashflows entered into the memory registers of the calculator, you need to inform the calculator of the *discount rate* you wish to use to convert these future values into a single present value. The T–Bar indicates that the discount rate i will be 0.10. Continue by keying–in:

10 i	10.00	enters 0.10 into register i

Now step 2:

You will notice that the top (gold) facet of key (1,3) is marked **NPV**. This stands for **Net Present Value**. It will also deliver the **Present Value** if 0 has been entered into **CFo**. This is the case in this example.

Therefore go ahead and solve for **(N)PV**:

solving

| f | | NPV | (1,3) | **481.59** |

Therefore the Present Value of this series of future cash payments of 100, 200 and 300, discounted at 10% per period, is 481.59.

Just how did the calculator arrive at this answer? – Just the way we demonstrated in the first chapter when we considered the relationship:

$$PV = \frac{FV}{(1 + i)^n}$$

$$PV = \frac{100}{(1+.10)^1} + \frac{200}{(1+.10)^2} + \frac{300}{(1+.10)^3}$$

$$PV = 90.91 + 165.29 + 225.39$$

$$PV = 481.59$$

Verifying Accuracy of Entries

You can check for the accuracy of your entries by recalling the various storage registers to verify what they contain. Recall the value in the **n** register:

<u>Key In</u>	<u>Display Shows</u>	<u>Comment</u>
RCL (4,5) n	3.00	Shows number of *different* CFjs

Recall the values in the various registers in which the calculator stored your **CFo** and **CFjs**. The memory cells used are in the numerical keypad, 0 through 3.

RCL 0	0.00	Shows 0.00 stored in memory cell 0
RCL 1	100.00	Shows 100.00 stored in memory 1
RCL 2	200.00	Shows 200.00 stored in memory 2
RCL 3	300.00	Shows 300.00 stored in memory 3

Now that you know *where* these values are stored, you can easily change them, if you need to, by "writing over" the stored value and entering the new value directly into the memory cell/register.

For example, suppose that the value 200 which you entered into memory cell 2 should have been 500. How can you change this single entry without having to re-enter all the values?

Key In	Display Shows	Comment
500 STO 2 (4,4)	500.00	Replaces the value of 200 in memory cell 2 with 500
solving		
f NPV	729.53	new Present Value

Adding Cashflows to a Series

If you wish to continue to add cashflows to this series, simply continue to enter the new ones from where you left off. (Don't enter 0 into **CFo** because this would reset **n** = 0). Let's add two additional cashflows: 600 and 750.

Key In	Display Shows	Comment
600 g CFj	600.00	Stores 600 in memory cell 4
750 g CFj	750.00	Stores 750 in memory cell 5
solving		
f NPV	1605.03	New PV

Using Nj To Indicate Repeating Cashflows

Cashflows frequently repeat themselves for a number of periods before changing. Consider a situation in which a cashflow of 1000 is received for <u>6</u> periods; then the cashflow increases to 1200 for <u>3</u> periods and finally rises to 1500 for the last <u>2</u> periods. What is this cashflow's presently worth (what is its **PV?**) to an investor who requires a 12% return per period on his money?

End of Period		(?)	
	1	1000	
	2	1000	
	3	1000	6 times
i = .12	4	1000	
	5	1000	
	6	1000	
	7	1200	
	8	1200	3 times
	9	1200	
	10	1500	
	11	1500	2 times

Key In	Display Shows	Comment
f CLX	0.00	Clears memory, sets n = 0
0 g CFo	0.00	sets the n register to 0 and installs 0 in memory cell 0
1000 g CFj	1,000.00	Stores 1000 in memory 1

Now you need to inform the calculator that this cashflow of 1000 occurs 6 times (in a row):

Key In	Display Shows	Comment
6 g Nj	6.00	Informs the calculator that this number occurs <u>6</u> times
1200 g CFj	1,200.00	Stores the second *different* cashflow in memory cell 2
3 g Nj	3.00	Informs the calculator that this cashflow occurs <u>3</u> times
1500 g CFj	1,500.00	Stores the third *different* cashflow in memory cell 3
2 g Nj	2.00	Informs the calculator that this cashflow occurs <u>2</u> times

Now inform the calculator regarding the discount rate you wish to use.

12 [i]   12.00   **Enters .12 into the i register**

Before solving for the answer, check to see how many *different* cashflows the calculator has stored. You have entered three *different* cashflows: one occurring 6 times, a second occurring 3 times, and the third occurring 2 times.

[RCL] [n]   3.00   **Shows that 3 <u>different</u> cashflows have been entered.**

Also, check to see that the value of each of the 3 different cashflows is correct:

[RCL] 1	1000.00	**Value stored in memory cell 1**
[RCL] 2	1200.00	**Value stored in memory cell 2**
[RCL] 3	1500.00	**Value stored in memory cell 3**

solving

[f] [NPV]   6,485.79   **The Present Value of <u>11</u> sequential cashflows in the amounts specified.**

Some Limitations on the Number of Cashflows

The calculator will accept 10 cashflows and store each in Registers 0 thru 9, and *up to* 10 more in additional registers .0 through .9.[1] Any one of these cashflows may be repeated a maximum of 99 times. Therefore if you had a certain cashflow, 180, which occurred 100 times, you could not enter 100 into Nj since it exceeds the calculator's limit of 99 per memory cell (register). You could, however, enter this cashflow as follows:

180 [g] [CFj]	180.00	
<u>98</u> [g] [Nj]	98.00	
180 [g] [CFj]	180.00	
<u>2</u> [g] [Nj]	2.00	

---

[1] The 12–C handbook defines these 20 storage registers as R_0 through R_9 and $R._0$ through $R._9$ Note the decimal points. You can examine the contents of any register by using the recall **RCL** key (4,5) followed by the cell you wish to see. There are times when some of these memory cells are used for other functions. In those cases, fewer than 20 storage cells will be available.

Any other combination of numbers (**Njs**) totaling **100** would do as well. But if you attempt to enter any one cashflow 100 times or more, the calculator will display an **Error Code (6)** message.

Adjusting for Incorrect Entries

Now and then you will make errors in entering cashflows. If the cashflow contains only a few entries, it's not terribly inconvenient to clear the memories and re-enter the data. But if there is a long series of **CFjs**, re-entering all the data from scratch can be time consuming and frustrating. Here's how to correct for data entry errors.

Wrong Amounts

If you have entered an incorrect amount in the series, simply key-in the correct amount, press STO (4,4) and deposit the corrected amount in the cell (R_X) in which it belongs.

For example, enter the following cashflow series in your calculator:

			(PV?)
End of Period	1		100
	2		400
i = .10	3		500

The second entry, 400, should have been 300. To make the correction, follow these steps:

Key In	Display Shows	Comment
300 STO 2	300.00	Over-rides the value in R_2 Changing it from 400 to 300

Re-solving

f NPV

If you make this correction properly, the **PV** of the series will change from 797.15 to 714.50.

Wrong Njs

Occasionally the number of times a unique cashflow occurs is mis-entered in **Nj**. For example, suppose that you entered this set of values:

		(PV?)	
End of Period	1	100	1
	2	**300**	
i = .10	3	**300**	2
	4	**300**	
	5	**300**	
	6	500	3
	7	700	4
	8	900	5

The error consists in the fact that the second, separate cashflow of 300 occurs <u>3</u> times not <u>4</u> times.[2] The T-Bar should have been:

		(?) <u>PV</u>	
End of Period	1	100	1
	2	**300**	
i = .10	3	**300**	2
	4	**300**	
	5	500	3
	6	700	4
	7	900	5

Here are the keystrokes to correct this error:

Key In	Display Shows	Comment
2 $\boxed{n}$	2.00	**Informs the calculator that a change is to be made affecting the second CFj entry**
3 $\boxed{g}\boxed{Nj}$	3.00	**Changes Nj from 4 to 3**
5 $\boxed{n}$	5.00	**Restores n to 5, the correct number of <u>separate</u> CFj entries**

Re-solving

$\boxed{f}$ $\boxed{NPV}$

---

[2] To check on Nj, enter the number of the cashflow you want to inspect into n, then $\boxed{RCL}$ $\boxed{g}$ $\boxed{Nj}$

If you have made these adjustments correctly, the **NPV** will change from 2,016.72 to 1,936.58. The difference is a loss of the Present Value of one entry of 300, which, however, is offset by the fact that the 3rd, 4th and 5th cashflows each advance one period in time.

The most common error made in revaluing **Nj** is to forget to restore the proper **n** value. Note, in this case, that **n** should be **= 5,** both before and after the correction. Recall **n** to verify this. If it is not **5,** make the necessary change.

Discounting Cashflows from Leases[3]

The ability to discount uneven cashflows is a requirement for the valuation of leases since almost all leases furnish uneven **PMTs** in the form of rents which change from period to period. Since leases can be bought and sold, and also used as collateral for loans, valuing a lease is a pre-condition of many financial transactions.

Consider this situation:

> You have just completed the leasing of a 24,000 s.f. industrial building to a credit tenant.[4] The tenant has contracted to pay rent as follows:
>
> First three years $12,000 per month
> Next two years   13,000 per month
> Last two years   14,000 per month
>
> As owner of the building, you are pressed for capital and would like to sell the lease (not the real property) to an investor. If the investor requires a 15% annual return, what is the likely (present) value of the lease to the investor?

---

[3] This initial example does not adjust for lease PMTs made in advance. This will be covered later in this chapter.

[4] A credit tenant is one whose net assets are sufficient to act as security for the entire amount due under the lease.

This is a problem which requires you to discount the future receipt of the monthly rent at a rate equivalent to 15% per year. Note that rent is paid monthly, while the required rate of return is expressed annually. (See footnote 3)

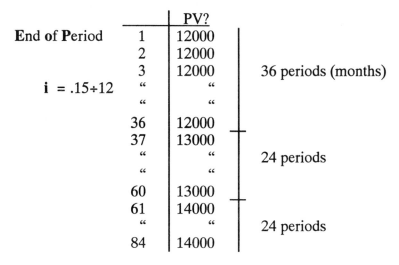

The keystrokes would be:

Key In	**Display Shows**	
0 CFo	0.00	
12000 g CFj	12000.00	
36 g Nj	36.00	
13000 g CFj	1300.00	
24 g Nj	24.00	
14000 g CFj	14000.00	
24 g Nj	24.00	
15 g i	1.25	
solving f NPV	654,628.74	Do not clear these entries.

If the investor pays exactly $654,628.74, and if the tenant pays the rent as scheduled, the investor will realize a 15% rate of return (yield) on his money over the term of the lease. If he pays *more* than $654,628.74, he will earn *less* than 15%, since a higher Present Value requires a lower discount rate. If he pays *less* than $654,628.74, he will have a *higher* yield since a lower Present Value requires the application of a higher discount rate.

The discount rate *is* the investor's yield.

The Concept of Net Present Value

Most investments involve up-front cash. These out-of-pocket, negative cashflows can be represented by entering the amount of the original investment in **CFo** as a negative number. The calculator stores **CFo** in register R_0 (in memory cell 0 on the keypad).

When you press *f*, NPV (1,3), after having entered a series of cashflows, the calculator responds by determining the Present Value of each individual cashflow, discounting each one back to a **PV** using the discount rate you entered in $\boxed{i}$. Then it adds the resulting present values together, including the value in register R_0. When the value in register R_0 (**CFo**) is 0, the result is not different from the total of the PV for all future cashflows. But when **CFo** is a negative number, indicating an out-of-pocket initial cashflow, the calculator adds the positive and negative results and displays the **Net Present Value. Therefore the summation** $(\sum)$[5] **of all the PVs + (– CFo) = Net** Present Value.

For example,

> Let's assume the buyer of the lease on the industrial building in the preceding example negotiated to acquire the lease for $580,000. What would be the **NPV** of this lease in the hands of this investor?

Hopefully, your calculator still retains the values from this recent problem. (If not, please re-enter them.) If so, you need only to "slip in" the **CFo** value into register R_0 in order to structure a Net Present Value calculation. Here are the keystrokes:

Key In	Display Shows	Comments
580000 $\boxed{\text{CHS}}$ $\boxed{\text{STO}}$ 0	-580,000.00	Changes the sign, stores –580,000 in memory cell R_0, the cell in which the CFo is stored. Using STO instead of $\boxed{g}$ $\boxed{\text{CFo}}$ avoids resetting the n counter.
$\boxed{f}$ $\boxed{\text{NPV}}$	74,628.74	The sum of the present value of 654,628.74 & –580,000.

---

[5] The symbol $\sum$, sigma, is used to designate the sum of a series of numbers

Usefulness of the NPV Method

Many financial professionals prefer the **NPV** method of ranking an investment over any other method. In theory, any number of alternative investments can be reduced to a **NPV** number and then prioritized or rank-ordered. Any investment which has a negative **NPV** would automatically be eliminated from consideration because the net present value of future returns (their present worth) would be less than the amount of the original investment.

Of those alternatives which result in a positive **NPV,** *and which carry comparable risks,* the investment which would deliver the highest **NPV** *may* be the logical choice.

If the investments carry dissimilar degrees of risk, ranking them according to their **NPVs** would be inappropriate *unless* the **NPV** of each investment were determined using a risk-adjusted discount rate.

Discount Rate Varies with Risk

We have said little about the **risk** associated with the probability of receiving future cash flows. The difference in risk associated with each financial alternative should be reflected in the selection of the discount rate. A higher risk calls for a higher discount rate, and, as you already know, a higher discount rate results in a <u>lower</u> Present Value. Therefore riskier investments usually have a lower **NPV** than a less risky one because the selection of a higher discount rate results in a lower **PV**. We will expand on the selection of a discount rate later.

Return on Investment (ROI) - a Profitability Index

A variation of the **NPV** method is to determine the Present Value of the future returns and divide this number by the amount of the original investment, the **CFo**. In the example above, the Return on Investment (**ROI**) for the investor would be:

$$\frac{\sum PVs}{CFo} = \frac{654,628.74}{580,000}$$

$$= 1.13$$

This indicates that the investor may recover 100% of his capital and an additional profit of 13% or (1+.13).

The NPV of an Income-Producing Real Property

As you know, the **NPV** of an income-producing property is also a function of the $\sum$ **PV** of all the future cashflows which may reasonably be expected to flow to the owner during his holding period. Let's identify the cashflows that can reasonably be anticipated.

The Initial Investment

The first cashflow in the typical real estate investment is a negative one: the total amount of the owner's cash necessary to acquire the property. This does not include the mortgage,[6] since mortgage funds flow from a lender's investment in the property, not the owner's.

> Let's assume that Brown has an opportunity to acquire a ten-unit apartment house. He expects to hold the property exactly 7 years. His analysis anticipates[7] the following after-tax cashflows[8] from the property:

End of Year		(?)
	1	50,000
	2	52,500
	3	55,000
i = ?	4	57,500
	5	60,000
	6	63,000
	7	68,750 + Net Proceeds on sale of $725,000

Notice that the net proceeds (after tax) from the sale, $725,000,[9] are scheduled to occur at the end of the 7th year. Therefore the cashflow at the end of the 7th year would be the sum of the after-tax cash[10] derived from operating the property in year 7, $68,750, **plus** the net after-tax sales proceeds of $725,000.

---

6 Those analyses which include the mortgage are referred to as "mortgage-equity" analyses

7 The value of all investments depends on the Principal of Anticipation.

8 The analysis can be either pre-tax or after-tax. But in the case of real estate investments, most analyses are done on an after-tax basis.

9 This is the Future Value of the investment & is often referred to as "reversionary income."

10 Don't mix apples and oranges in your analysis. If the net proceeds are to be expressed as an after-tax number, then the PMTs during the holding period must also be after-tax numbers. Analyses of income-producing real property which are before-tax analyses ignore the depreciation and interest deductions attached to the real estate.

The point is that this last-year total cashflow occurs at the <u>end of the 7th year</u>. Do not make the mistake of entering the net sales proceeds as one more cashflow (at the end of the 8th year). This would distort the financial chronology of the cashflows by adding an additional period **n** and would produce an incorrect result. Let's enter these data into the calculator:

<u>Key In</u>	<u>Display Shows</u>	
f CLX	0.00	
0 g CFo	0.00	
50000 g CFj	50,000.00	
52500 g CFj	52,500.00	
55000 g CFj	55,000.00	
57500 g CFj	57,500.00	
60000 g CFj	60,000.00	
63000 g CFj	63,000.00	
68750 Enter	68,750.00	(last 2 lines are additions)
725000 + g CFj	793,750.00	

Brown considers these cashflows to be very secure because the property is located in a city which will no longer permit new apartment houses to be built; the area is convenient to transportation, attractive and well-maintained, and there is a strong demand for apartments units, which demand is not expected to abate. Inspection shows the property is well-constructed. Because of these factors, Brown is willing to accept a 12% annual return on his investment.[11]

Therefore he seeks to discount the future receipt of these cashflows using a (**discount**) **rate, i,** of 12% to arrive at the property's **Present Value**. Therefore inform the calculator that $i = 12$:

	12 i	12.00
solving	f NPV (1,3)	587,201.30

You can readily see that if Brown pays exactly $587,201.30 for this property, he will attain an investment yield of exactly 12% on his original cash investment. If he pays less than this amount, his yield will rise; if he pays more than this amount, his yield will decline.

But what would his yield be if he paid exactly $500,000 for this property?

---

[11] If this property carried negative characteristics, the market would increase the discount rate to reflect the additional risk. As a result, its market value (Present Value or Present Worth) would decline. The reason that less desirable properties command lower market prices is because investors apply higher discounts rates to their cashflows.

It would be logical of you to assume that you could enter –500,000 in **CFo** and then push the $\boxed{\text{i}}$ key (1,2) to ask the calculator to solve for **i, the yield.** Let's try it:

Key In	Display Shows
500000 $\boxed{\text{CHS}}$ $\boxed{\text{g}}$ $\boxed{\text{CFo}}$	**-500,000.00**
solving	
$\boxed{\text{i}}$	--- $\boxed{\text{Error 5}}$ ---

Unfortunately, as you can see, this is not the way. Instead, reset **n** = 7 and enter these keystrokes:

$\boxed{\text{f}}$ $\boxed{\text{IRR}}$ (1,5)   **15.32**

This is the discount rate, 15.32%, which will exactly produce a **NPV** of zero. (Prove this to yourself by solving for **NPV**.) We could also say that this discount rate, when applied to all the future cashflows, will result in a $\sum$ **PV** (total Present Value) which is exactly equal to the original investment, **CFo**, $500,000. This unique discount rate is known as the **Internal Rate of Return**.

The Internal Rate of Return, (IRR)

The *single* discount rate which will produce a Net Present Value = 0 is called the Internal Rate of Return (IRR). Because the IRR is an important measure of investment performance, we will defer any detailed discussion of it to Chapter 3. But before we leave this section, let's address a few anomalies.

Negative Cashflows

Other than the initial cashflow, **CFo**, all of our examples have used positive cashflows occurring in later periods. But there are many circumstances in which negative cashflows occur in financial investments. When you discount a negative future cashflow (or **PMT**) the result is a negative Present Value:

$$\frac{-FV}{(1+i)^n} = -PV$$

Contrary to popular opinion, negative cashflows in and of themselves are not necessarily indicative of a poor investment. Consider a situation in which a $1,000 investment is scheduled to return the following cashflows:

	CFo	(1,000)
End of Period	1	100
	2	200
i = .10	3	1200

If the initial $1,000 is in one lump sum at the beginning of the investment period, the **NPV** of this investment is:

1000 [CHS] [g] [CFo]	**-1,000.00**
100 [g] [CFj]	**100.00**
200 [g] [CFj]	**200.00**
1200 [g] [CFj]	**1,200.00**
10 [i]	**10.00**
solving	
[f] [NPV]	**157.78**

You can also *simultaneously* solve for the IRR:

[f] [IRR] (1,5)	**16.16**

But if the initial $1,000 could be paid in two annual (EOP) installments of $500, note the effect on the **NPV**:

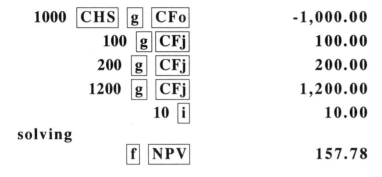

	NPV= CFo **0** + ∑PV
End of Period 1	-500 + 100 = –400
2	-500 + 200 = –300
i = .10 3	1200

translating

Key In	**Display Shows**
0 g CFo	**0.00**
400 CHS g CFj	**-400.00**
300 CHS g CFj	**-300.00**
1200 g CFj	**1,200.00**
10 i	**10.00**
solving	
f NPV	**290.01**[12]

---

[12] Partnership contributions are often "staged" or made over time in order to make the investment more affordable to many investors.

The effect on the IRR is also dramatic:

$$\boxed{f} \quad \boxed{IRR} \qquad\qquad 39.72$$

Many limited partnership interests are sold using "staged" investor contributions. These initial payments are negative (out-of-pocket) payments which may occur simultaneously with return payouts (if any) from operations. The net cashflow position can be depicted by adding the T-bars representing both cashflows:

	Staged Investment	Operating Returns	Net Cashflow
	0	0	0
EOP 1	(1,500)	590	(910)
EOP 2	(1,500)	640	(860)

Although staged initial investments may improve the investor's yield, the General Partner will charge interest on the deferred amounts, thereby reducing the payback. These interest payments should be included as negative cashflows in the periods in which they are payable.

PMTs Occurring at the Beginning of the Period

When we worked with even **PMT**s and the horizontal financial register, we had the ability to select the timing of the **PMT**, either at the **BEGIN**ing (1,7) or at the **END** (1,8) of the period. Unfortunately, the HP–12C does not provide this option when working with uneven **PMT**s. Regardless of whether the calculator is set to BEGIN or END, the calculator delivers the **NPV** of uneven cashflows as though the cashflows *always* occur at the **END** of each period. But there are many circumstances in which the the cashflows are paid in advance, such as in real property leases, equipment and automobile leases, and partnership contributions, to name a few.

Therefore the answer to the problem presented earlier, involving the value of the industrial lease, though accurately determined, is not probable because **PMT**s under the lease would undoubtedly[13] be made in advance, at the beginning of the rental period. Since the calculator cannot be adapted to make this change, you will have to make it.

The problem can be solved easily by removing the first cashflow and solving the problem as though the second cashflow occurred at the end of period one – which is so close to the beginning of the second period that we can consider them to be simultaneous. When the Present Value has been determined, the first cashflow is added back at full value since it is received at the beginning of the investment and is therefore not subject to a discount.

---

[13] They don't <u>have</u> to paid in advance. You are free to construct any arrangement satisfactory to both parties.

After omitting the first cashflow, proceed to solve the problem:

As Originally Presented				**As It Should Be**			
			(?)				(?)
EOP	1	12000		EOP	1	12000
	2	12000			2	12000
	3	12000			3	12000
i = .15÷12	'	"		i = .15÷12	'	"
	'	"			35	12000
	36	12000			36	13000
	37	13000			'	"
	'	"			'	"
	'	"			59	13000
	60	13000			60	14000
	61	14000			'	"
	'	"			'	"
	'	"			83	14000
	84	14000				

The first series of cashflows now consists of $12,000 paid 35 times. We extracted the first **PMT** of $12,000; as a result, all the succeeding **CFj** s advance one period in time.

The keystrokes are:

Key In	**Display Shows**
0 g CFo	0.00
12000 g CFj	12,000.00
35 g Nj	35.00
13000 g CFj	13,000.00
24 g Nj	24.00
14000 g CFj	14,000.00
24 g Nj	24.00
15 g i	1.25

solving

| *f* NPV | 650,811.59 |

(Now add back the initial cashflow of $12,000 which was removed)

| 12000 ⊞ | 662,811.59 |

Therefore the lease for this building, which calls for payments in advance, and using a 15% discount rate, has a **Present Value** which is $8,182.85 ($662,811.59 - 654,628.74) greater than the same lease which calls for **PMTs** at the **END** of the period.

Now that you understand how to handle the first payment when it occurs at the very beginning of the cashflow series, why not let the calculator do the addition for you.

You can do this by placing the first **PMT** in **CFo** as a <u>positive</u> number. The calculator treats the series as it does in the **NPV** example: it will determine the $\sum$ **PV** of the series and then add it to the value stored in **CFo**. Presto!

This method of handling payments which are made at the beginning of the investment is also applicable to computer spreadsheets. (=NPV(rate,nper,PMT) + **CFo**)

Handling Constant Growth Cashflows Which Exceed Calculator Memory

There are many instances when you will be called upon to determine the Present Value of a capital sum which grows at a constant rate over very long periods of time. For example:

> Determine the present value of an annuity of $1,000 which grows at a constant rate of 4.5% per annum over 50 years. Payments are received at the EOP, and the applicable discount rate is 8%.

This situation presents two problems: first to determine the 50 annual cashflows increased at the rate of 4.5% p.a., and then to enter these fifty different cashflows into a calculator which will accept only 20 distinct entries.

The solution is much more easily handled by applying the formula , presented in Chapter 1, for the **PV** of a finite annuity, growing at a constant rate **g,** for **n** periods, **PMTs** at EOP:

$$PV = \frac{C}{(i\text{-}g)}\left(1 - \frac{(1+g)^n}{(1+i)^n}\right)$$

$$PV = \frac{\$1000}{(.08\text{-}.045)}\left(1 - \frac{(1+.045)^{50}}{(1+.08)^{50}}\right)$$

PV =$28571.43 * .80741

PV = $23,068.95

Varying the Discount Rate

The selection of a single discount rate implies that the risk of receiving future payments from an investment will remain constant. In most circumstances this will not be so. As we attempt to anticipate farther into the future, the margin for error increases, as does the risk of not receiving our return cashflows.

For example, it is quite common to value the worth of small business ventures by *varying* the discount rate applied to the future cashflows which can be anticipated from the operation of the business. Unfortunately there is no convenient way[14] to instruct the calculator to vary the discount rate to be applied to a series of future cashflows. If different discount rates are to be used, the **PV** of each future cashflow must be determined using that particular discount rate. Then the total of all the resulting individual **PV**s, the $\sum$ **PV**, can be determined by simple addition.

An example of this occurs in the valuation of small business opportunities. Consider this situation:

> John Bleachsuds is considering the purchase of a well-located coin-operated laundromat in a newly developing section of town. The laundromat has been in operation for just two years and is doing quite well. An examination of the operating records, together with estimates of increased usage by a growing local population, lead Bleachsuds to believe that the laundromat could produce significant gains. In particular, a new apartment house is to be constructed only a few blocks from this location within the next year and will be in operation in two years. If this happens, Bleachsuds estimates the following amounts of net cash from operations:
>
> | | |
> |---|---|
> | Year 1 | $35,000 |
> | Year 2 | 38,500 |
> | Year 3 | 60,000 |
> | Year 4 | 65,000 |
> | Year 5 | 70,000 |
>
> Bleachsuds is comfortable with discounting the first year's income @ 25%, and the second year's income @30%. But confidence in his own estimates of income for the outyears is shakier, and he feels that he must have a 50% return to justify the risk that the apartment house may never be built.

---

[14] Yes, the calculator can be programmed to perform this kind of calculation, but programming a hand-held calculator is, at best, cumbersome in comparison to solving this kind of problem on a computer spreadsheet

This is the kind of problem which cannot be solved on a financial calculator in one operation. But we can solve the problem by breaking it down into its component parts, determining the PV for each part and then adding the PVs together:

Let's construct three T-Bars:

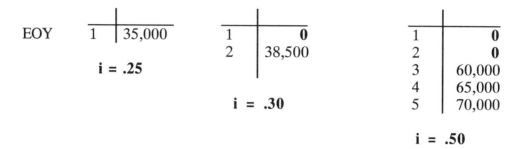

Notice that zeros have been inserted in the second and third T-Bars to maintain the time relationships among the payments. (If you were to add these three T-Bars horizontally, the result would be the cashflow originally described.)

By applying the methods we have already described, the following PVs are calculated:

PV Year 1 @ 25%............$28,000
PV Year 2 @ 30%..............22,781
PV Yrs. 3,4,5 @ 50%............39,835
$\sum$ PV $90,616

The great difficulty in determining the value of a small business opportunity is the task of ascertaining accurate, present-income numbers, as well as estimating the business' potential for future growth. For this reason, discount rates, reflecting increased uncertainty (risk), are usually quite high.

Chapter Summary

1. Whenever PMTs are unequal in amount or sign, the determination of the Present Value of a cashflow must be made by using the CFo, CFj and Nj registers.

2. The determination of the Present Value of an uneven cashflow (EOP) follows the same formula used in the determination of the PV of even cashflows:

$$PV = \frac{C_1}{(1+i)^1} + \frac{C_2}{(1+i)^2} + \frac{C_3}{(1+i)^3} + \frac{C_4}{(1+i)^4} = \frac{C_5}{(1+i)^5} \ ....$$

3. The HP-12C can never accommodate more than 20 *separate* cashflow entries, and at times less than 20. Each separate cashflow, however, may be repeated up to 99 times per storage register.

4. There is no button to adjust uneven cashflows for BEGIN or END of period. When the first cashflow occurs at the beginning of the period it should be removed from the cashflow stream, the PV of the remaining cashflows determined, and then the original cashflow added back.

5. Discounting all future cashflows and totaling their numbers results in the Present Value of an investment. If the original cash invested is then subtracted, the result is the Net Present Value of an Investment. If no initial cash were invested, the result would simply be the Present Value of the investment.

6. That single discount rate which, when applied to all future cashflows results in a total PV exactly equal to the original investment, is called the Internal Rate of Return.

7. Risk is the likelihood that a beneficial future event (reward) may never happen. High risk situations indicate the use of high discount rates, **i.** Risk runs with reward.

8. Discounting a Future Value (or PMT) which is negative results in a negative Present Value.

9. In those instances when different discount rates are to be applied to a cashflow series, the separate PVs must be determined for each discount rate. The resulting PVs can then be added together.

10. The value of income-producing property depends on the Principle of Anticipation: the owner of the property anticipates the future receipt of cashflows and, by discounting them, places a Present Value on his property.

   The Present Value of *any* investment, in fact, is equal to the discounted value of all anticipated cash returns.

Chapter 3
The Internal
Rate of Return

The IRR is undoubtedly the most arcane of all the indices of financial performance. Few investors outside the institutional investment community use the IRR. The average investor has only a muddy understanding of it, if at all, and is typically not motivated to study its usefulness. Yet, properly understood and used, it is an excellent yardstick of *overall* investment performance since it measures investment performance over the entire holding period.

We have already defined the IRR in Chapter 2 in the section dealing with uneven cashflows. The IRR is a discount rate, but a very special and unique discount rate. The IRR is:

> ...that certain, *single* discount rate, which - when applied to all future cashflows - results in Present Values whose total is exactly equal to the initial investment.[1]

IRR Under Different Aliases

Bankers have a special name for their IRR[2]: they call it "yield." The true interest rate charged to borrowers (which, under federal Regulation Z, a lender must disclose to a borrower) is more commonly known as the APR: the <u>A</u>nnual <u>P</u>ercentage <u>R</u>ate.

When next you enter a bank lobby and see a stanchion sign advertising a Certificate of Deposit rate as "4% (4.38% APR)," you will recognize that the stated, or *nominal*, rate of

---

[1] If $\sum PV = CFo$, and CFo is made negative, then $\sum PV + CFo = 0$.

[2] Also known as the "Infernal Rate of Return."

interest paid by that depository is 4%, but that as a result of compounding, the yield, or the *effective* rate of interest, to the depositor is 4.38%.

IRR, Yield and APR are all one and the same measuring stick under different brand aliases. A banker's "yield" = automobile dealer's "APR" on auto leases = investor's "IRR" on an apartment house.

IRR - a Calculator or Computer Supplied Discount Rate

By this time you should be comfortable in your ability to discount a series of cashflows if *given* a discount rate. Oftentimes an investment problem does not supply an initial cash investment (CFo); it's up the analyst to determine an appropriate discount rate and apply it to future cashflows to determine the Present Value of the cashflow.

At other times, however, the cash initially required for the investment is specified, and the subsequent cashflows are estimated based on economic and financial assumptions and projections of future performance.[3] The problem then becomes to determine the IRR on the investment *given these particular cashflows*. Given the required data, the calculator – not the investor – supplies the discount rate, or yield.

Let's take a very simple situation to demonstrate the **IRR**.

In the preceding chapter, you worked through an example of valuing a small business opportunity (the coin-operated laundry) using different discount rates for different periods in the cashflow.

Let's examine this kind of structure again (but using small and simpler numbers):

		(125)
End of Period	1	50
	2	60
	3	70

Let's assume that the receipt of 50 at the end of period 1 may be quite secure and we would be justified in using a 10% discount rate against the first **PMT**. But because the receipt of the second **PMT**, 60, is less likely, a discount rate of 15% is more appropriate. Lastly, because the receipt of the third **PMT**, 70, is even less likely, a discount rate of 20% is used.

---

[3] A pro-forma

[4] In fact, this is the method commonly used to evaluate the worth of small businesses. Their future net operating income is estimated and then discounted, typically at increasing annual rates, over a period of future years. The $\sum PV$ of the NOIs becomes the asking price of the business.

There is no way that we can enter all three **PMTs** in the calculator and discount each one, in one operation, using different discount rates. That's a task for the computer.[5] But we can determine the Present Value for each separate **PMT**, using its appropriate discount rate, and then add the sum of the **PVs** together to determine $\sum$ **PV**. Let's do that:

$$(1) \quad PV_1 \quad = \quad \frac{50}{(1+.10)^1} \quad = \quad 45.45$$

$$(2) \quad PV_2 \quad = \quad \frac{60}{(1+.15)^2} \quad = \quad 45.37$$

$$(3) \quad PV_3 \quad = \quad \frac{70}{(1+.20)^3} \quad = \quad \underline{40.51}$$

$$\sum PV \quad = \quad 131.33$$

But if it is *given* that the **CFo** of this investment is 125, the task becomes to determine that *single* discount rate which will cause the $\sum$**PV** of the three **PMTs,** when added together, to total 125, not 131.33. We begin by entering the cashflows as we have previously:

Key In	Display Shows	Comments
f CLX	0.00	Clears registers
125 CHS g CFo	-125.00	Stores CFo in R_0; sets n = 0
50 g CFj	50.00	Stores value in R_1
60 g CFJ	60.00	Stores value in R_2
70 g CFJ	70.00	Stores value in R_3
solving		
f IRR (1,5)	19.44	the IRR of this cashflow

Iteration

You probably noticed that the calculator flashed "..**running**.." and that it took some time to find the answer. The reason for this is that there is no pre-programmed formula built into a calculator (or computer) chip which will lead directly to the IRR. Instead, the calculator proposes a discount rate to itself and "tests and fits"[6] to see whether this discount rate will result in an $\sum$PV which, when added to the –**CFo,**[7] will exactly total zero.

---

[5] Most of the principles and techniques covered in this text can easily be translated to the computer using Excel® or Lotus 1-2-3®. Both contain financial functions that are pre-programmed to perform these calculations.

[6] This repetitive process is called Iteration.

If the result is less than zero (negative), the calculator chose too high a discount rate.[8] If the addition of $\sum$PV and –CFo results in a value greater than zero (positive), the discount rate was too low. In either case, the calculator "tests and fits" a discount rate until it discovers that *single rate* which will produce a $\sum$PV which, when added to the –CFo will net precisely to zero. That rate is the Internal Rate of Return for this cashflow series. You can readily see why the **IRR** is alternately defined *as that single discount rate which will cause the Net Present Value of a cashflow to equal zero.*

Your calculator now contains the **IRR** which is stored in $\boxed{i}$. Leave it there for the following computations. Now, using the **IRR** stored in **i** as the discount rate,[9] determine the **PV** for each of the cashflows and add them up.

$$(1) \quad \mathbf{PV}_1 = \frac{50}{(1+.1944)^1} = 41.86$$

$$(2) \quad \mathbf{PV}_2 = \frac{60}{(1+.1944)^2} = 42.06$$

$$(3) \quad \mathbf{PV}_3 = \frac{70}{(1+.1944)^3} = \underline{41.08}$$

$$\sum \mathbf{PV} = 125.00 \quad \text{(the CFo)}$$

This proves that the single discount rate which we computed, 19.44%, when applied to each future cash flow, will produce three **PV**s, the sum of which is exactly equal to our original investment of $125.00. **That single discount rate *is* the IRR.**

The IRR by Construction

Another way we might determine the IRR is by *construction.*. You may have once solved problems in geometry by constructing physical models of the problem and then *measuring* to find the answer. Examine the following cashflow, then plot the Net Present Values, using as discount rates, 12%, 14%, 16%, 18%, 20%, 22% and 24%.[10]

---

7 The addition results in zero because the CFo is entered as a negative number.

8 See–Saw Marjorie Daw: Discount rates sit on one end of a teeter-board and Present Values on the other.

9 Retrieve the IRR from **i**, add one to it, store it in 9 and use it as the denominator of the fraction.

10 Enter the cashflows only once; then change the discount rate in **i** to obtain the NPV

		−1,000
End of Period	1	200
	2	300
i = as above	3	400
	4	500
	5	600

You should have obtained the Net Present Values in the table at the right for each discount rate.

If you plot the Net Present Value against the Discount Rate, you can see where the curve will cross the x (horizontal) axis. This point on the curve (where NPV = 0) represents the IRR.

As you can see, the curve crosses the **x** axis about half way between 22% and 24%. The actual IRR is 23.3%.

% Discount Rate	Net Present Value
12	361
14	284
16	213
18	149
20	89
22	33
24	-18

The IRR is that discount rate which causes the NPV = 0

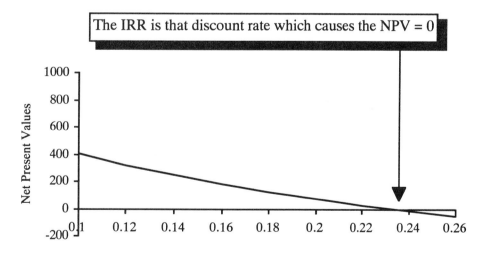

Discount Rate Applied to Cash Flow

Therefore, if you can construct a few points which represent a number of Net Present Values which decline and eventually turn from positive to negative (cross the x axis), you can probably "sketch in" the curve as it crosses the x axis, and then make a very useable estimate of the IRR.

The IRR By Interpolation

NPV   Discount Rate

```
+33 _|           |_____ 22%
     |           |
     |           |
     |           |
   0 _|           |_____ 23.3%
     |           |
     |           |
 -18 _|           |_____ 24%
```

There is still another way to arrive at this special number. Notice in the diagram to the left, that the Net Present Values (left) cross the zero NPV line from positive to negative between the NPVs points of +33 and −18. These NPVs correspond to discount rates (on the right) of 22% and 24% respectively.

The absolute distance between 33 and -18 is 51. A Net Present Value of zero, therefore, would lie 33/51 along a line proceeding from 22 to 24, an absolute distance of 2. But 33/51 of 2 = 1.30. Therefore the IRR lies at a point which is 1.30 along the line from 22% to 24%, or 22.0%+1.30% = 23.3%.

What Does The IRR Tell Us ?

These graphic examples of the **IRR** are meant to emphasize that the IRR is a particular discount rate: It is that *single discount rate* which will render the NPV of a cashflow equal to 0. Since the discount rate is also a yield, the IRR is the *yield* which can be expected if the investment is held *for the entire length of time indicated by n.* If one period is added or lost, or if any single cashflow is changed, you can see that the **IRR** must also change.

What the IRR really tells us is the rate at which we are accumulating wealth on the cash *remaining* in the investment, *measured over the entire life of the investment.* In most cases, the cash which we have remaining in an investment, at any one moment, is our *net equity* in the investment. Therefore one use of the IRR may be to help us choose, from investment opportunities of similar risk, that investment most likely to render us the greatest yield on invested equity.

In addition to helping make an initial investment decision, the IRR can also help quantify the result of changes made in our investment strategy. For example, what effect on future yield can be anticipated as the result of refinancing an investment? When should an investment be sold? Is the indicated IRR return commensurate with the discernable risk in a particular investment which may be offered to us? The IRR is a valuable tool, but there are some limitations.

Limitations to the IRR

The investment which produces the highest **IRR** may not always be the best investment, either from the point of risk[11] or from a financial point of view.

Consider this cashflow:

		(1,000)
End of Period	1	0
	2	0
i = ?	3	2500

Key In	Display Shows	Comments
f CLX	0.00	Clears all memory
1000 CHS g CFo	-1000.00	Stores value in R0
0 g CFj	0.00	Stores 0 in R1
2 g Nj	2.00	0 PMT occurs twice
2500 g CFj	2,500.00	Last PMT into R2
solve f IRR	35.72	The IRR for this series

This percentage return would be considered excellent by most investors. But the fact that the entire cash return occurs at the end of the investment period suggests there may be significant risk associated with this investment.[12] The old adage *"..a bird in hand is worth two in the bush..."* was probably coined following someone's sobering investment experience in which a significant pay-off, promised far in the future, never materialized.

The second caution to be exercised in selecting an investment based on the **IRR** alone is that the discount rate, or percentage yield, ought not be the sole objective of investing. The objective is *dollars* gained over the distance run, not percentage rates achieved.[13]

To illustrate, let's propose two investment opportunities available to an investor with $50,000. The first requires an initial investment of $45,000 and returns the following cashflow:

---

[11] The IRR is a number *derived* from other numbers at hand. It is not a discount rate *selected* as the result of careful risk assessment. Therefore the IRR neither measures nor accurately reflects risk.

[12] The investor must wait three periods to finds out if the investment will pay off.

[13] This is precisely why most wealthy investors eventually avoid high-risk/high yield investments. Smaller percentage returns on large capital investments return very satisfactory dollar results.

End of Period		-45,000
	1	10,000
	2	20,000
	3	30,000

The **IRR** of this investment is 13.3% and will return a raw total of $60,000 over 3 periods. But the investor will have $5,000 extra which he has not yet invested.

The second investment consumes the investor's entire $50,000 and generates the following cashflow:

End of Period		-50,000
	1	8,000
	2	15,000
	3	45,000

The **IRR** for this investment is less, 13.0%. But it will return a raw total of $68,000.

Unless the investor, after making the first investment of $45,000, can invest the remaining $5,000 of his cash in an investment which can earn 16.96%,[14] he may favor the second investment even though it may be somewhat more risky and carries a lower IRR. The second investment simply returns more (quantity) money in the same time frame. "Percentages" are not the sole selection standard of a "good" investment, nor do they pay rent.

Multiple IRRs for the Same Cashflow

A popular pastime for financial academes is to point out that more than one **IRR** may exist for the same cashflow.[15]

The following example is illustrative only. There are very few instances in the real world when multiple **IRR** solutions become a business problem.[16]

End of Period		- 10,000
	1	60,000
	2	(110,000)
	3	60,000

---

[14] $5,000 invested for three years requires a 16.96% annual return rate to yield $8,000.

[15] Following Descartes "rule of signs," there are as many solutions to a polynomial as there are changes of sign.

[16] One great financial skill worth cultivating is the ability to step back from a situation and ask "Does this result make sense?"

$$CFo = \frac{PMT}{(1+i)^{\wedge}1} + \frac{PMT}{(1+i)^{\wedge}2} + \frac{PMT}{(1+i)^{\wedge}3}$$

$$10{,}000 = \frac{60000}{(1+i)^{\wedge}1} + \frac{(110000)}{(1+i)^{\wedge}2} + \frac{60000}{(1+i)^{\wedge}3}$$

There are three possible solutions for **i** : 0%, 100% and 200%.

1) At 0% $10{,}000 = \dfrac{60000}{(1+0)^{\wedge}1} + \dfrac{(110000)}{(1+0)^{\wedge}2} + \dfrac{60000}{(1+0)^{\wedge}3}$

$$= \quad 60{,}000 \quad - \quad 110{,}000 \quad + \quad 60{,}000$$
$$= \quad 10{,}000$$

2) At 100% $10{,}000 = \dfrac{60000}{(1+1)^{\wedge}1} + \dfrac{(110000)}{(1+1)^{\wedge}2} + \dfrac{60000}{(1+1)^{\wedge}3}$

$$= \quad \frac{60000}{2} \quad + \quad \frac{(110000)}{4} \quad + \quad \frac{60000}{8}$$

$$= \quad 30{,}000 \quad - \quad 27{,}500 \quad + \quad 7{,}500$$
$$= \quad 10{,}000$$

3) At 200% $10{,}000 = \dfrac{60000}{(1+2)^{\wedge}1} + \dfrac{(110000)}{(1+2)^{\wedge}2} + \dfrac{60000}{(1+2)^{\wedge}3}$

$$= \quad \frac{60000}{3} \quad + \quad \frac{(110000)}{9} \quad + \quad \frac{60000}{27}$$

$$= \quad 20{,}000 \quad - \quad 12{,}222 \quad + \quad 2{,}222$$
$$= \quad 10{,}000$$

Reinvestment Rate of Payments – Does It Matter?

Another frequently asserted limitation of the **IRR** is that the attainment of the Internal Rate of Return depends upon a reinvestment, at a rate of return equal to the IRR, of the **PMT**s flowing *from* the investment. Some contend that unless the **PMT**s derived from the investment can be reinvested at the same **IRR**, then the **IRR** is illusory.

Consider this T-Bar and tabulation of a cashflow showing the progress of an initial investment of $479.59. The **PMT**s (100, 125 ...etc.) are cashflows produced by, and removed from, the investment as they occur. The **IRR** of this cashflow is 15%.

		(479.59)
End of Period	1	100
	2	125
IRR = 15%	3	150
	4	175
	5	200

You will recall that a discount rate and an interest rate are opposite sides of the same coin. The IRR *is* a discount rate. Therefore the IRR can also be treated as an interest rate.

The table below depicts the progress of the investment as the cash, *remaining in the investment after withdrawal of the PMTs,* earns interest at the IRR rate:

Beginning Balance	Interest Rate	Principal Plus Interest	Withdrawal (PMT)	Remaining Balance
479.59	0.15	551.53	**-100**	451.53
451.53	0.15	519.26	**-125**	394.26
394.26	0.15	453.40	**-150**	303.40
303.40	0.15	348.91	**-175**	173.91
173.91	0.15	200.00	**-200**	0.00

The table shows that the net balance of the investment (NPV) will be zero at the end of the holding period. During the period of the investment, the *remaining balances* earn interest at the **IRR** rate. The rate at which the **PMTs** could be reinvested does not affect the **IRR** of this cashflow. Therefore the contention that the **IRR** depends upon the reinvestment rate of the **PMTs** is not valid.

But since the IRR measures the rate of return on cash *remaining* in the investment, what happens to the PMTs may affect the overall performance of the investor's *portfolio* – and this is probably what some financial pundits seek to establish. Investing the *payments* from this investment at rates either higher or lower than the IRR of this investment will not change the IRR of this investment, but investing the proceeds at a certain rate will definitely have an influence on the overall *portfolio* return. Logic which proposes that an investment yielding a high IRR should be rejected solely because the cash flowing from the investment cannot be reinvested at the same attractive rate is pure financial sophistry.

Aside from these limitations, some consider that the **N**et **P**resent **V**alue of an investment to be a better measuring stick because it : 1) deals with cash returns and not percentages; 2) forces the investor to address the issue of risk by requiring the *active selection* of a discount rate rather than forcing one mathematically; 3) offers the opportunity to assign different discount rates for different periods of the investment.

The IRR and the Problem of Negative Cashflows

The **IRR** calculation handles negative cashflows which may occur in the investment series in exactly the same way it does positive payments: it discounts them back and produces a negative –PV. These negative PVs are added to the positive PVs to produce the $\sum$ **PV**.

Consider this cashflow:

		(50,000)
End of Year	1	10,000
	2	-5,000
	3	85,000

The **IRR** of this investment is 23.45% The investor in this situation is being called upon to supply an additional $5,000 at the end of year 2. One assumption implicit in this financial structure is that the investor can invest a certain sum at the beginning of the investment (an additional **CFo**) at the same internal return rate of 23.45% for 2 years in order to accumulate cash to cover this future negative **PMT**. How many investments abound which offer an interest rate of 23.45% each year for two years?

The Modified Internal Rate of Return: (MIRR)

This distortion in the **IRR** is the reason for Modifying the **IRR** to produce the **MIRR**: the Modified Internal Rate of Return – or, as some would have it, the **FMRR** (Financial Management Rate of Return).

For those who wish to use the **IRR** method for cashflows containing significant negative **PMTs**, the MIRR method provides adjustments to compensate for the fact that the IRR discounts negative sums at the same rate as for positive sums. The financial reality is that it is extremely difficult to invest small initial sums (PVs) at a large interest rate. Let's reconsider the previous example:

		(50,000)
End of Year	1	10,000
	2	-5,000
	3	85,000

The **IRR** of this investment is 23.45%.

This investment requires two negative **PMTs** from the investor: one at the very beginning in the amount of –$50,000 (the **CFo**), and a second, –$5,000, at the end of the second period. The Present Value of the second negative **PMT**, discounted at the **IRR** of 23.45% is –$3,280.86.

Since the probability of being able to invest so small an amount, $3,280.86, at so great a rate of return, 23.45%, for so short a period, is usually quite low, we need to adjust this cashflow to reflect a more conservative (and realistic) estimate of return.

One method of covering this future cash requirement would be to set aside an additional amount up-front (in addition to the $50,000) which, invested at a conservative rate of interest, say 5%, would grow to $5,000 at the end of the second period. The availability of this cash would offset the negative **PMT** at the end of the second period.

This amount would be:

	n	**i**	**PV**	**PMT**	**FV**
	2	5	?	0	5,000.00
solving			:		
			−4,535.15		

Our adjusted T-Bar would look like this:

End of Period		(50,000) − 4,535.15 = (54,535.15)
	1	10,000
	2	0
	3	85,000

The **MIRR** of this cashflow is 22.39%, a reduction from the original **IRR** of 23.45%. (Solve for the MIRR exactly as you would for the IRR.)

A second approach would be to reinvest the $10,000 which will be available at the end of period 1 in a conservative investment of low risk in order to have cash available to make the second negative **PMT**. If we could invest $10,000 for one period @ 5% interest, the revised T-Bar would show:

End of Period		(50,000)
	1	0 ¬
	2	-5,000 + 10,500 = **5,500**
	3	85,000

or,

End of Period		(50,000)
	1	0
	2	**5,500**
	3	85,000

Now if we solve for the **MIRR** of this cashflow, we obtain 22.42%, a slightly higher yield than the previous solution.

But it is unnecessary to use all the $10,000, since only a portion of it, invested for one period @ 5%, would yield enough to cover the negative cashflow at the end of the second period. How much, then, of the $10,000 needs to be carried forward for one period in an investment earning 5% to yield $5,000?

	n	i	PV	PMT	FV
solving	1	5	?	0	5,000.00
			:		
			−4,761.90		

The T–Bar now becomes,

		(50,000)
End of Period	1	10,000 − 4,762 ¬ = 5,238
	2	-5,000 + 5,000 = **0**
	3	85,000

The MIRR of this series is 22.94%, the best yield of all three methods.

From a practical standpoint, large negative **PMT**s occurring well down in the cashflow sequence are best taken managed by planning to reinvest *sufficient* previous **PMT**s at a conservative interest rate to cover the future negative **PMT**. This would be cash-sparing since it would require no additional up-front investment. If the negative **PMT**s occur early in the cashflow, however, there may be no choice but to provide for them by an additional **CFo** invested separately in a low-risk investment at a conservative rate of interest. In any case, the MIRR will *always* be less than the IRR.

Providing most efficiently for the future negative cashflows which may be encountered in an otherwise attractive investment is a hallmark of good cashflow management.

Note: The HP–12C handbook suggests discounting, at the safe rate, all negative cashflows back to present value, and compounding all positive cashflows forward at the "re-investment rate"; then to solve for the IRR. This method will always result in a lower investment yield than the method described here. The HP method is also one source of the commonly heard "the IRR depends on the re-investment rate." If one chooses the re-investment rate, why bother determining the IRR or MIRR? Use the NPV method instead.

Chapter Summary

1. The Internal Rate of Return is that single discount rate which will convert all future payments to present values whose sum will be exactly equal to the cash originally invested.

2. The IRR is <u>not an average</u> of periodic rates of return, but rather a single discount rate, and therefore a yield, expressed on a per period basis, which may be realized if the investment delivers the projected cashflows and is held for all the planned number of periods.

3. The calculations necessary to determine the **IRR** <u>do not</u> involve risk assessment, although a high IRR may suggest risk. Therefore the investor or financial analyst may wish also to compute the Net Present Value of the investment, a process which requires the discount rate to be selected with due consideration given to risk.

4. There are certain technical limitations to the **IRR**, such as the possibility of multiple solutions. Though real, the possibility is considered remote when dealing with real-world investments. Nevertheless, the investor/analyst should be alert when dealing with cashflows whose **PMT**s change sign (+ –) frequently. There will potentially be as many separate IRR solutions as there are changes in sign.

5. While the calculation of the **IRR** is mathematically precise, the estimates of future **PMT**s upon which the **IRR** is based may be moderate, conservative or highly optimistic. Therefore expressing an **IRR** to the second decimal point may be grossly misleading by implying a degree of precision to the whole exercise which is inconsistent with the precision of underlying assumptions.

6. The Modified Internal Rate of Return, **MIRR (or Financial Management Rate of Return - FMRR)**, overcomes some of the problems posed by negative **PMT**s which occur in a cashflow series. In order to maintain the highest possible rate of return, *sufficient* cash flowing from a previous period should be reinvested at a conservative rate to cover future negative cashflows.

7. The calculated **IRR** is not at all dependent upon the rate at which outflowing **PMT**s can be reinvested in a subsequent investment. But prudent <u>portfolio</u> management will take into consideration the options available for the reinvestment of funds in managing the entire amount available for investment.

Chapter 4
Cashflows from Stocks and Bonds

Stocks and bonds comprise an important part of a well-balanced portfolio, so it is essential to understand how these financial investments return cash to the investor and how a rate of return on this cash can be measured.

An analysis of the cashflows produced by stocks and bonds, however, is not the equivalent of an analysis of the economic fundamentals which produce these cashflows. That's a task for the stock or bond analyst. But given economic projections relevant to an issue, and the cashflows they imply, it's our task to measure and rate the returns which can be anticipated from ownership.

Cashflows from Stocks

Many investors buy stocks on their past record. But today's value of any financial investment is not measured by what has already happened, but rather by what is likely to happen in the future. Most of these same investors would not buy a 20–year old racehorse because of the number of races he has already won; they would probably be more interested to know how many races he *can* win in the future.

Stocks, too, depend for their present market value on their future cashflows. These future cashflows can be separated into two neat piles: first, the dividends which a stock will pay over the contemplated holding period, and, second, the amount of gain – or loss – it will produce when sold at the end of the holding period.

The dividend which a stock pays can be regarded as a periodic **PMT.** For the most part, companies which pay dividends increase and decrease their dividend amounts depending on current earnings and the firm's forecasted requirement for cash to fund future projects. The gain (or loss) involved in the valuation also includes the amount of appreciation (or loss) in value which the investor will experience when he sells the stock. The final cashflow, the gain or loss, is exactly equivalent to our concept of the reversionary value, or Future Value. But in order to maintain touch with the subject matter, we will use **DVD** to represent the periodic PMT, and P_n to represent the final price (FV) when the stock is sold in **year$_n$**.

Market Capitalization Rate

We can express the rate of return, $\boxed{r}$, which can be expected from the ownership of a stock over a single period as:

$$r = \frac{DVD_1 + (P_1 - P_0)}{P_0}$$

where P_0 is the original price paid and P_1 is the sale price obtained one period (year) later. This rate of return, $\boxed{r}$, is known as the stock's **Market Capitalization Rate.** It is the *yield* which the market expects from the future cashflows. It is identical to the discount rate $\boxed{i}$ with which we are already very familiar:

For example,

> An industry analyst forecasts that the stock of ABC Tek, currently selling for $50 per share, will earn $6.25 per share in the coming year, and that the price will advance to $55. The dividend is also expected to be increased to $2.50, in line with the company's current dividend policy of distributing 40% of earnings to shareholders.
>
> What is the expected rate of return on this future cashflow?

The expected market capitalization rate is:

$$r = \frac{\$2.50 + (\$55 - 50)}{\$50}$$

$$r = .15 = 15\%$$

Current Stock Price When Cap Rate Is Known

If the average market capitalization rate for companies *of similar risk* in this particular industry were already known – say 15% – the present price[1] (P_0) of ABC Tek could also have been determined using the forecasted dividend and estimate of future price:

$$r = \frac{DVD_1 + P_1 - P_0}{P_0}$$

$$P_0 * r = DVD_1 + P_1 - P_0$$

$$P_0 + P_0 * r = DVD_1 + P_1$$

$$P_0 = \frac{DVD_1 + P_1}{1+r}$$

$$P_0 = \frac{\$2.50 + 55.00}{1.15}$$

$$P_0 = \$50.00$$

And in Subsequent Years....

If we accept that both the dividend and current price of ABC Tek will grow at a 10% annual rate during the second year of ownership, we can calculate the Present Value of ABC Tek's stock at the beginning of the second year by dividing the cashflows by (1 + market capitalization rate)

$$P_1 = \frac{DVD_2 + P_2}{(1+r)}$$

$$P_1 = \frac{\$2.50 * 1.10 + \$55.00 * 1.10}{(1.15)}$$

$$P_1 = \$55$$

We can also express the current (P_0) market value of the stock by reference to the discounted value of the first year's dividend *plus* the discounted value of next year's price, P_1.

$$P_0 = \frac{DVD_1}{1.15} + \frac{P_1}{(1.15)}$$

$$P_0 = \frac{\$2.50}{1.15} + \frac{\$55}{(1.15)}$$

$$P_0 = \$2.17 + \$47.83 = \$50.00$$

---

[1] Not "price" but "value," actually, since stocks often trade above and below their true value.

We can, in fact, continue to express the present price of ABC Tek in terms of the discounted value of all the future dividends together with the discounted value of the final sales price at the end of holding period **n**.

$$P_0 = \frac{DVD_1}{1.15^1} + \frac{DVD_2}{1.15^2} + \frac{DVD_3}{1.15^3} + \frac{DVD_4}{1.15^4} \cdots\cdots \frac{DVD_n + P_n}{(1.15)^n}$$

If we assume that the stock will be held in perpetuity, we can disregard the final sales price since its Present Value diminishes to an insignificant sum.

We can show this to be true by determining the cumulative Present Value of all future dividends and the Present Value of the final sales price (both increasing 10% per year) over a very long period of time. For all practical purposes, 100 years can be equated to a perpetuity.[2] The table below shows the respective contributions of the dividends and the final price to total Present Value over a holding period of 100 years. Note that the sum of the two present values always totals $50.00.

YEAR	FUTURE VALUES		PV OF DIVIDEND	PRESENT VALUES OF ...		TOTAL PV
	DIVIDEND	PRICE		CUMULATIVE. DIVIDEND	PRICE	
0		$50.00	$0.00	$0.00	$50.00	$50.00
1	$2.50	$55.00	$2.17	$2.17	$47.83	$50.00
2	$2.75	$60.50	$2.08	$4.25	$45.75	$50.00
3	$3.03	$66.55	$1.99	$6.24	$43.76	$50.00
4	$3.33	$73.21	$1.90	$8.14	$41.86	$50.00
-						
10	$6.48	$129.69	$1.60	$17.94	$32.06	$50.00
-						
50	$293.48	$5,869.54	$0.27	$44.58	$5.42	$50.00
-						
100	$34,451.53	$689,030.62	$0.03	$49.41	$0.59	$50.00

---

[2] Core States Financial, founded in 1781 as Philadelphia National, has paid dividends continuously since 1844. It is one of a group of 200 U.S. firms that are at least 100 years old.

Therefore the current (PV) value of a stock to be held over a long period may be expressed as the sum total of an infinite series of **DVDs**, discounted (capitalized) at the market capitalization rate, **r** :

$$P_0 = \sum_{n=1}^{\infty} \frac{DVDn}{(1+r)^n} = \frac{DVD}{r}$$

This, of course, assumes no growth, or setback, in the dividend.

Current Price When Dividends Grow

If ABC Tek were to make no investments in future growth, the rate of growth, g, would equal zero, and it would undoubtedly distribute most, if not all, its earnings per share (EPS) as dividends. The market might value the stock by capitalizing its fully distributed earnings as it would any annuity projected to continue in perpetuity:

$$P_0 = \frac{DVD}{r} = \frac{EPS}{r} = \frac{\$6.25}{0.15} = \$41.67$$

But we have postulated that ABC Tek will not distribute all its earnings, but rather will re-invest a portion of them in projects which will result in earnings and dividends growing at the rate of 10% (given a consistent dividend policy). Therefore, the value of the stock, with earnings and dividends growing at the rate of 10% and operating in a market environment which capitalizes cashflows at 15%, becomes:

$$P_0 = \frac{DVD}{r-g} = \frac{\$2.50}{.15-.10} = \$50.00 \qquad (\text{Compare to } PV = \frac{PMT}{(i-g)})$$

Stock Price Combines PV of Present & Future Earnings

If the valuation of ABC Tek's stock without growth is $41.67, and the value with growth is $50.00, then the present value of future growth must be the difference between the two:

1. The PV with Future Growth	$50.00
2. The PV without Future Growth	41.67
Present Value of Future Growth	$8.33

But how can we account for this component of total price?

The Contribution of Future Earnings to Present Value

In Chapter 1 it was shown that the Present Value of an infinite series of identical cashflows can be expressed as :

$$PV = \frac{C}{i}$$

If we express the same formula in terms of stocks, we have:

$$P_0 = \frac{DVD}{r}$$

The Present Value of a series of stock cashflows subject to a constant growth rate is:

$$P_0 = \frac{DVD}{r-g}$$

If it is true that –

$$P_0 = \frac{DVD}{(r-g)} \quad \text{then it is also true that} \quad r = \frac{DVD}{P_0} + g$$

or,

Market Capitalization Rate = Dividend Yield Rate + Dividend Growth Rate.[3]

If the company maintains a consistent dividend policy, paying out the same portion of earnings as current dividend, then the growth rate in earnings will equal the growth rate in dividends. This growth component, **g**, of the total return rate, **r**, is a product of a company's **Re-investment Ratio** and its rate of **Return on Equity (ROE)** or,

g (growth rate) = Re-investment Ratio * ROE

Let's take a closer look at these two important elements of the growth rate, the re-investment ratio and the return-on-equity.

The Re-investment Ratio

The portion of current net earnings (EPS) which a company earmarks as dividends is its **Dividend Ratio,** which is $= \frac{DVD}{EPS}$. That portion of retained earnings devoted to funding projects for future growth[4] is its **Re-investment Ratio** $= 1 - \frac{DVD}{EPS}$

The amount of *new* earnings which will flow from the re-investment of a portion of earnings will depend upon the rate, or yield (IRR), at which these re-invested earnings earn

---

[3] This formula holds only so long as g is less than r.

[4] On the assumption that all retained earnings are re-invested. But this is frequently not the case.

new cash. This rate may be equal to, above, but hopefully not below, the company's current Return on Equity.

Return on Equity, a Management Report Card

There is no guaranty that reinvested retained earnings will yield a targeted rate of return. Undoubtedly management will carefully weigh each new potential growth opportunity to develop an estimate of yield (IRR) on the new cash to be invested. Some companies evaluate these new opportunities by posting a required return rate (IRR), or "hurdle rate," and then calculate the Net Present Value of the project. Those projects with a negative NPV are rejected.

The average stockholder, however, may not be privy to all the details about new growth opportunities and future yields, and thus is often forced to assume that the race horse will run in the future as it has in the *recent* past.[5] He will attempt to measure the Return on Equity which management has produced *recently*. To do that he must collect relevant information about costs, profits, earnings and the number of shares currently outstanding. He will use these data to estimate a **Return on Equity**.[6] One estimate of ROE will be:

$$\textbf{Book Equity per share} = \frac{\text{Shareholder investment + retained earnings}}{\text{Total number of shares outstanding}}$$

$$\textbf{ROE} = \frac{\text{Earnings per Share}}{\text{Book Equity per share}}$$

In the case of ABC Tek, we see that it will distribute as dividends 40% ($2.50) of anticipated earnings and re-invest the difference, 60% ($3.75) in growth opportunities. Recent data from ABC Tek's financial reports indicate that it has an ROE of 16.67%. This accounts for the growth rate, **g**:

$$\textbf{g} = \text{Reinvestment Ratio * Return on Equity}$$
$$\textbf{g} = 60\% * 16.67\% = 10\%$$

But in terms of *dollars* of new earning, the result would be:

$$\text{New Earnings} = \underline{\text{EPS(\$6.25)}} * 60\% * 16.67\% = \$0.625 \text{ per share}$$

---

[5] In contrast to the professional investor who concentrates on prospects for future earnings.

[6] In his approach to Value Investing, Warren Buffet starts with "owners' equity" which he defines as "net owner earnings," i.e. reported earnings *plus* depreciation and amortization minus new capital investment. This amount is known as "free cashflow." His valuations are based on this number.

The Present Value of these new earnings, however, must take into account the portion of current earnings re-invested to produce the new cashflow. Therefore we are really interested in the **Net** Present Value of new earnings:

$$\underline{N}PV = -\$3.75 + \frac{\$0.625}{.15} = \$.41667$$

Assuming an annual growth rate of 10%, the market will capitalize these new earnings and add the resulting Present Value to the Present Value of existing earnings.

$$P_0 = \frac{\$6.25}{0.15} + \frac{\$0.41667}{.15 - .10}$$

$$P_0 = \$41.67 + \$8.33 = \mathbf{\$50.00}$$

Therefore, the market may assign a value, P_0, to the stock as a combination of the the *present value of a constant stream of no-growth earnings* plus the *net present value of future earnings.*

It is important to note that the value of a growth stock is not simply equal to the discounted value of all future earnings since future earnings depend on the reinvestment of a portion of current earnings. We cannot recognize all future earnings without also recognizing all the reinvestment amounts needed to produce them. This is why we solved for the Net Present Value rather than the Present Value.

Free Cashflow Per Share

The term "Free Cash Flow" signifies the amount of net after-tax earnings, after adding back depreciation and amortization deductions, <u>which are not retained and reinvested</u> in the business. Therefore Free Cash Flow refers to <u>distributable</u> cash per share.[7]

Therefore the value of a stock can also be expressed as a function of its Free Cash Flow:

$$P_0 = \sum \frac{(\text{Free Cash Flow})_t}{(1+r)^t} = \sum_{t=1}^{\infty} \frac{\text{Free Cash Flow}}{r}$$

---

[7] This is a useful distinction since not all retained earnings may be used to fund growth opportunities.

Conditions For Growth

From the company's point of view, one with good prospects for growth will retain earnings so long as the rate of return on new investment is in excess of the market capitalization rate. Stockholders will accept this strategy this so long as the ROI of new projects is in excess of the market capitalization rate, resulting in price appreciation. They are also encouraged to invest in growth companies when the long term capital gains tax rate is significantly less than the rate on ordinary income (dividends).

For example:

> As Chairman and CEO of ABC Tek, your firm has projected earnings at $6.25 per share. Industry earnings are capitalized at 15%.
>
> Your New Product Development VP, however, presents a new opportunity well within the company's resource capabilities. His projections estimate the the new project will yield (IRR) 15.0% on invested cash (re-invested equity). He asks that you allocate 60% of current EPS to the project.
>
> Should you?

If all projections and performance expectations are met:

ROE * Retained Earning = New Earnings per Share
15% * $3.75 = $0.5625 additional *new* earnings per share

The *Net* Present Value of the new earnings will be:

$$\text{NPV} = -\$3.75 + \frac{\$0.5625}{0.15} = \$0.00$$

Since the project will have a Net Present Value of zero, you would probably not approve the project,[8] nor would you be likely to approve any other new project <u>whose indicated yield would be less than the market capitalization rate of 15%,</u> or which would have a negative NPV; to do so would lower total earnings and the market value of your stock.[9]

If, on the other hand, a different project were offered which indicated a potential yield of 20% on re-invested earnings (higher than current ROE), and subsequent growth of 10% p.a., the contribution to long-term stock value would be attractive:

---

[8] Since there is no additional return, why take the risk?

[9] Any new project with an IRR less than current ROE will result in a loss in stock value, but a project yielding less than the market capitalization rate would depress price below fully distributed earnings.

ROE * Retained Earning = New Earnings per Share

$20\% * 3.75 = \$0.75$

NPV of New Earnings $= -\$3.75 + \dfrac{\$0.75}{0.15} = \$1.25$

$P_0 = \dfrac{\$6.25}{.15} + \dfrac{\$1.25}{.15-10} = \$66.67$

It is easy to see why the leader of the business is always looking for growth opportunities whose yields are projected to be in excess of current Return on Equity.

When Growth is Limited or Nearly Absent

Those companies whose growth prospects are very limited are confined to distributing sufficient earnings in the form of dividends to support the stock's current price. Utility companies, for example, are in a near-constant process of applying for rate increases to increase dividends and maintain share value. Because of the time delay in obtaining such increases, utilities tend to lose market favor during times of significant inflation because they carry below market yields. During times of deflation, they tend to regain investors' favor because their yields are high in relation to current market rates.

Companies which have available to them very excellent opportunities for new investment, with yields in excess of their current market capitalization rates, often retain all, or nearly all, current earnings for future growth. Many of the high-growth technology stocks of the 1990's paid no dividends whatsoever. Investors appear content to have all earned income re-invested for rapid capital appreciation.

When Growth Slows

Wall Street has a saying that *no tree grows to the sky.* Many growth companies reach a point when they can no longer find new investment opportunities promising the high IRRs they achieved when their company (and industry) was young. In these cases, they often increase dividends and buy back large blocks of their outstanding shares in order to support market value per share. In other words, they slowly transform themselves from growth stock companies to income stock companies.

Tendency For ROE To Decline

In the case of ABC Tek, which presently has a satisfactory[10] ROE rate of 16.7% in a very competitive industry, it may be difficult to continually reinvest 60% of its earnings in projects which will yield at least 15%, the market capitalization rate. Let us assume that *after* 5 years its yield on newly invested cash (ROE) decreases to 14% and management increases the dividend payout to 50.0% of EPS. The growth factor, **g**, also declines, as does the stock price, P_0:

g = ROE * Reinvestment Ratio
g = .14 * .50 = .07 = 7.0%

At the <u>end of year 5</u> its P_5 will become:

$$P_5 = \frac{DVD_6}{(r - .07)} \quad \text{and its price, } P_0 \text{, will become:}$$

$$P_0 = \frac{DVD_1}{1+r^1} + \frac{DVD_2}{1+r^2} + \frac{DVD_3}{1+r^3} + \frac{DVD_4}{1+r^4} + \frac{DVD_5}{1+r^5} + \frac{DVD_6}{(1+r)^5*(r-.07)}$$

$$P_0 = \frac{2.50}{(1.15)^1} + \frac{2.75}{(1.15)^2} + \frac{3.02}{(1.15)^3} + \frac{3.33}{(1.15)^4} + \frac{3.66}{(1.15)^5} + \left(\frac{5.03}{(1.15)^5(.15-.07)}\right)$$

$$P_0 = \$41.22$$

As you can see, the Present Value of growth stocks is very sensitive to changes in both the ROE and the Reinvestment Ratios. The so-called "high-flyers" are often stocks which are in very high growth-rate industries, pay little or no dividends, and reinvest all, or almost all, retained earnings in new ventures whose yields are projected to exceed current market capitalization rates. You can conceptualize a high-growth rate stock as:

$$P_0 = \frac{DVD}{r} + g, \quad \text{where} \quad \frac{DVD}{r} = 0$$

Therefore, $P_0 = g$

In contrast, income stocks look like,

$$P_0 = \frac{DVD}{r} + 0.$$

---

[10] Subjective

Stock Value in the Absence of Dividends

When a stock pays no dividends, its Present Value is the discounted value of an estimate of its future price, since there is no source of cashflow other than **F V**.

P/E Ratios, Relationship of Price to Earnings

The P/E ratio used by stock dealers is the quotient produced by dividing a stock's current price by its last reported annual earnings. A stock currently selling for $20 and earning $1.25 last year would have a P/E ratio of 16. If we turn this ratio upside down we have the earnings/price ratio, or market capitalization rate, *which is applicable only to stocks with no (or very little) growth potential.*

$$P_0 = \frac{EPS}{r} + (g = 0)$$

Because it cannot discriminate between stocks which have no growth and stocks with low current earnings but with excellent growth prospects, the P/E ratio based on past earnings has limited usefulness for many investors seeking appreciation. But a more serious limitation of the P/E ratio is that it relies on *past* earnings to indicate value. And if nothing else is clear, it *is* clear that buying a 20-year old race horse is a much different bet from buying a filly whose time trials late last night indicated that she can beat every other horse in tomorrow morning's race.

While it may be somewhat satisfying to understand the basic financial theory underlying cashflow valuation of stocks, the devil is in the details. Here are some things to ponder.

> * Current earnings which are capitalized at the market capitalization rate are not guaranteed to infinity. Core businesses are also subject to risk, to change and to competition. Increased industry competition increases risk perception and tends to raise market capitalization rates and lower stock prices.
> * The market changes its perception of risk associated with a company's prospects for growth. High yields, especially in industries with low thresholds of entry, invariably invite competition which reduces market share, lowers prices, lowers profits, lowers earnings and eventually shareholder value.
> * A company may retain a significant portion of its earnings for a "rainy day." This is especially true in cyclic industries such as autos and housing which frequently adopt a defensive posture as a means of self-preservation. These retained earnings, which are not invested at the company's market capitalization rate, increase net assets and tend to reduce return on net equity.
> * High growth rates in new industries are difficult to sustain, not only because of increased competition but also because of rapidly changing technology. The growth factor, **g**, becomes harder and harder to accomplish.

Bonds

Bonds are essentially different from equities (stocks) in that they represent no ownership interest in the company; they are, in fact, I.O.U.s made by the issuing entity and secured by assets of one sort or another.[11]

Bonds take on a nomenclature related to the issuing entity: those issued by a city or state are "municipal" bonds; those issued by corporations are "corporate" bonds, while those issued either by the federal government, or an agency of the federal government, are "federal" or "agency" bonds.

There are many other sub-classifications of bonds which have very significant import for investors and financial planners. Those interested in this *anything-but-dry* subject of *bonds* are encouraged to investigate and read further. For our part, we want to look carefully at how the value of bonds is determined in anticipation of the *cashflows* they promise to the investor.

Bond Value Predicated on Anticipated Cashflows

The value of *all* financial investments depends on the *Present Value* of cashflows which the owner can reasonably anticipate during his period of ownership.[12] Bonds are no exception. Bonds are somewhat unique, however, in that they *almost always* combine a series of payments, PMTs, with a reversionary value, FV. Bonds are often (and accurately) described as mortgages, but unlike mortgages which typically amortize to zero value,[13] bonds seldom amortize to zero value: they customarily have a reversionary value at term of $1,000 and act like interest-only $1,000 promissory notes.

In the case of bonds, the PMTs are the *interest* payments to be received during the holding period, while the Future Value (FV) is the amount of cash which the holder of the bond will receive when the bond is redeemed.

---

[11] "Bonds" are debt instruments secured by a pledge of assets; "Debentures" are unsecured debt instruments.

[12] A recurrent theme.

[13] Or at least are *scheduled* to do so.

Timing and Reversionary Value of Bonds

Most bonds issued in the United States are designed to pay interest semi-annually, in arrears. Therefore the last PMT which the bond holder receives at maturity is a combination of the redemption value of the bond *plus* the last interest payment.

In Chapter 2, we stressed the need for caution in characterizing the timing of the cashflows. You will recall that many reversionary sums (FVs) are due at the end of the holding period along with the last cashflow from operations, or – in the case of mortgages – with the last payment due in the schedule. Bonds fit this note of caution since the redemption value (FV) will always be made concurrently with the last interest payment. Do not schedule the last interest payment (PMT) and then schedule the redemption value (FV) one period later. Doing so will distort your calculations regarding the true yield-to-maturity.

When Bonds Are "Called"

We are hedging the point a bit when we refer to the last payment as the reversionary value rather than simply referring to a par value of $1,000. This is because many issuers reserve the right to "call," or redeem, the bond before its scheduled maturity date. In these cases, the "call" price is always greater than the par value of the bond.

Bond "Coupon" Rate and Maturity Date

The *coupon* [14] *rate* of the bond is the rate of interest stated in the bond document at the time of issuance. This is the annual interest rate which will be paid <u>over the life of the bond</u>. Therefore a bond issued with a 7% "coupon" will pay:

Coupon Rate x Face Value = Annual Interest Payment

.07   x $1,000   = $70.00

The PMT, $70 in this case, will almost *never change*. Almost all bonds issued in the United States are designed to pay interest *semi-annually, in arrears*. Therefore the actual amount received by the bond holder in the example above will be $35.00 every six months.

The maturity date stated in the bond document is the date on which the issuer will fund the redemption value of the bond (FV). Federal and federal agency bonds tend to have the longest maturity dates (30-40 years), although some private (corporate) bonds have been

---

[14] Derives from the fact the bond document once had detachable coupons which were intended to be torn off and remitted to the issuer for periodic payment. No longer used.

issued with maturity dates as long as 100 years.[15] These super-long-term bonds, as the reader can readily appreciate by now, behave like perpetual annuities ($PV = \dfrac{PMT}{i}$) .

Bond Terminology

In order to work through a consistent example, let's choose two United States Treasury obligations listed as follows:[16]

	Rate	**Mo/Yr**	**Bid**	**Ask**	**Ask/Yld**
#1)	3 1/2	Nov 98	98:13	99:13	3.71
#2)	5 1/2	Nov 98**n**	99:27	99:29	5.53

The **rate** indicates the "coupon rate" for the bond. Therefore bond #1 pays 3.5% of $1,000 annually, or $17.50 every <u>six</u> months. Bond #2 pays $27.50 every six months.

The **Mo/Yr** indicates that both instruments will mature in November 1998. The small **n** indicates that the second "bond" is really a "note."[17] The fact that both instruments mature at the same time but carry different (original) interest rates indicates that they were issued at different times, bond #1 when rates were slightly lower, and bond #2 when rates were somewhat higher.

The **Bid** is the price offered for these instruments at the end of the trading day. All bonds are quoted as a percent of the current bid price. Treasury bonds, however, use "ticks" to represent a fraction of 1%: one "tick" equals 1/32 of 1%. Thirty-two ticks equal 1%.

In our pricing example of a Treasury bond, the colon between 98 and 13 indicates that the bond is priced at 98 **percent** of $1000 plus 13 "ticks," or 13/32nds of a percentage point. This price, 98:13, means 98+13/32%, or 98.40625% of $1,000, or $984.0625.[18] Both Treasury notes and bonds are quoted using "ticks," but "bills" are quoted using hundredths of a point. Corporate bonds are quoted in fractions: e.g. 98 1/2 = 98.5% of $1,000, or $985.00

---

[15] In 1995, Columbia/HCA Healthcare issued $200 million of debt due in 100 years. Other recent issuers of century debt are: Disney (1993), Coca-Cola (1994) and ABN Amro (1994). Bonds with very long maturity dates may be subject to re-classification as equities by the government, thus eliminating the deducibility of interest payments made to bond holders.

[16] As listed in Barron's, Nov 27, 1995. Other publications may follow different formats.

[17] "Bills" refer to instruments with a maturity date of 1 year or less; "Notes" refers to instruments with a maturity of from 1 year to 10 years; "Bonds" refers to instruments with a maturity of 10 years or more. But they are all <u>bonds</u>.

[18] To convert the bond quote to price, simply multiply by ten: divide by 100 to convert to decimals and multiply by $1,000 to represent face value.

The **Ask** is the price last asked by a seller of the instrument on this trading day. Yield-To-Maturity rates are calculated on **Ask** prices.

The **Ask/Yld** is the yield (IRR) which the buyer of the instrument would realize if he paid the Ask price and held the note to maturity (redemption) in November 1998.

Calculating Bond Yields

We can easily construct two T-Bars to represent the cashflows from these instruments from today to maturity. For the sake of convenience, let's assume that both instruments mature on the very same day, three years from Nov. 1, 1995.

Bond #1

		(994.0625)[19]
	1	17.50
	2	17.50
$r = ?$	3	17.50
	4	17.50
	5	17.50
	6	17.50 + 1,000

The Net Present Value of these cashflows can be depicted as:

$$\text{NPV} = -994.0625 + \frac{17.50}{(1+r)^1} + \frac{17.50}{(1+r)^2} + \frac{17.50}{(1+r)^3} + \frac{17.50}{(1+r)^4} + \frac{17.50}{(1+r)^5} + \frac{1017.50}{(1+r)^6}$$

We are looking here for the value of **r** which will render the NPV = 0. We are looking for the IRR.

Yield = 1.85548% per six months, or 3.71097 % per year.

(To determine the necessary keystrokes, consult Chapter 2 dealing with uneven cashflows.)

---

[19] Price converted from 99 + 13 ticks

Bond #2

		(999.0625)
	1	27.50
	2	27.50
$r = ?$	3	27.50
	4	27.50
	5	27.50
	6	27.50 + 1,000

Yield (r) = 2.76717% per six months, or 5.53435% per year.

Using the Calculator to Determine Yield-To-Maturity

The HP 12-C provides a convenient system to determine Yields-to-Maturity (**YTM**), and given a desired YTM, the Price. The on-board program of the HP 12-C is particularly useful when the time to maturity is irregular, i.e. not measured in even months or years.

Let's first consider its facility in calculating YTM.

> A bond bearing a coupon of 7.75% matures on Nov. 10, 2005. Its current Ask price is 96.5.
>
> What is this bond's current **YTM** if purchased on Dec. 1, 1999 at the Ask price?

You already know that bond prices are quoted as a percent of $1,000. But the HP is already programmed to allow for this, so you need make no conversion from percent to dollars.

<u>Key In</u>	<u>Display Shows</u>	<u>Comments</u>
96.5 PV	96.50	**Enters today's asking price**
7.75 PMT	7.75	**Enters coupon rate**
12.011999 Enter	12.01	**The settlement (purchase) date**[20]

solving

11.102005 f YTM	8.51	**The Yield to Maturity (IRR)**

---

[20] Notice that the format for the date is M.DY (2,8). When this format is used, no date notation appears in the calculator's window. When the format D.MY is used (2,7), a notation of the format does appear in the window. The entire format may be viewed by setting the decimal place to f 7

Observe the date format (**M.DY**) carefully . Note that although the first of the month was used in the settlement date, the formatted date still reserved two places for the day, i.e. 12.**01**1999. The other date format, **D.MY**, key (2,7) could also have been use to format both dates with identical results.

Determining Bond Price, Given YTM

When you are attempting to determine the current value of a bond, the procedure is equally simple:

> A bond bearing a coupon of 7.75% matures on Nov. 10, 2005. The settlement date is Dec.1, 1999.
>
> What is this bond's current value to an investor who requires an 8.51% return rate?

Key In	Display Shows	Comments
7.75 PMT	7.75	Enters coupon rate
8.51 i	8.51	Enters desired YTM
12.011999 Enter	12.01	The settlement (purchase) date[21]

solving

11.102005 f Price	96.5037	The price as a % of $1,000

Now press

x≈y (4,4)	0.44712	The amount (% of $1,000) of accrued interest due the prior owner of the bond.

In those cases in which the settlement date does not fall on a dividend date, the purchaser will need to reimburse the seller for the amount of interest which the seller has accrued up to the settlement date.

In this case, the calculator assumes that the maturity date of the bond is on Nov. 10, 2005. It then counts back in six month intervals to the purchase (settlement) date, Dec. 1, 1999,

---

[21] Notice that the format for the date is M.DY (2,8). When this format is used, no date notation appears in the window. When the format D.MY is used (2,7), a notation of the format appears in the window. The entire date may be viewed by setting the decimal place to f 7

assuming that each six month interval will mark a dividend date. Therefore it marks Nov. 10, 1999 as a dividend date. The purchaser will receive the next full dividend of $77.50/2 on May 10, 2000 but will not have owned the bond for the entire period covered by the dividend payment. The accrued interest is the interest earned by the prior owner from Nov.10, 1999 to Dec. 1, 1999, the settlement date. The interest for this period will be $4.47 due the previous owner. Therefore the accrued interest due the previous owner is added to the indicated price:

Continuing with the keystrokes,

| + | **96.95089** | **Indicating price of $969.51 including accrued interest.** |

When Call Dates Are Involved

When a bond contains a call provision (the issuer's right to redeem the bond before its maturity date), the YTM of the bond is determined in one of two ways: if the coupon rate is *above* current market rates, the YTM is calculated to to the call date; when the coupon rate is *below* market rates, the YTM is calculated to the maturity date.

Call prices are always above par ($1,000), but the HP-12C is pre-programmed to assume that the FV of all bonds at maturity will always be $1,000. There is no way to override this maturity price to enter a value greater than par, such as a call price.

For example:

> A bond which carries a 7.75% coupon rate and a maturity date of Dec.1, 2005 also specifies a call date on Dec.1, 2002 at 105.
>
> What will be the YTM for an investor who purchases the bond on Dec. 1, 1999 @ 96.5, if the bond is called?

Determining the YTM of this bond to its call date is made difficult because there is no way to inform the calculator that the call price is 105. But we can use a device to approximate the price.

We know that the investor is to receive 6 future semi-annual interest payments, including the last payment. Each of these will be equal to $38.75 ($77.50/2). Instead of delivering the $50 call premium at the end of the cashflow, we can adjust the periodic interest payments to include an amount which would be the financial equivalent of $50 over the next 6 payments, using the coupon rate of 7.75% as the interest rate.

What would these PMTs need to be?

	n	i	PV	PMT	FV
	6	7.75/2	0	?	50.00
solving				:	
				−7.561282	

Therefore the receipt of an extra $7.561282 every six months has a Future Value of $50, the amount of the call premium. By including this payment with the regularly scheduled interest payment, we can provide the financial equivalent of $50 at the call date. In other words, the receipt of $46.31182 ($38.75 + 7.561282 = $46.31182) for the remaining six payments has the same <u>Future Value</u> as the receipt of $38.75 for six payments with a final premium payment of $50.00.

We can now employ the HP-12C to determine the YTM by use of a "new" annual coupon rate, which is double the six-month rate:[22]

<u>Key In</u>	<u>Display Shows</u>	<u>Comments</u>
96.5 PV	96.50	**Enters today's asking price**
9.26236 PMT	9.26	**Enters "new" annual coupon rate**
12.011999 Enter	12.01	**The settlement (purchase) date[23]**
solving		
12.012002 f YTM	10.66	**The Yield to Call Date (IRR)**

Determining the Value of a Bond Using Call Price

Now that we own this quiet subterfuge, we can turn it around to determine the Price (PV) of a bond involving a call premium.

For example:

> A bond which carries a 7.75% coupon rate and a maturity
> date of Dec.1, 2005 also specifies a call date on Dec.1, 2002 at 105.
>
> What is the maximum price an investor should pay in order to realize
> a 10.65% yield if the settlement date will be Dec. 1, 1999?

---

[22] The calculator automatically halves the annual coupon rate.

[23] Notice that the format for the date is M.DY (2,8). When this format is used, no date notation appears in the window. When the format D.MY is used (2,7), a notation of the format appears in the window. The entire date may be viewed by setting the decimal place to f 7

Key In	Display Shows	Comments
9.26236 [PMT]	9.26	Enters adjusted coupon rate
10.66 [i]	10.66	Enters desired yield (YTM)
12.011999 [Enter]	12.01	The settlement (purchase) date[24]
solving		
12.012002 [f] [Price]	96.5	Value if called

Unfortunately, this device works only when the settlement date falls on the anniversary of a dividend date (6 months or 12 months), in order to avoid the problem of accrued interest. If they do not coincide in this way, the HP–12C will not deliver an accurate YTM or price.[25]

Does Yield Determine Price or Vice-Versa?

It is commonly held that the current yield (IRR) determines the current price when, in fact, it is the current price which determines the yield. It is valid to apply the current yield for one bond to determine the value of another only when their maturity dates are the same and their coupon rates are the same.

If the current price must be fashioned before we can calculate the yield, then the question posed is "What fashions the current price?" The answer is the spot rate for money.

Term Structure of Interest Rates, Yield Curves

The difficulty in considering the yield–to–maturity rate (the IRR) as *the* value for r for each future period to the maturity date of the bond, is that we already know that as the receipt of cash gets pushed farther and farther into the future its Present Value declines. A single r value (IRR) does not show these differences. It is much more accurate to depict the PV of the bonds in question by the following amounts:

$$PV = \frac{PMT}{(1+r_1)^1} + \frac{PMT}{(1+r_2)^2} + \frac{PMT}{(1+r_3)^3} + \frac{PMT}{(1+r_4)^4} + \frac{PMT}{(1+r_5)^5} + \frac{PMT}{(1+r_6)^6}$$

---

[24] Notice that the format for the date is M.DY (2,8). When this format is used, no date notation appears in the window. When the format D.MY is used (2,7), a notation of the format appears in the window. The entire date may be viewed by setting the decimal place to [f] 7

[25] Some models of financial calculators do provide for the specification of a call price other than $1,000.

where the values r_1 to r_6 are different – generally increasing to reflect the additional risk of time to receipt.[26] These values are not set by computers, but rather by the **market.** They reflect investors' collective judgments regarding the risk of inflation, and the risk that the PMT or the principal value may never be realized.[27] The phrase "term structure of interest rates" refers to the relationship between interest **rates** and the **time** to maturity.

It is important to recognize that there are many different yield curves, depending upon the class of security represented by the curve. Most financial media publish the U.S. Treasury yield curve for U.S. securities of varying maturities. While not risk-free, US Treasuries represent the lowest risk, and therefore act as a a <u>base</u> from which other interest rates, adjusted for the additional risk, may be calculated.[28]

The "normal" yield curve depicts steadily rising interest rates with increasing maturity. Nevertheless, yield curves may be flat, or actually negatively sloped (descending) during times when interest rates are high but when investors foresee a substantial drop in future rates. A slightly inverted yield curve for US Treasuries, which occured on Dec. 8, 1995, is depicted in the following graph:

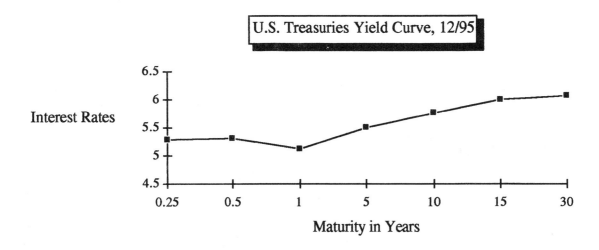

U.S. Treasuries Yield Curve, 12/95

---

[26] The value of r could also decrease if the investor anticipated a decline in interest rates.

[27] In the case of "junk" bonds of low rating, the value r is quite high to reward the buyer for the inherent risk of default. High r values depress current PV.

[28] The U.S. Treasury has inaugurated bonds whose maturity value will be adjusted for inflation, thereby preserving the purchasing power of the principal. These bonds bear lower coupon rates reflecting lower (zero?) risk, and may come to be regarded as bearing the risk-free interest rate.

Bond Duration – A Measure of Price Volatility

One of the more important questions which arises for bond investors is the degree to which the price of a bond changes in response to changes in current market interest rates (yield). One might expect that a given percentage change in the yield rate would result in a correspondingly equal percentage change in the price, or value, of the bond This is, however, not the case.

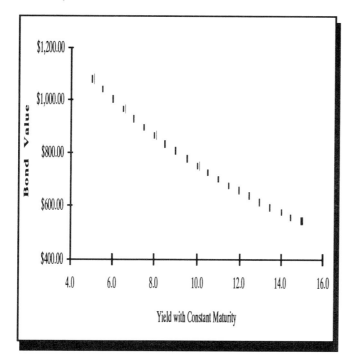

For example, consider the value of a 6% coupon bond with constant maturity as yield ranges from 5% to 15%. The chart at the left traces bond value as the market yield changes. The points on the chart do not describe a straight line - value is influenced not only by changes in yields but also by the bond's coupon rate and time-to-maturity.

Bond Duration is a measurement tool which enables the investor to estimate the sensitivity of bond value to changes in market yield rates, taking into account a specific coupon rate and a specific time to maturity.

Derivation of Bond Duration

We already know that the (Present) Value of any investment is the sum total of all future financial benefits, each discounted at a rate commensurate with the perceived risk. We know, too, that as the receipt of a cash benefit is pushed farther and farther into the future, the present value of that benefit diminishes. Bonds are no exception. Therefore the risk of recovering the full reversionary value of the bond is increased with the time to maturity. But in the interim, cash (and, therefore, a percent of the purchase price) may be recovered as a function of the coupon rate of the bond: a bond with a higher coupon rate – say 10%, or $100 per year - will return a higher percentage of the bond's current market value over a given number of years when compared to a bond of similar maturity but with a lower coupon rate. The calculation of Bond Duration brings all these factors together in one number, allowing us to have a measurement of a bond's price sensitivity (volatility) to changes in market interest rates.

We can represent the present value, or current market price, of the bond as:

$$\text{Value} = \sum_{t=1}^{n} \frac{CF_t}{(1+i)^t}$$

where   CF = coupon payment per period
                      i = current market yield rate per period of time
                      t = time (expressed in 6-month periods)
                     n = number of time periods to maturity

If we seek to measure the sensitivity of the Value (V) of the bond to changes in market yield rates (i), we need only to take the first derivative of **V** with respect to **i** :

$$\frac{dV}{di} = \sum \frac{-t * CF_t}{(1+i)^{t+1}}$$

When the value of **i** is small, as will be the case when shifts in yield rates are small, the expression $\frac{1}{(1+i)}$ substantially equates to 1. To simplify the matter, let's remove $\frac{1}{(1+i)^t}$ from the summation:

$$\frac{dV}{di} = \frac{1}{(1+i)} \sum \frac{-t * CF_t}{(1+i)^t}$$

Therefore,

$$\frac{dV}{di} \approx 1 * \sum \frac{-t * CF_t}{(1+i)^t} = \sum \frac{-t * CF_t}{(1+i)^t}$$

But the expression $\frac{CF_t}{(1+i)^t}$ represents the Present Value of the particular cashflow CF_t.

Therefore we can restate the equation as approximately :

$$\frac{dV}{di} \approx \sum -PVCF_t * t$$

In 1938, Frederick R. Macauly defined Duration as the total weighted average time for recovery of the payments and principal in relation to (i.e. divided by) the current market price of the bond. Bond Duration, therefore, is

$$\text{Duration} = \sum_{t=1}^{n} \frac{-(PVCF_t * t)}{\text{Market Price}},$$

where $\textbf{Market Price} = \sum_{t=1}^{n} \frac{CF_t}{(1+i)^t}$ and $\textbf{PVCF}_t =$ the present value of cashflow t .

Calculating Bond Duration

The calculation of a bond's Duration was a time–consuming task in Macauly's day. Today the computer makes the measurement of bond value as a result in a change in market yield – or any other variable – a relatively minor chore. Following Macauly's formula, Bond Duration for a 5 year bond, bearing a 6% coupon and a market yield of 10%, can be calculated as:

Year	Pmt #	Coupon$	PV Factor[29]	$PV	PV/Price	Duration[30]
0.50	1.00	$30.00	0.952381	$28.57	0.0338	0.01689
1.00	2.00	$30.00	0.907029	$27.21	0.0322	0.03218
1.50	3.00	$30.00	0.863838	$25.92	0.0306	0.04597
2.00	4.00	$30.00	0.822702	$24.68	0.0292	0.05838
2.50	5.00	$30.00	0.783526	$23.51	0.0278	0.06950
3.00	6.00	$30.00	0.746215	$22.39	0.0265	0.07943
3.50	7.00	$30.00	0.710681	$21.32	0.0252	0.08825
4.00	8.00	$30.00	0.676839	$20.31	0.0240	0.09605
4.50	9.00	$30.00	0.644609	$19.34	0.0229	0.10292
5.00	10.00	$1,030.00	0.613913	$632.33	0.7478	3.73910

Market Price = $845.57[31]   1.0000   **4.3287**

Therefore this bond with a current value of $845.57 has a current absolute[32] Duration of **4.3287**

---

[29] The discount rate used here is 10%/2, the rate per period.

[30] Bond Duration is the product of **PV/Price** * the value under column **Year**. It is measured in years, but it is not a measure of time required to recover the price of the bond.

[31] The Market Price is the summation of all the separate PVs in the cashflow.

[32] Duration carries a negative sign.

The steps in calculating the absolute Duration as it appears above are:

1. Determine the coupon rate. The coupon rate/2 * $1000 = PMT (Coupon$).
2. Determine the PV factor using the yield: $1/(1+i)^t$ where **t** is the PMT #.
3. Multiply the PV factor * Coupon$
4. Divide result of #3 by the current market value of the bond.
5. Multiply this factor by the years in column 1.

The sum of all final values in the right-hand column is the absolute **Duration.**

Determinants of Duration

As we can see from the equations above, coupon rate (which determines the size of the periodic cashflow), yield (which determines present value of the periodic cashflow), and time-to-maturity (which weights each cashflow) all contribute to Duration.

Holding coupon rate and maturity constant –

* Increases in market yield rates cause a decrease in the present value factors of each cashflow. Since Duration is a product of the present value of each cashflow and time, higher yield rates also lower Duration. Therefore Duration varies inversely with yield rates.

Holding yield rate and maturity constant –

* Increases in coupon rates raise the present value of each periodic cashflow and therefore the market price. This higher market price lowers Duration. Therefore Duration varies inversely to coupon rate.

Holding yield rate and coupon rate constant –

* Increases in maturity lower market price and therefore increases Duration. Duration varies directly with time-to-maturity (t).

Using Duration to Approximate Value Changes

The magnitude of the Duration is an index to the sensitivity of the bond to changes in market interest rates. Bonds with high Duration factors experience greater increases in value when rates decline, and greater losses in value when rates increase, compared to bonds with lower Duration factors.

In order to *approximate* the percent change in market value as the result of a percent change in yield, Macauly derived **Modified Duration**, which is simply Duration times the factor which we removed from the formula for Duration above.

$$\text{Modified Duration } (-D_M) = -\text{Duration} * \frac{1}{(1+i)} = -D_M$$

In the example above, where Duration is 4.3287, the Modified Duration is:

$$\text{Modified Duration } (-D_M) = -4.3287 * \frac{1}{(1+\frac{.10}{2})} = -4.12257$$

Macauly used this Modified Duration, $-D_M$, to *approximate* the percent change in bond value for a given percent change in yield.

Percent change in bond value ≈ $-D_M$ * percent change in yield.

If yield rates rose from 10% to 10.5%, a 0.5% increase in rates, Macauly's formula would predict a percent change in Value as:

$$\text{Percent change in bond value} \approx -D_M * \text{percent change in yield.}[32]$$
$$\approx -4.12257 * +0.5$$
$$\approx -2.0613\%$$

The price change calculated by Duration would be $845.57 * -2.0631\% = -\$17.43$ The new bond price would be approximately $845.57 - \$17.43 = \$828.14$. We can confirm the percent change and new price by entering these data into a spreadsheet:

Year	Pmt #	Coupon	PV Factor	$PV	$PV÷Price	Duration
0.50	1	$30.00	0.950119	$28.50	0.03441	0.017205
1.00	2	$30.00	0.902726	$27.08	0.032694	0.032694
1.50	3	$30.00	0.857697	$25.73	0.031063	0.046594
2.00	4	$30.00	0.814914	$24.45	0.029513	0.059027
2.50	5	$30.00	0.774265	$23.23	0.028041	0.070103
3.00	6	$30.00	0.735643	$22.07	0.026642	0.079927
3.50	7	$30.00	0.698949	$20.97	0.025313	0.088597
4.00	8	$30.00	0.664084	$19.92	0.024051	0.096203
4.50	9	$30.00	0.630959	$18.93	0.022851	0.10283
5.00	10	$1,030.00	0.599486	$617.47	0.745421	3.727106
			Price	**$828.35**	1.00000	**4.320286**
				New Modified Duration		**4.104785**

---

[32] Since Modified Duration is a negative value, a decrease in yield rate results in an increase in bond value. Multiplying the negative Duration * a reduction in yield results in an increase in bond value.

As you can see, the computer indicates a decline in value from $845.57 to $828.35, a loss of $17.22 vs. $17.43 as predicted by Macauly's approximation. If the Duration of our example bond were in the order 8 or 12, a reduction of 0.5 % in interest rates would indicate a loss of approximately 4% ($33.82)[33] and 6% ($50.73), respectively.

This difference in the answer we have obtained is caused by the convexity of the bond value curve. Macauly's formula describes a straight line, but bond value in response to yield changes describes a slight curve. When yield changes are small, the difference in value change is negligible, but when these differences are substantial ($\geq 0.5\%$) then the differences in value increase. Therefore the use of Duration to estimate change results in a reasonable *approximation*, especially when the changes in interest rates are not too large.

Significance of Duration

In the pre-computer days of Macauly, Duration was conceived as a short-hand method of estimating price volatility as the result of changes in yield. Today, the value of Duration is somewhat less evident, since computer price programs can be easily written which indicate precisely the value of a bond with respect to all the important financial variables: coupon, yield and time. Still, Duration can be used by the bond investor to implement his investment strategy. If the investor believes that market yields are going to decline, he may wish to shift his portfolio to bonds carrying longer Durations. If an increase in yields is expected, he may elect to change the mix to include bonds of shorter Duration.

Obviously bonds are subject to risk beyond changes in the coupon-yield-matuity variables, e.g. the risk of default, but Duration was not intended to reflect this kind of risk.

Duration and the Bond Portfolio

Perhaps the most significant use of Duration today is as a short-hand method of estimating the changes in the value of a bond portfolio. Assume that a portfolio consists of (for simplicity) three bonds carrying the following current prices and Modified Durations:

Bond	Current Price	Mod. Duration
A	$845.57	4.12257
B	$625.95	7.3523
C	$884.17	4.04855

On a given day the market yield rate increases 20 basis points (+.2%). What effect will this have on the value of this portfolio?

---

[33] $845.57 * 8 *.005 = $33.82

Fortunately, the HP–12C has a set of statistical registers which will calculate a weighted mean. Here are the keystrokes (set decimal to f 5):

Key In	Display Shows	Comments
4.12257 [Enter]	4.12257	
.2 [%]	0.00825	
845.57 [Σ+]	1.00000	
7.3523 [Enter]	7.3523	
.2 [%]	0.01470	
$625.95 [Σ+]	2.00000	
4.04855 [Enter]	4.04855	
.2 [%]	0.00810	
$884.17 [Σ+]	3.00000 .	

Now, by recalling R_2 (2,8), you will retrieve the total of all the original bond prices:

[RCL] 2	2,355.69	The total of the original prices
[RCL] 6	23.33540	The sum of the loss in value. (This is a loss since the rate increased)
[−]	2,332.3546	New value of portfolio
[f] 2	$2,332.35	

Use of Zero Coupon Bonds – A Trade Or Investment?

"Zero Coupon Bonds" refers to bonds which are "stripped" of their coupons (dividends). The most popular of the "strips' are U.S. Treasury bonds,[34] which are not stripped by the federal government, but rather by security dealers who buy the complete bonds and separate out the coupon interest payments from the reversionary value ($1,000). One can buy both the stripped interest coupons and/or the stripped principal. The Wall Street Journal denotes the former as **ci**, while the stripped principals are earmarked **bp.**

---

[34] Corporate bonds are also available as "strips."

Zero Coupon bonds (bps) are very volatile short-term investments popular with those who prefer to bet on changes in long-term interest rates.

For example, assume that current long-term (30-year) rates are at 9.5%. The Present Value (Ask) of a stripped-coupon Treasury maturing in 29 years is quoted at 7:22, meaning 7.6875, or $76.875 (per $1000 of reversionary value).

A trader foresees long–term interest rates declining to the 7.5% range within three years. Therefore the receipt of $1,000 in 26 years (29 minus 3), discounted semi-annually at 7.5% will be:

n	i	PV	PMT	FV
26*2	7.5÷2	?	0	1,000

solving :
−$147.44

This will represent an annual yield in three years of:

n	i	PV	PMT	FV
6	?	-76.875	0	147.44

solving :
11.46 x 2 = 22.92%

A yield such as this is very tempting. But the door swings to and fro. Suppose that yield rates increase 2% in three years. The results demonstrate the reward and the risk of the high leverage implicit in Zeros:

n	i	PV	PMT	FV
52	11.5÷2	?	0	1,000

solving :
54.63

The yield now becomes:

n	i	PV	PMT	FV
6	?	-76.875	0	54.63

solving :
-5.53*2 = −11.06%

Duration Of Zero Coupon Bonds

This volatility in Zero Coupon bonds can also be seen in their Duration. Since there are no coupon payments, the entire Duration is a function of the last payment, which is the principal. In the case of a 30-year Zero Coupon bond, discounted over 30 years (60 periods) @10% (5% per period), the Duration is:

Year	Pmt #	Coupon	PV Factor	$ PV	$PV÷Price	Duration
30	60	1000.00	0.05354	$53.54	1.00	30.00

For all practical purposes then, the Duration of a Zero Coupon Bond, is approximately equal to its maturity (in years). The longer the maturity, the higher the Duration. A high Duration factor indicates that long-term Zero Coupon bonds are *very* sensitive to changes in market rates. An absolute change of only 0.5% in interest rates would result in approximately a 15% variation in value for a 30-year bond.

Zeros As an Investment & Planning Tool

If, on the other hand, U.S. Treasury Zero Coupon bonds are acquired for <u>long-term purposes</u> <u>without the need for intermediate liquidity</u>, they can be important <u>low-risk</u> instruments with which to fund future cashflow requirements.

For example:

> An assessment of future income requirements for an education fund indicates that $250,000 will be required in 18 years. Zero Treasuries which will mature in 18 years are currently priced at 34:21, or $346.5625 at a time when long term interest rates are 6.06%. Two hundred fifty of these strips are acquired today at a cost of $86,640.
>
> What is the risk of loss of principal in year 18 if interest rates rise to 8.06% at the time of redemption ?

The answer is <u>zero risk</u>, since the bonds will be redeemed at $1,000 per bond. The risk inherent in this scenario is the calculation of the amount which will be required in year 18. This calculation must anticipate a reasonable inflation rate, since tuition fees in 18 years will not be at today's prices. But if held to maturity, there is virtually no risk in receiving the par value of a Treasury bond. The purchasing power of the recovered principal, however, is another matter.

Chapter Summary

1. Stocks and bonds, as do all other investments, derive their Present Value from the discounted value of the cashflows realized over the intended holding period.
2. Investments in stocks cover a broad range of yield sources: growth stocks tend to deliver an acceptable yield from profits expected from future investments. Income stocks derive their value largely from the Present Value of their dividends. The bulk of the remainder combine yields from dividends and from growth opportunities in varying proportions.
3. The market capitalization rate of a stock is equal to its dividend yield plus growth rate.
4. The growth rate of a stock is a product of its re-investment ratio, or portion of earnings plowed back into new opportunities, and its anticipated rate of return on the new venture. High growth stocks tend to re-invest all, or nearly all, earnings into future projects which promise a rate of return above the market capitalization rate of the stock.
5. For investors who are not privy to the IRR of a firm's future investment opportunities, the best course may be to anticipate that the firm will produce a rate of return equal to its current return on equity.
6. Over time, growth companies tend to find it difficult to re-invest earnings in highly yielding new projects. As a result, they generally increase dividend payout, but may also buy back quantities of their own stock, or reduce debt.
7. Except for those stocks whose values are determined mainly from the PV of future dividends, the Price-Earnings ratio is a poor indicator of present worth.
8. Bonds are interest-bearing instruments whose price varies inversely to the current market rate interest for securities of equal risk and maturity.
9. The Yield-To-Maturity rate of a bond is its IRR, which tends to conceal the time-maturity rate of return inherent in the pricing of bonds.
10. Zero Coupon bonds are derivative instruments of bonds.They are highly sensitive to changes in market interest rates.
11. Bonds with "call" dates are valued to the call dates when the coupon rate exceeds the market rate, and to the maturity date when the coupon rate is below the market.
12. The YTM of a bond can be more easily calculated by adding to the remaining interest payments an amount necessary to amortize the call premium.
13. The term "Free Cash Flow" refers to distributed net earnings before deductions for depreciation and amortization, but after deductions for retained earnings.
14. Bond Duration is a sensitivity tool which can be used to approximate the change in bond price as the result of a change in yield rates. It is particularly useful in estimating the impact of yield rate changes on a portfolio of bonds.
15. The Duration of a Zero Coupon Bond is approximately equal to its maturity, measured in years.

Chapter 5
Promissory Notes & Mortgages

In this section we will evaluate cashflows arising from mortgages and promissory notes. Before we begin, it may be helpful to define some new terms and delineate a few important concepts related to promissory notes and mortgages.

The most common financial method of acquiring real estate, as you know, is by combining owner funds (equity) with borrowed funds (debt). When stocks or bonds are acquired with borrowed funds, they are said to be bought "on margin." In either case, these two initial cashflows taken together equal the acquisition price.

Distinguishing Mortgages & Trust Deed Loans

In eastern states, lenders commonly use an instrument called a Mortgage to secure their loans. The Mortgage is an instrument recordable against the owner's title and acts as a *security device* in the event of a failure of the borrower to repay the debt or otherwise fail to uphold the loan agreement. The borrower executes a promissory note as *legal evidence* of the debt. Many Mortgage forms combine the two instruments, the security instrument and the promissory note, in a single document.

In western states, and some southern states, Mortgages are not used for reasons which reduce to the fact that they are legally cumbersome. In these states, the promissory note also acts as legal evidence of the debt, but the security device – which is always a separate, recordable instrument – is known as a Trust Deed. A Trust Deed *is* a recordable instrument, whereas a promissory note *is not* recordable.

In those states in which Mortgages are used, the relationship is a two-party arrangement between lender and borrower with the borrower (mortgagor) retaining full title to his property.

In those states in which Trust Deeds are used, the relationship is a three-party arrangement among 1) the borrower (trustor), 2) the lender (beneficiary) and 3) a trustee (a neutral third party).

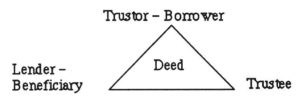

In executing the Trust Deed, the Borrower-Trustor establishes a Trust and appoints the Trustee[1] as guardian of that which is to be placed in Trust – the deed to the Borrower's property. This deed, however, does not carry with it any rights to use or possess the property, only the right for the Trustee to sell the property under carefully proscribed legal conditions.[2] If the Borrower-Trustor breaches his agreement with the Lender-Beneficiary, the Lender notifies the Trustee to initiate a *foreclosure* action to sell the property under a **Power of Sale** clause contained in the Trust Deed. To give public notice to whomever may be interested that the title to the property is encumbered by a lien,[3] the Beneficiary requires that the Trust Deed be officially recorded against the title to the Trustor's property.

Time of Recording Establishes Priority

When more than one Trust Deed is recorded against a Borrower's title, the order in which the Trust Deeds are recorded establishes which is the "First Trust Deed," "Second Trust Deed." and so on... Each Trust Deed recorded is stamped with the exact time (hour and minute) of recording, and also assigned a sequential Document Number, by the recording clerk. If one wishes to determine whether a certain Trust Deed is a First, Second or Third Trust Deed, it is necessary to examine the actual document and note the time of recordation and the Document Number for each Trust Deed. The Trust Deed document itself gives no other indication of its priority. Trust Deeds which are recorded earlier than others are said to be "senior" notes, while those recorded later are "junior" notes. *Senior* and *junior* refer to the time-priority of the Trust Deeds and not to the value of the corresponding promissory notes which they secure.

These matters are relevant because they relate to investment risk.

If a lender forecloses under a Trust Deed which is senior to other Trust Deeds recorded on the same property, the lender takes full title to the property *in the condition in which it existed at the very time (hour and minute) his Trust Deed was recorded.* All junior Trust

---

[1] Usually, but not necessarily, a corporation created and owned by the title company which insures the title.

[2] Which are listed in the Trust Deed document itself, and, in most states, in its Civil Code.

[3] An encumbrance involving money.

Deeds are automatically expunged from the title.[4] This fact creates **risk** for junior lien holders, and this risk is factored into the interest rates charged by lenders who make loans secured by junior Trust Deeds. This helps explain why second and third Trust Deed loans[5] command higher interest rates.

If the reader seeks more information, he or she may wish to consult a book dealing with real estate principles or finance, since there is considerable misinformation about the workings of this important aspect of investment financing.

One particular area of confusion derives from the fact that many people use the term "Trust Deed" when they are referring to the loan or to the promissory note. The two are different; and it is more than just academic hair-splitting to want to maintain the distinction.[6]

Promissory notes are very commonly bought and sold in secondary and tertiary financial markets. Trust Deeds never are.[7] It is the promissory note which not only *evidences* the debt, but also recites the term of the loan (**n**), the amount of the payment (**PMT**) and its due date, the interest rate (**i**), the principal amount (**PV**), and – in some cases – the amount due at maturity (**FV**), as well as other important conditions of the loan. While recorded Trust Deeds cite some terms of the loan (**PV**, **PMT**, due date), they usually do not recite all the terms of the Promissory Note.

Our interest is not in the Trust Deed (nor in the Mortgage) especially, but in the terms of the *Promissory Note,* because it is from the note that cashflows arise, not the Trust Deed.

Lastly, be aware that many individuals use the term "*mortgage* " (lower case) to equal *loan,* or "*trust deed*" to equal *loan.* There's no way to discern what they mean except by patient inquiry.

In the following sections of this chapter we will discuss a number of common loan constructions and examine the cashflows which flow between borrower and lender.

It is helpful to understand that lenders change loan programs change frequently, adjusting the terms of loans in seemingly limitless ways, all designed to gain a marketing and financial advantage. Therefore, as you progress through these sections, be mindful of how the conventional elements of loans can be put together in unconventional ways and the effects of these structures and terms on cashflows. A thorough understanding of the key elements of loan cashflows will help you evaluate a wide variety of existing loan programs, loan programs yet to be concocted, and, perhaps, enable you to solve many financing problems using innovative cashflow techniques.

---

4   Tax liens, however, are given automatic precedence over trust deeds.
5   Loans secured by junior Trust Deeds
6   If the Promissory Note can be separated from the Trust Deed, then some Promissory Notes
    can be securitized with instruments other than a Trust Deed on the subject property.
7   When a promissory note is sold, any Trust Deed which acts as security for the note automatically
    transfers, by operation of the law, to the owner of the note. No action by the new owner is required.

The Amortizing Loan

The word *amortizing* derives from *a morte*, which means, literally, "to (the) death." This pertains to the fact that if the required loan payment is made each period, the balance of the loan will eventually be paid down to zero (i.e. killed off).

In terms of cashflows, this means that the Future Value (**FV**) of *every* fully amortizing loan will eventually become zero. This is true even if only a few pennies from the regular **PMT** are available to reduce the principal.

The Amortization Schedule

The length of time required for the balance of an amortizing loan to reach zero is called the *amortization schedule* of the loan. The graph below illustrates the progress of a loan which will amortize over a 30-year period, and shows the cash from the payment devoted to interest vs. the cash devoted to reduction of the loan balance (the equity portion[8] of the payment). At any point in the progress of a fixed-rate amortizing loan, the addition of the interest and equity portions of the payment will always total to the same number. Therefore the hallmark of a *fixed-payment* amortizing loan is an *equal* payment over the entire schedule of the loan.

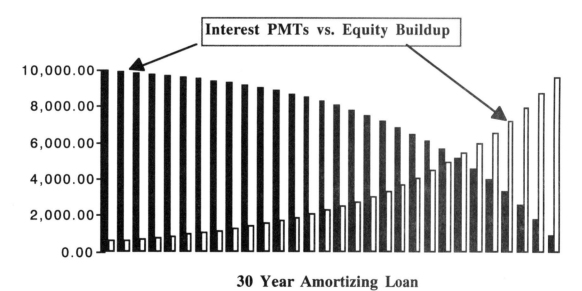

30 Year Amortizing Loan

---

[8] "Equity Portion" because it lowers the outstanding debt and increases the owner's cash position in his property.

Most commercial and residential amortizing loans are scheduled to be reduced to a zero balance over a period of from 15 to 40 years.[9] Since the payments needed to reduce the loan to zero are typically (but not always) made on a <u>monthly</u> basis, it would be more accurate to refer to these loans as loans which will amortize over 180-360 <u>months</u>. (Loans structured to amortize as the result of yearly payments require different PMTs.) Nevertheless, these loans are commonly referred to as 15-*year* or 30-*year* amortizing loans.

Amortization Schedule vs. Due Date

The advantage of loans which are constructed to amortize over long periods of time (30-40 years) is that the required payments are kept relatively low. But long amortization schedules place the lender of a fixed-rate loan at risk to rising interest rates. Therefore lenders will commonly schedule the loan as though it were to last 25, 30 or 40 years – but "call"[10] the loan at the end of the 5th, or 7th or 10th year in the schedule.

This kind of loan is commonly used in connection with income-producing properties and less frequently, but not infrequently, with residential properties. Whenever a loan calls for a payment which is more than twice any of the preceding six regularly scheduled payments, that payment is called a **balloon payment.** Therefore all loans set up on fully amortizing schedules, but which require an early payoff by the borrower, contain balloon payments. Loans requiring a balloon payment must often meet certain legal obligations for notification to the borrower of the impending due date .

Only Fixed-Rate Loans Offer Constant Payments

Payments of the same amount, month-in and month-out, were once the hallmark of every amortizing loan. In terms of the calculator, we mean that the amount of the payment (**PMT**) never changed over the life of the loan. Since the late 1970's, however, interest *rates* on certain kinds of amortizing loans periodically do change – and therefore the **PMT** necessary to "kill off" the balance of the loan, over the amortization schedule originally selected, also changes from time to time.

In order to distinguish between the two types, we now refer to amortizing mortgages whose **PMT**s never change as **fixed-rate mortgages,** and to those whose **PMT**s change from time to time (as the result of a change in interest rates) as **Adjustable-Rate Mortgages**, or **ARM**s. Creative mortgage types have even created the hybrid - the adjustable rate mortgage which later converts to a fixed-rate mortgage. If you guessed that these loans are now called **convertible mortgages**, you are right.

---

9   Although other schedules are frequently encountered.
10   Require that the loan be paid in full before the end of its amortization schedule.

The Fixed–Rate, Amortizing Loan

The elements of this loan are the same as for all cashflow problems:

n   **denotes** the number of *periods* over which a payment will be made. The total number of periods = the amortization schedule.

i   **denotes** the interest *rate* of the loan, expressed to correspond to the same time interval as **n.**

PV   **denotes** the Present **Value** of the loan at any point in its schedule.

PMT   **denotes** the payment per period **n** which is required to reduce the remaining balance of the loan to zero.

FV   **denotes** the Future Value, or balance of the loan, at any point in its amortization schedule. For the *fully* amortizing loan, this amount , by definition, will always be zero at the end of the amortization schedule.

These five financial variables and their symbols are used by all financial calculators and by all financial (computer) spreadsheets.They are represented on the HP-12C by the same keys (1,1) through (1,5) which we used in solving cashflow problems in previous chapters.

n	i	PV	PMT	FV

Determining the Payment Necessary to Fully Amortize a Loan

<u>Problem:</u>

> Calculate the monthly payment (**PMT**) necessary to amortize a loan of $100,000 (**PV**) over a period (**n**) of 30 years, if the lender charges an annual interest rate (**i**) of 10%.

Remember that the time span of **n, PMT** and **i** must all be the same. This problem, however, expresses **n** in years, **PMT** in months, and **i** in years. Since we are going to solve for the *monthly* **PMT**, we must first translate **n** into *months* and **i** into a *monthly* rate of interest to maintain time consistency among these cashflow variables.

The hard way to do this is to key-in 30 (years), multiply by 12 (months/year) and enter the result (360) into the **n** register (key (1,1). An easier way is to use the blue key ⌐g⌐ (4,3).

Key–In	Display Shows
30 ⌐g⌐ ⌐n⌐	**360.00**

This installs 360 (months) into the **n** register by <u>automatically</u> *multiplying* 30 x 12.

Similarly, we can conveniently convert the annual interest rate (10) into a monthly rate by using the blue key ⌐g⌐ as a prefix to the ⌐i⌐ entry:

Key–In	Display Shows
10 ⌐g⌐ ⌐i⌐	**0.83**

In this case, using the blue key ⌐g⌐ before entering 10 into **i** <u>automatically</u> *divides* 10 by 12, = 0.83

We have now filled two of the Registers, **n** and **i.**

n	i	PV	PMT	FV
360	0.83			

Now enter the Present Value (in this case the original loan amount, $100,000) into **PV:**

Press	Display Shows	Comment
100000 CHS PV	-100,000.00	**Pressing the CHS key (1,6) changes the sign of the number in the display**

We have now filled three of the Registers, **n , i** and **PV.**

n	i	PV	PMT	FV
360	0.83	-100,000.00		

Notice that the figure 100,000 was entered as a negative number. We did this by first keying-in the number 100000, then keying **CHS** (1,6) to change the sign, and then entering the result into **PV.** Had we not changed the sign, the payment (**PMT**) would be a negative number. There's nothing wrong with this, but you may wish to make it a general rule to enter all **PV** loan values – whenever appropriate – as a negative (from the lender's point of view) and read out all **PMT**s as positive. The sign convention requirement of this machine requires that at least one of the cash entries must be a negative number.[11] This requirement is also true for computer spreadsheets.

Now we need to enter something into the Future Value register. Since this loan will be a completely amortizing loan, we know that in 360 months **FV** *must*, by definition, be zero. Therefore we enter **0** into **FV**.

n	i	PV	PMT	FV
360	0.83	-100,000	?	0

Now all we need to do is to call for the answer by pressing PMT , the unknown:

	n	i	PV	PMT	FV
	360	0.83	-100,000	?	0[12]
solving				:	
				877.57	

Therefore the **PMT** necessary to amortize a **$100,000** fixed-rate loan over **360 months,** with **monthly PMT**s including interest calculated at the rate of **10%** per annum but applied monthly, is **$877.57 per month.**

Problem:

> Suppose that you wish to determine the **PMT** for a loan of this amount, with an identical interest rate, but amortized over a 15-year schedule (180 months).
>
> What **PMT** would be required?

---

[11] Cash must flow out *and* in.

[12] Due to the calculator's continuous memory feature, a number from a previous problem will hang over in FV and result in an incorrect answer. Therefore whenever you intend that 0 should be in FV, <u>put it there</u> by keying 0 into FV. This kind of error most often occurs when you have not used the calculator for an interval following a previous problem that involved a value in FV.

The only value in the registers which needs to be changed is the value in the **n** register. There is no need to clear the entire calculator and re-enter all the other values. (Don't worry about the value in **PMT**.) Simply *write-over* the value in **n** and re-solve for **PMT**:

	Key–In	Display Shows
solving	15 [g] [n]	180.00
	[PMT]	**1,074.61**

This solution says that a monthly payment of $1,074.61, which includes monthly interest at the annual rate of 10%, will completely amortize a $100,000 loan in 15 years (180 months). Not all loans are institutional loans, as you well know. Many are made by private investors. Consider this situation:

Problem:

> Suppose that you are involved in the sale of a property whose owner has agreed to carry back a note in the amount of $15,000 as part of the purchase price. He requires, however, that he receive **PMT**s such that the note will be completely paid off (amortized) in 8 years, and he will settle for nothing less than 9% annual interest on the note. He also requires that the **PMT**s be made monthly. What **PMT** can he expect to receive?

Here's how to solve for **PMT** in this common situation:

n	will be 8 x 12	(expressed in months)
i	will be 9 ÷ 12 %	(expressed in months)
PV	will be –15000	
PMT	?	(will be answered in PMT per month)
FV	will be 0	(the loan fully amortizes in 8 years)

The calculator key-strokes are:

	Key–In	Display Shows
	f CLX	0.00
	8 g n	96.00
	9 g i	0.75
	15000 CHS PV	-15,000.00
	0 FV	0.00
solving	[PMT]	219.75

Solving for n, the Number of Periods

Unfortunately you find that Buyer in the preceding problem cannot make this high a payment ($219.75). Following a discussion, the Buyer determines that he could make a PMT of not more than $200.00 per month. How long will it take for this PMT of $200 to amortize the loan?

n	will be ?
i	will be 9÷12 %
PV	will be -15000
PMT	200.00
FV	will be 0

Key–In	Display Shows
f CLX	0.00
9 g i	0.75
15000 CHS PV	−15000.00
200 PMT	200.00
0 FV	0.00

solving

$\boxed{\text{n}}$	111.00

Therefore a **PMT** of $200 will completely amortize this debt *within* 111 months.

As previously discussed, one of the idiosyncrasies of the HP-12C calculator when it attempts to solve for **n** is that the answer is *always* given in integers (no decimal places). In almost all cases, the **PMT** made for **n** periods will overpay the loan. Therefore when solving for **n** always check for an overpayment by re-solving for **FV**. Enter these values:

Key–In	Display Shows
9 g i	0.75
15000 CHS PV	−15000.00
200 PMT	200.00
0 FV	0.00
n	111.00

solving

$\boxed{\text{FV}}$	-72.50

In this case, the calculator tells you that a full **PMT** of $200.00 per month in the **111th** month will overpay the loan by $72.50.[13] Therefore the last **PMT** should be $127.50 ($200.00 - 72.50).

Solving for a Balloon PMT

Continuing with the Problem:

> Unfortunately, the Seller refuses to carry this note that long. By way of compromise, the Buyer agrees to pay a balloon payment at the end of the 8th year, if the Seller would agree to the $200 per month payment and if the balloon payment is limited to not more than $2,500. We already know that a **PMT** less than $219.75 will not amortize this loan in 8 years at the given interest rate. But what will the balloon payment be?

n	will be 8 x 12
i	will be 9÷12 %
PV	will be -15000
PMT	200.00
FV	will be **?**

n	i	PV	PMT	FV
96.00	0.75	-15,000.00	200.00	?

Here are the keystrokes:

Key–In	Display Shows
8 g n	96.00
9 g i	0.75
15000 CHS PV	-15000.00
200 PMT	200.00
solving FV	2,762.59

---

13 The negative sign in FV indicates that the balance of the loan is less than zero.

Solving for the Interest Rate, i

Continuing with the Problem:

> Since the balloon payment of $2,762.59 would exceed the Buyer's limit of $2,500, the Buyer refuses to agree to these terms. As a compromise, you negotiate a modification whereby the Buyer will agree to a balloon payment of up to $2,500 *if* the Seller will lower the interest rate not more than one-half percent.
>
> What will the interest rate **i** be?

```
n    = 96
i    = ? %
PV   = –15000
PMT  = 200.00
FV   = 2,500
```

Key–In	Display Shows
8 g n	96.00
15000 CHS PV	-15,000.00
200 PMT	200.00
FV	2,500.00

solving

	Key	Display	
	i	0.73	(Monthly interest rate)
	12 x	8.78	

The Seller agrees to this rate, 8.78%, as an acceptable alternative to not selling his property. Your negotiation is successfully concluded. Congratulations!

Payments When the Period is Not Monthly

Problem:

> You are negotiating the sale of a small retail center whose owner has agreed to carry back a note as part of the purchase price. She requires a 10% annual interest rate but has agreed to *quarterly* payments. If the amount of the note is $60,000 and the required annual interest rate is 10%, what quarterly **PMT** will be required to amortize this note over a 7-year term?

The key to this kind of problem, involving something other than *monthly* **PMT**s, is to recognize that you must key-in both the number of periods, n, and the interest rate per period, i, in quarters of a year, and not in months. Therefore:

$$
\begin{aligned}
\mathbf{n} \quad &= 7 \times 4 \ (\text{quarters/year}) = 28 \\
\mathbf{i} \quad &= 10 \div 4 \ (\text{quarters/year}) = 2.5 \\
\mathbf{PV} \quad &= -60{,}000 \\
\mathbf{FV} \quad &= 0 \\
\mathbf{PMT} \quad &= ?
\end{aligned}
$$

Key-In	Display Shows
7 [Enter]	7.00
4 [x] [n]	28.00z
10 [Enter]	10.00
4 [÷] [i]	2.50
60000 [CHS] [PV]	-60,000.00
0 [FV]	0.00

solving

[PMT]	3,005.28

The *total annual* payments under this note would be 4 times the quarterly payments of $3.005.28, or $12.021.10.

Continuing,

4 [x]	12,021.10

Note: The blue key **g** is <u>not</u> used as a prefix to key-in either the interest rate **i** or the number of periods **n** since **g**, **i** divides by 12 and **g**, **n** multiplies by 12. It cannot be used when the period is <u>not</u> 12.

Let's turn this problem around so that you can see how to handle the determination of the annual interest rate when the loan is not payable monthly.

Problem:

> The owner of the retail center has agreed to carry back a note for $60,000 payable $$3,005.28 per quarter for 7 years. She agrees that these payments will be considered to fully amortize the promissory note. What interest will she realize on the note?

Solving for i

n	will be 7 x 4 = 28
i	= ?
P V	= –60000
F V	= 0
PMT	= 3,005.28

<u>Key–In</u>	<u>Display Shows</u>
7 Enter	7.00
4 x n	28.00
600000 CHS PV	–600000.00
3005.28 PMT	3,005.28
0 FV	0.00
solving	
i	2.50

But the interest rate, 2.50%, is the rate *per quarter*. This answer must be multiplied by 4 to express the annual rate.

Continuing,

4 x	10.00

Remember! Always keep the time-frame for **n**, **i**, and **PMT** the same – in this case quarterly.

Generating an Amortization Schedule for a Fixed–Rate Loan

An amortization schedule is simply a numerical record of the progress of an amortizing loan as it proceeds toward a zero ending balance. The schedule typically shows periodic payment, the starting and ending balances of the loan per period, together with the interest paid and equity buildup (loan paydown).

These schedules come in handy whenever it is necessary to calculate the interest paid over a number of consecutive payments, or the amount of loan reduction which takes place over an interval of time, or the remaining balance of a loan after a certain number of payments have been made.

For example, you may need to know how much tax-deductible interest you have paid on your home mortgage during the last tax year. Or you may need to know how much principal reduction will occur in a certain mortgage over the next three years. Or you may want to know what the balance of your mortgage will be in five years, when you intend to sell or refinance the loan.

Many financial professionals have access to "canned" computer programs which prompt the user for the required data and then produce a printed amortization schedule over the time period specified. But every financial professional should be able to generate an amortization schedule without a "canned" program. An understanding of amortization schedules makes it easy to construct one on a computer's spreadsheet, which can be printed out for third–party use.

Mortgage Interest is Paid in Arrears

One important fact about the typical amortizing mortgage is that the interest is paid in arrears. This means that the payment for the use of the money during the month is paid at the end of the month – not in advance at the beginning of the month.[14]

First–time home buyers are often confused about this because they are accustomed to paying apartment rent in advance at the beginning of the month. When they secure a purchase money mortgage through escrow, the escrow officer is directed by the lender to collect interest on the mortgage money from the day it is credited to their account to the first of the next month. The first payment on the mortgage is usually due one month <u>after</u> <u>that.</u>

For example, suppose a sale escrow closes on the 16th of June. A purchase loan is funded through the same escrow at closing. The lender will typically instruct the escrow officer to collect interest on the total mortgage funds from the 16th of June through June 30th. These funds will be remitted by the escrow holder to the lender following the closing[15] and will appear on the buyer's closing statement as (prepaid) interest.[16] The first full, regularly scheduled payment on the mortgage, however, will not be due until August 1, and will pay interest in arrears for the month of July, together with a small additional sum to begin to reduce, or amortize, the loan.

Let's consider the amortization schedule for the first two months of a loan. Let's also assume that the loan is in the original amount of $100,000, payable monthly over 30 years and bearing interest at the rate of 10% per annum.

Before creating an amortization schedule on the calculator, let's construct a **hand-made** amortization schedule for the first two months so that you can understand the process.

---

[14] Contrast this to lease payments which are typically paid in advance.
[15] These interest charges will appear on the buyer's closing statement and not on the lender's mortgage statement.
[16] A tax deduction frequently overlooked.

	Beginning Balance	Payment	Interest	Equity (Paydown)	Remaining Balance
(1)	100,000.00	877.57	833.33	44.24	99,955.76
(2)	99955.76	877.57	832.96	44.61	99,911.15

Here's how these numbers were determined:

The **Interest** for the first period is equal to $100,000 x (.10 ÷ 12.) (The interest rate per month = .10 ÷ 12)

Key-In	Display Shows	Comment
f 4	0.0000	Set decimal places to 4[17]
100000 Enter	100,000.0000	
0.10 Enter	0.1000	
12 ÷	0.0083	
x	833.3333	Interest for month #1

But the payment made was $877.57. Therefore the excess, $44.24 ($877.57 - 833.33), was available to reduce the **Beginning Balance** of the mortgage: $100,000 - 44.24 = $99,955.76, Continuing,

877.57 x<>y	833.3333	
−	44.2367	

The amount by which the mortgage is reduced, $44.24, is referred to by some as the **mortgage paydown** , and by others as the owner's **equity buildup**. Both terms are common and either is acceptable.

The Beginning Balance of the mortgage on the first day of the *second* month is equal to the Remaining (ending) Balance from the previous month. The payment for the second period does not change. (Constant, even payments are the hallmark of the fixed-rate amortizing loan.) But the interest for the second month is less because the Present Value of the loan has been reduced.

---

[17] Decimal set to 4 places to show interest rate to be 0.0083 rather than 0.01

Key-In	Display Shows
f 2	**Returns decimal setting to 2 places**
99,955.76 Enter	**99,955.76**
0.10 Enter	**0.10**
12 ÷	**0.01**
x	**832.96**
(chaining)	
877.57 x<>y	**832.96**
−	**44.61**

Therefore the Remaining Balance after the second **PMT** = ($99,955.76 – 44.61) = $99,911.15. This sequence – which can easily be entered into a spreadsheet – continues in exactly the same fashion until the last **PMT** when the remaining balance should be zero.[18]

Amortization Schedules Using the HP-12C

The 12-C makes developing amortization schedules easy.

Problem:

> Recreate the two-period amortization schedule above using the calculator.

First, set up the loan in the calculator and *solve* for **PMT**. *Solving* for the **PMT** rather than keying-in the **PMT** improves the accuracy because the machine will calculate the **PMT** using 9 decimal places. You would probably key-in only 2.

	n	i	PV	PMT	FV
	360	0.83	–100,000.00	?	0
solving				877.57 (877.57157)	

---

[18] Now that you understand how the loan amortization schedule is constructed, it should be a relatively simple matter for you to reproduce these calculations on a computer spreadsheet and have your own print-out capability.

Now reset **n** to **0** by simply "writing over" the value (360) which is now in the **n** register. *Do not change any other register values.*

Press	**Display Shows**
0 [n]	**0.00**

Your register should now look like this:

n	**i**	**PV**	**PMT**	**FV**
0	**0.83**	**–100,000.00**	**877.57**	**0**

To amortize the loan <u>one</u> (1) period, follow these steps:

Press	**Display Shows**	**Comment**
1 [f] [amort][19]	**833.33**	The interest for the first period
[x<>y] (3,4)	**44.24**	The paydown for the first period
[RCL] [PV]	**-99,955.76**	The Remaining Bal. after one **PMT**

To amortize for five (5) *additional* periods:

Press	**Display Shows**	
5 [f] [amort]	**4,161.07**	The <u>total</u> interest for these <u>five</u> periods
[x<>y][20]	**226.78**	The paydown for these <u>five</u> periods
[RCL] [PV]	**-99,728.98**	The Remaining Bal. after <u>six</u> **PMT**s

This means that if you desire to determine the interest and paydown *for* the 120th **PMT** in a schedule, and the remaining balance *after* the 120th **PMT** in the schedule, you must first amortize 119 periods, and then amortize one additional period. If you amortize 120 periods directly, the interest you obtain would be for the entire 120 periods, and the paydown would be the entire paydown for 120 periods. The remaining balance, however, would be correct.

---

[19] The [amort] function is printed in gold over button (1,1)

[20] This is key (3,4)

Determining Remaining Balances

If you have no need to know the interest amount, but simply want to know the remaining balance of a loan, there are two short-cuts you may want to use. These depend on the following two financial facts:

1. The remaining balance of an amortizing loan is equal to the **FV** of all the **made** **PMT**s, and,
2. The remaining balance of an amortizing loan is equal to the **PV** of all the **unmade PMT**s.

Problem:

> What is the remaining balance after the 36th **PMT** on a loan in the original amount of $100,000, amortized over 30 years, bearing interest at the annual rate of 10% and payable monthly?

Set up this loan in your calculator as before:

	n	i	PV	PMT	FV
	360	0.83	−100,000.00	?	0
solving				:	
				877.57	

Since 36 **PMT**s will have been **made**, follow these simple steps:

	Key In	Display Shows
	36 [n]	36.00
solving		
	[FV]	98,151.65

or,

Since 324 (360 - 36) **PMT**s remain **un**made, follow this solution *after resetting the calculator:*

	n	i	PV	PMT	FV
	324	0.83	?	877.57	0
solving					
			-98,151.65		

	Key In	**Display Shows**
solving	**324 n**	**324.00**
	PV	**-98,151.65**

Perhaps the following T-Bars will help show you why both these methods are correct.

The first T-Bar represents a $100,000 loan on which PMTs have been made for three years (36 **PMT**s). The second segment of the T-Bar, represents the **PMT**s needed to be made over the remaining life of the loan (324).

$$\begin{array}{c|l} n & (100{,}000) = \textbf{(PV)} \\ \hline 1 & 877.57 \end{array}$$

$\boxed{i = .10 \div 12}$

$$\begin{array}{c|l} 36 & 877.57 + \textbf{FV} = \begin{array}{c|l} & 98{,}151.65 = \textbf{(PV)} \\ \hline 37 & 877.57 \end{array} \end{array}$$

$$\begin{array}{c|l} 360 & 877.57 + \textbf{FV} = 0 \end{array}$$

As you can see, the Remaining Balance (FV) of the loan at the end of 36 months is $98,151.65. This number can also be considered to be the Beginning Balance (PV) of a new loan, amortized over the remaining schedule (n = 324) at the same interest rate.

This structure will be very meaningful when we consider Adjustable Rate Mortgages, since we could easily change the interest rate at the end of the 36th period and calculate a new **PMT** to carry on the amortization to zero. This is, in fact, exactly what the lender does when it changes the interest rate on an Adjustable Rate Mortgage.

Segment Summary

1. An **amortizing** loan is one in which the payment made will eventually reduce the balance of the loan to zero.

2. Some amortizing loans feature fixed payments for the life of the loan. Others vary the payments to accommodate changing interest rates. The latter are known as **ARMs** (Adjustable Rate Mortgages).

3. The amortization period represents the number of periods, **n**, over which a payment must be made to reduce the loan balance to zero.

4. Some loans call for at least one payment which is at least twice as large as the any of the preceding six payments in the schedule. These payments are known as **balloon** payments.

5. Amortization *schedules* chronicle the progress of the loan and depict the beginning balance, the payment made, amount of interest paid per period, equity buildup per period and remaining balance.

6. The **remaining balance** of an amortizing loan is equal to the **present value of all the unmade payments.**

7. The **remaining balance** of an amortizing loan is also equal to the **future value of all the made payments.**

8. Interest on amortizing loans is usually paid **in arrears.**

II. The Adjustable–Rate Loan

The adjustable–rate loan (**ARM**) is a financial device by which the lender transfers to the borrower most of the risk of an increase in future interest rates.

It is the **interest** rate which is adjusted in an **ARM**. But in order to maintain the same amortization schedule, the **PMT** also changes to keep the loan on its course to a zero balance over the years specified in the original schedule of the loan.

The lender, in constructing this type mortgage, selects an interest rate base **Index**, then adds to the index a **margin**, or **spread**, to arrive at the total effective interest rate. The interest rate on an **ARM** mortgage is always equal to the index rate plus the spread rate.

Periodically, the lender adjusts the total interest rate applied to the loan to reflect changes in the underlying base index rate which, in turn, reflect changes in market rates of interest. In this way, the total **ARM** interest rate increases when the base index rate rises, and decreases when the base index rate falls. But in either case, the lender is always assured of his spread, or margin, regardless of the ups and downs in market interest rates. As the total interest rate changes, the monthly amount necessary to amortize the mortgage over the years remaining in the original schedule also changes. The actual change in the **PMT**, however, usually lags the change in the interest rate in order to permit the borrower to follow some semblance of a budget.

This temporary discrepancy between the amount of the payment necessary to amortize the loan under the original schedule and the amount actually paid each month may create negative variations in the balance of the mortgage as compared to a fixed–rate mortgage. For example, when rates rise, the **PMT** made for a number of months may be insufficient to continue to amortize the remaining balance of the mortgage. Rather than decrease, the balance of the mortgage may actually (though not always) increase. This increase is sometimes referred to as a **negatively amortizing mortgage.**[1]

Because part (most) of the risk of rising interest rates is transferred to the borrower, issuers of **ARM** mortgages are generally content with a lower total interest rate. If market interest rates rise, the **ARM** lender can pass along the increase to the borrower according to the terms of the **ARM** loan document, whereas in the case of a fixed-rate mortgage, the lender must absorb the added cost of increasing market interest rates and therefore settle for a lower profit, or even a loss, on his mortgage investment. If a borrower opts for a fixed-rate mortgage, the lender will increase the total interest rate to provide room for the possibility of a future increase in market rates. If the borrower is willing to accept an **ARM** – which involves the lender's right to change the interest rate – the lender can afford to charge a lower rate because he is not exposed to the risk of higher rates.

---

[1] The term "negatively amortizing" is an oxymoron.

Selection of a Base Index

Lenders of Adjustable Rate–Adjustable Payment Loans are required to declare in the loan document the Base Index which will determine the total interest charged. The lender is also restricted in the amount of the interest rate by the imposition of "caps" in the spread, or margin, he may apply. ARMs carry lifetime caps on the rate as well as annual caps.

Different lenders select different Indices to use as the base **Index**. The following list depicts some of the Indices which are in current use by many **ARM** lenders:

1-year Treasury Bill...............	a U.S. Treasury security maturing in 1 year
3-year Treasury Note.............	a U.S. Treasury security maturing in 3 years
5-year Treasury Note	a U.S. Treasury security maturing in 5 years
10-year Treasury Bond	a U.S. Treasury security maturing in 10 years
National Average Mortgage Rates	Published by Freddie Mac[2]
LIBOR rate........................	the average of interbank offered rates for dollar deposits in the London market based on quotations at five major banks.
Cost Of Funds Index..............	the average cost of deposits to financial institutions affiliated with the Federal Home Loan Bank Board located within a designated District or region.
Index of U.S. Treasury Securities Adjusted to Constant Maturity of One Year	Average yield on a basketful of Treasury notes that will fall due over the coming year. Used in approx. 50% of ARMs.

Many other Indices are possible and a few others are used. In some cases, which are almost always restricted to commercial loans, the index used is the "prime rate."[3]

The point is that each index establishes a base reference, or *link,* to current market interest rates. The lender's spread is added to the base to result in the effective rate for the **ARM** instrument. Since the indices vary quite a bit, the amount of the spread will also vary in order for the effective interest rate to reach competitive market levels. Therefore one cannot judge the acceptability of an **ARM** mortgage rate solely by the index used nor by the amount of the spread. The higher the index, the lower the spread; the lower the index, the higher the spread. The lender will add sufficient spread to any index it chooses to bring the total interest charged to the level of current, comparable mortgage rates.

The choice of the Index should be made by other parameters. Some lenders prefer to index their **ARM** rates to short-term **T**(reasury)-**Bills**. The advantage here is that short term rates respond rapidly to changes in market interest rates. When interest rates are rising, short

---

[2] Freddie Mac = Federal Home Loan Mortgage Corporation
[3] The interest rate which lenders extend to major customers.

term T-Bill rates will rise quickly. A mortgage rate tied to these T-Bills will also rise rapidly, preventing any significant loss in market-rate interest to the lender.

But mortgage rates and payments which change rapidly, and sometimes sharply, wreak havoc with the average borrower's budgeting process. Surveys have shown that most informed consumers prefer to have their mortgage tied to an index which changes slowly – either up or down. Gradual changes help in budgeting.

The longer term Treasury **Notes** and the 10-year Treasury **Bond** tend to be somewhat less volatile, but the best index to select to achieve low volatility is the **Cost of Funds Index** (COFI). This Index is the average of the last four months of the cost of depository funds acquired by member institutions in the particular Federal Home Loan Bank District. In California, for example, the 11th District Federal Home Loan Bank's cost of funds is used; hence the acronym, 11th District **COFI**. The COFI is the average of the last four months[4] of interest rates paid by institutions to attract funds. When a new rate becomes available, the oldest of the four monthly rates is dropped and the latest added. In this way, the curve is smoothed considerably. This explains why interest rates on **ARM**s do not decline as rapidly when general market rates are declining. But the converse is true also: rates tied to COFI also do not rise as rapidly when general rates are rising, and in some cases may even continue to decline for a short time.

It is difficult to construct a prospective amortization schedule for an **ARM** because the changes in interest rate cannot be predicted. The best one can do is to assume that the initial *stabilized* rate will be constant, and then to develop a schedule using that rate. This is not to say, however, that an ARM mortgage should not be examined for the payments which would become due under the most severe interest rate increases permissible under the terms of the loan. It should, and that technique is covered below.

Teaser Rates

We say adjustable mortgage *stabilized* rate, because some lenders, as an inducement to the borrower to take an **ARM** rather than a fixed-rate loan, will offer an introductory **teaser rate**. This rate is often substantially below the rate which currently applies to borrowers within the portfolio of the same lender. Teaser rates are marketing ploys and most often do not last more than a few (1-6) months. In order to curb abusive and misleading use of teaser rates, many states have now enacted laws prohibiting the use of teaser rates which understate the stabilized rate by more than a small margin (1-2 percentage points).

It is possible retrospectively to reconstruct the progress of an ARM, but in order to do so you must have the initial terms of the loan (index used, spread, amortization schedule), and the months during which the interest rate changed and the months in which the **PMT** changed. No financial calculator can do this; it is even a daunting task on a computer.

---

[4] A moving average

ARMS Subject To Significant Lender Errors

As the result of studies by the General Accounting Office, Office of Thrift Supervision, National Credit Union Association and others, it has been estimated that mortgage lenders in the United States may have already overcharged borrowers as much as $10 billion in payments connected with **ARM**s. Most overpayments are associated with a lender's applying the wrong Index or the wrong spread rate to a mortgage. Those who have the skill to monitor the periodic changes in an adjustable rate mortgage are well advised to do so.

The Progress of an ARM

In order to demonstrate, as best we can, the amortization of an **ARM**, let's consider a brand new **ARM** offered under the following terms:

Principal Amount (**PV**)	$100,000	
Amortization Schedule (**n**)	30 years	
Beginning (teaser) Rate (**i**)	5.5%	Note that this is less than index+ spread rate
Index Rate	4.0%	
Spread Rate	2.5%	(250 basis points[5])

A reading of the loan agreement indicates that the Beginning Rate will apply for the first <u>3</u> months of the loan. Beginning with the 4th month, and every month thereafter, the interest rate will adjust to the sum of the index rate + spread rate. <u>The **PMT**, however, will remain constant for the first 6 months</u> and then adjust in the seventh month and every six months thereafter to that amount necessary to amortize the then remaining balance of the loan over the time remaining in the *original* schedule.

This is a very typical ARM but you must be careful not to assume that all ARMs are the same. The variations are almost endless and *only a careful reading of the terms of the loan document can reveal the exact terms of any particular mortgage instrument.*

The initial PMT is determined as it would be for a fixed-rate loan:

	n	i	PV	PMT	FV
	360	5.5÷12	-100,000	?	0
solving				:	
				567.79	

---

[5] A basis point = 1/100 of one percent. Therefore there are 100 basis points in 1%.

The amortization schedule follows the typical format:

Period	Beginning Balance.	Payment	Interest	Paydown	Remaining Balance
(1)	100,000.00	567.79	458.33	109.46	99,890.54
(2)	99,890.54	567.79	457.83	109.96	99,780.58
(3)	99,780.69	567.79	457.33	110.46	99,670.12

At this point in the progress of the loan, the interest rate will adjust upward to 6.5%, although the **PMT** will not yet change. Note the effect on the Interest paid, the Paydown and the progress of the Remaining Balance.

(4)	99,670.23	567.79	539.88	27.91	99,642.21
(5)	99,642.32	567.79	539.73	28.06	99,614.15
(6)	99,614.26	567.79	539.58	28.21	99,585.94

At this point the loan will be recast in order that it may be amortized over the remaining 354 months in the schedule. Let's assume that the interest rate also changes in this month and increases from 6.5% to 6.625%. Again, note the effect on the Interest paid, the Paydown and the Remaining Balance.

	n	i	PV	PMT	FV
solve	354	0.5521	-99,585.94	?	0
				641.10	

(7)	99,585.94	641.10	549.80	91.30	99,494.64

You can see that determining the balance of an amortizing loan which has been amortizing for a number of years can be a very challenging task. No doubt that the HP–12C could be programmed to handle an amortizing loan given entry stops to supply the various new rates and the interval of the PMTs. Except for some unique and unusual purpose, perhaps, such an exercise would be mental gymnastics at best, with little practical value. If the task seriously presents itself (and it does), it is much more easily accomplished (and saved) on a computer spreadsheet.

Determining Maximum Interest Rate Exposure - "Caps"

ARMs transfer most, but not all, of the of the interest rate risk. Most **ARM** lenders offer "caps" on the maximum interest rate which can ever be charged on the loan.[6] These "caps," known as "lifetime caps" are commonly in the order of 5-6% over the starting rate but can, and do, differ from lender to lender.

Many clients are interested to know at the outset the maximum amount of payment to which they could ever be exposed if interest rates increased dramatically. Since most ARMs limit the maximum <u>annual</u> increase in interest rates (usually to 2%), it is unlikely that the payor on the note would be faced with the need to pay the maximum interest rate increase represented by the "cap" in any one year.

For example, if the ARM given as an example above carried a maximum interest rate cap of 6% over the starting rate (5.5%) the payor could never be required to service the loan with an interest rate greater than 11.5% (6% + 5.5%). But even if the interest rates increased dramatically in any one year, the maximum *annual* increase would be limited to 7.5% (5.5% + 2.0%). The lender could and would, apply increases the following year, and the year after that, in order to reach the 11.5% maximum limit.

In order to determine the maximum exposure, in terms of monthly **PMT**s under the loan, we need only to substitute the maximum chargeable interest rate for the starting rate:

	n	i	PV	PMT	FV
	360	11.5÷12	-100,000	?	0
solving				:	
				990.29	

Limit On Payment Increases Under ARMs

And additional safeguard available to the **ARM** borrower is a "cap" on the amount by which the annual **PMT** may increase, regardless of the increase in the interest rate. For example, in our example **ARM** the interest rate *could* increase as much as 2% in any one year.

---

[6] In some states the lender is required by law to place a lifetime cap on the interest rate which
    may be charged on this type loan. California is one such state.

Therefore the **PMT** based on this increase in interest rate would be:

	n	i	PV	PMT	FV
	360	0.63	-100,000	?	0
solving				:	
				699.21	

In this calculation we have added the annual cap in the interest rate, 2.0%, to the starting rate of 5.5%. Our monthly interest would be (5.5+2.0)/ 12 = 0.63.

But even this rate produces a **PMT** of $699.21 which is higher that the starting **PMT** of $567.79. How much higher?

Key–In	Display Shows
567.79 [Enter]	567.79
699.21 [Δ%] (2,4)	23.15

Most **ARM**s specify that the **PMT** may not be increased more than 7.5% in any one year. Since 23.15% is far greater than the maximum allowable percentage increase in the **PMT**, the 7.5% limit , in this case, determines the maximum **PMT**:

Key–In	Display Shows
567.79 [Enter]	567.79
1.075 [x] (2,10)	610.37

Therefore the maximum allowable **PMT** for that year will be $610.37, which is 7.5% higher than the previous **PMT**.

Does that mean that the interest rate is also limited? No! The interest rate will remain at 7.5% (5.5% + 2.0%). The question is: "Is this higher **PMT** sufficient to amortize the loan over the remaining months in the schedule?"

If this dramatic increase occurred at the end of the second month (refer to amortization schedule above) let's determine the effect on the loan:

Beginning Bal.	Payment	Interest	Paydown	Remaining Balance
(1) 100,000.00	567.79	458.33	109.46	99,890.54
(2) 99,890.54	567.79	457.83	109.96	99,780.58
(3) 99,780.58	610.37	623.63	-13.26	99,793.84

In this situation, the maximum allowable **PMT** is insufficient to amortize the loan. In this case, the unpaid interest ($13.26) is added to the previous balance (of $99,780.58) resulting in a Remaining Balance at the end of the third period which is higher than the loan balance at the beginning of the same month. This is referred to as "negative amortization." When this occurs, the borrower usually has a number of remedies: 1) he has the right to voluntarily increase the amount of the monthly **PMT**, or 2) to pay off the remaining balance of the loan without fees or penalties (to refinance), or 3) to convert to a fixed-rate mortgage, or 4) to increase the schedule of the loan not to exceed 40 years.

ARM PMTs May Not Decline In Step With Rates

ARM payments may not decline even when interest rates decline if an annual "cap" in the interest rate has restricted the lender's right to collect the full amount of an increased **PMT**, as the result of past increases in interest rates. The **PMT** may even *increase* under these circumstances until the lender has recovered all the interest which he was not able to collect due to the annual "cap." Information regarding this important point will be contained in the loan documents the borrower is asked to sign.

Recasting an ARM

In order to protect the lender against loans which could possibly grow to amounts which threaten the lender's security in the property, most ARMs specify an absolute limit beyond which the Remaining Balance may not grow, e.g. 100% to 125% of the original amount. If this limit is reached, the lender has the right to "recast" the loan and start all over again with a higher **PMT**.

In most cases, the ARM is recast over the months remaining in the original schedule of the loan, but some lenders may be amenable to recasting the loan over a period equal to the original amortization schedule. Should this occur, the remedies (above) available to the borrower apply.

When To Choose an ARM Over a Fixed-Rate Mortgage

If one could predict the future of interest rates, it would be a relatively simple matter to choose between an **ARM** and a fixed-rate mortgage.

Interest rates are affected by a myriad number of economic factors, but invariably begin to rise with recovery from economic slumps. As the economic recovery becomes more robust, interest rates tend to rise even more, eventually flattening out when the economy begins to slow under the weight of increasingly expensive capital. With the onset of recession, demand for capital usually wanes and interest rates historically recede, bottoming out six to nine months before the end of the recessionary period of the cycle.

Unfortunately, economic cycles, which used to run in approximately four year periods, have not been very predictable in the last 10-12 years. The recession that began in the United States in late 1990 did not followed a typical pattern of recovery. Recovery was slow and erratic, and interest rates remained quite low for a period of years.

It is probably a wise course to make a judgment regarding the selection of an **ARM** first by measuring your ability to sustain an increase in mortgage rates to the level represented at the maximum permissible interest rate and payment caps. If these increases could not be met, an **ARM** should not be seriously considered. If these caps can be met, then one may elect to gamble on the future direction of interest rates depending on where you believes you are in the present economic cycle. If you believe the economy is set for sustained growth, you may wish to "lock in" a low, fixed-rate mortgage. If you believe the economy is entering into a recessionary period, you may wish to gamble on a future interest rate decline by selecting an **ARM**.

For more specific information regarding ARMs (which is beyond the scope of this text), consult "Consumer Handbook on Adjustable Mortgages," available from any lending institution which is a member of the Federal Reserve Board, or the Federal Home Loan Bank Board.

Segment Summary

1. ARMs are mortgages which are designed to transfer the risk of rising interest rates to the borrower rather than to the lender. By guaranteeing itself a "spread" over the underlying Index rate, the lender locks-in a dependable profit margin.

2. ARMs provide for periodic adjustments to the effective interest rate by linking the mortgage rate to an index reflective of general interest rates in the economy.

3. Lenders use a number of indices as the base for their mortgage rate computations, but those indices which are slower to change afford more stability to the borrower and enhance the ability to budget outflows.

4. Interest rates in ARMs contain "caps" which limit the annual increase the lender may charge, and also the absolute increase the lender may charge over the entire life of the loan.

5. Payment changes, which are generally subject to change every six to twelve months, are also subject to "caps." Many ARMs limit the annual change in a payment to a maximum increase of 7.5% over the highest payment in the preceding 12 months.

6. If a limit on a payment results in a payment too low to pay the higher interest on the debt, the unpaid interest will be added to principal.

7. "Teaser" rates are low rates made by the lender to induce a borrower to select an ARM. These rates seldom last more than a few months.

8. Real estate and mortgage professionals should test the capacity of the borrower to service an ARM if the maximum interest rate is applied, and inform the potential borrower of the results.

9. It is difficult to check on the historical accuracy of a lender's adjustments to an existing ARM. Therefore most real estate professionals should be able to confirm the accuracy of each adjustment to the payment and the interest rate as they occur. Keeping track of an ARM on a computer spread sheet would be an excellent method of double-checking for accuracy.

10. The selection of an ARM instead of a fixed-rate mortgage is an exercise in predicting the future of interest rates.

III Buydown Mortgages

Economic cycles in the United States have historically averaged four years. As interest rates rise, approaching the peak of the economic cycle, real estate (an interest-rate sensitive industry) begins to feel the pinch, and property sales typically decline. Buydown Mortgages are particularly useful during the part of the economic cycle when interest rates are high and when the buyer's ability to qualify for a loan is temporarily impaired.

A Buydown Mortgage is a common marketing device whereby the seller (usually, but not always, a developer) agrees to underwrite the buyer's mortgage by contributing to the mortgage payments for a specified period of time. The amount contributed is taken from the developer's profits, so it is not uncommon to see prices raised slightly to make room for a "buydown."

3-2-1s ... and other Arrangements

A "3-2-1" buydown, for example, indicates that the seller will "buydown" the mortgage the equivalent of 3 interest points[1] the first period, 2 interest points the second period, and 1 interest point the third period. The "period" typically is one year, but some builders arrange buydowns in which the buydown period is only six months. A "2-1" buydown indicates that the seller will contribute the cash equivalent of 2 interest points the first period and 1 interest point the second period. Any combination or schedule is possible.

A Builder's Buydown

> For example, NewStuds Inc. finishes a tract of $350,000 homes just as the economic cycle peaks and home mortgage interest rates reach 12% per year. Sales are depressed. The marketing department suggests a 2-1 buydown to stimulate sales. A 20% downpayment is required.
>
> What will be the buyer's payment , and how much will the builder contribute?

Under this arrangement, the lender will still receive payments reflecting a mortgage bearing 12% annual interest payable monthly, but the builder will contribute sufficient cash to reduce the monthly payment for the buyer *to the equivalent of* a 10% (12%-2%) mortgage the first year and an 11% (12%-1%) mortgage the second year. Beginning with the third year, the buyer will shoulder the **PMTs** alone.

---

[1] A "point" usually refers to one percent of the loan amount. But here we mean a reduction of 1% in the interest rate.

The T-Bars for the NewStuds Inc. mortgage buydown look like this:

Bank Receives			Buyer Pays			Builder Pays	
	(280,000)						
1	**2,880.12**	−	1	**2,457.20**	=	1	**422.92**
:	:		:	:		:	:
12	2,880.12		12	2,457.20		12	422.92
13	2,880.12		13	2,666.51		13	213.61
:	:		:	:		:	:
24	2,880.12		13	2,666.51		13	213.61
25	2,880.12		25	2,880.12		25	0

As you can see, during the first year (12 payments) the buyer makes payments on his mortgage as though the interest rate were 10% per annum. The builder supplies the balance of the monthly payment necessary to support the actual 12% annual interest rate. At the beginning of the second year, the buyer's monthly payment increases to an amount necessary to support an 11% mortgage. The builder continues to supplement the payment to a 12% level. At the beginning of the third year (payment #25), the buydown ends and the buyer assumes the full burden of the payments at the interest rate stated in the note.

Some buydowns are constructed using **ARMs** rather than fixed-rate mortgages with the expectancy that the economic cycle will have turned $180°$ and interest rates will generally be lower when the buydown expires.[2]

Developer "Buys Out"

Most banks and all prudent buyers recognize that some developer/sellers may not be around for two years to continue to make these supplementary payments.[3] Therefore the developer pays an up-front, lump sum amount to the lender to implement the buydown.

This lump sum is the **Present Value** of the payments which the builder is obligated to make under the buydown arrangement, discounted at a rate acceptable to the lender. If the lender, in the example above, discounted the builder's future **PMTs** using **i = 12%**, the mortgage rate, the lender may break even. If the lender discounts the builder's payments by something less than 12%, the **Present Value** (amount demanded of builder) will be higher, and the lender may make an additional profit on the buydown.

---

[2] Real estate traditionally leads the economy into a recession and also leads it out of a recession as interest rates fall.

[3] Developers have a high mortality risk

Determining Builder's Paydown

A T-Bar constructed to represent the builder's payments over the two year period looks like:

		(PV ?)
	1	422.92
	:	:
i = .12÷12	12	422.92
	13	213.61
	:	:
	24	213.61

The keystrokes for the solution are as for any uneven cashflow:

	f CLX	0.00
	0 g CFo	0.00
	422.92 g CFj	422.92
	12 g Nj	12.00
	213.61 g CFj	213.61
	12 g Nj	12.00
	12 g i	1.00
solving		
	f NPV	6,893.60

Therefore the builder may be relieved of his future obligation to supplement the mortgage under the buydown contract by making a lump sum payment to the lender in the amount of $6,893.60. If the lender agrees to discount the builder's obligation by 10% per annum, calculated for monthly payments, how much would the builder be required to pay?

	Key In	**Display Shows**
	f CLX	0.00
	0 g CFo	0.00
	422.92 g CFj	422.92
	12 g Nj	12.00
	213.61 g CFj	213.61
	12 g Nj	12.00
	10 g i	0.83
solving		
	f NPV	7,009.91

Since buydowns may be tied to **ARM**s, lenders may not be willing to discount the future payments by the current market interest rate on the loan, in order hedge a potential increase in market interest rates.

Buydowns – A Small Price To Pay

As a percentage of the selling price, buydown mortgages are often a small price to pay to make an otherwise difficult-to-sell property financially attractive. A reduction in price of less than 3 or 4% cannot be expected to have much impact on the buyer, and a price reduction always has a measurable impact on profits since all the reduction comes from profits. But the cost of a buydown is often much less than the cost of an effective price reduction, and often much more effective.

For example, in the case above, what percent of the selling price of $350,000 is represented by the buydown amount for a 12% discount rate from the lender?

Key In	Display Shows
350000 Enter	350,000.00
6893.60 %T (1,3)	1.97

Buydown Available to Private Homesellers

While most buydowns are used by developers and builders, there is no reason why they cannot also be used by the individual owner/seller to help make a property more marketable, especially during times of high interest rates. Many lenders now offer such programs for buyers of resale properties. As you can see, a buydown such as the 2-1 buydown depicted above represents only a 1.97% reduction in price, yet may be far more effective in obtaining a sale than an equivalent price reduction because lenders are willing to qualify the buyer at the beginning rate.

There is no reason why a buydown could not also be used with secondary (carry-back) financing. But in those cases in which a homeseller wishes to do this, professional assistance in drawing the note and terms of the purchase agreement should be seriously considered.

Knowing how to analyze the lender's buydown program enables the financial professional to help either the buyer or the seller to select the most favorable buydown mortgage.

A Variation on the Buydown Theme

Certain lenders have created "Buydowns" which entail "no buydown costs and no points." They also claim "no deferred interest added to your loan balance."

Consider a fixed-rate mortgage carrying a current interest rate of 7.75%, payable monthly over a 30–year term. In order to convert this fixed-payment, market-rate loan to a 2-1 Buydown in which the "lender pays the buydown," the lender establishes a starter rate of 6.75% for the first year, then adds 1 interest point for second year. Beginning with the third year, and continuing for the remaining period of the original schedule, the interest rate is set at 2 points over the starting rate, or 8.75% (one full interest point over the conventional rate). The final payment schedule is based on these rates:

First year rate	6.75%
Second year rate	7.75%
Remaining years' rate	8.75%

Since there are no points and no fees, it is a relatively simple matter to calculate the Annual Percentage Rate (APR) or this loan.[4] Let's assume $100,000 of loan amount and determine what the payments will be for each year of the loan:

Keystrokes	Display	Comment
100000 CHS PV	-100,000	Original amount of loan
6.75 g i	0.56	Enters interest rate, first yr.
30 g n	360.00	Amortization period
0 FV	0.00	Fully amortized loan
PMT	648.60	Payment/month, year 1
12 n FV	98,934.25	Remaining balance, year 1
CHS PV	-98,934.25	Beginning balance, year 2
7.75 g i	0.65	Interest rate, year 2
348 n	348.00	Amortization time remaining
0 FV	0.00	Fully amortized
PMT	715.05	Payment/month, year 2
12 n FV	97,987.87	Remaining balance, year 2
CHS PV	-97,987.87	Beginning balance, year 3
8.75 g i	0.73	Enters interest rate, yrs. 28-30
28 g n	336.00	Amortization time remaining
0 FV	0.00	Fully amortized
PMT	782.63	Payment/month, years 28-30

---

[4] The true cost of the loan to the borrower, reflecting all loan charges and points paid.

Having identified what the payments will be for each year of the "Buydown," we can enter these PMTs into an uneven cashflow format and solve for the Internal Rate of Return.

100000 CHS g CFo	**-100,000.00**	**Starting balance of loan**
648.60 g CFj	**648.60**	**Year 1 PMT**
12 g Nj	**12.00**	**12 PMTs first year**
715.05 g CFj	**715.05**	**Year 2 PMT**
12 g Nj	**12.00**	**12 PMTs second year**
782.63 g CFj	**782.63**	**PMT for Years 28-30**
99 g Nj	**99.00**	
782.63 g CFj	**782.63**	
99 g Nj	**99.00**	**(Calculator can only store**
782.63 g CFj	**782.63**	**99 entries in any one cell.)**
99 g Nj	**99.00**	**Total 99+99+99+39 = 336**
782.63 g CFj	**782.63**	
39 g Nj	**39.00**	
RCL n	**6.00**	**Checks for # of entries**

solving

f IRR	**0.70**	**Monthly yield**
12 x	**8.44**	**Annual yield = APR**

The lender can afford to advertise no points and no costs since his yield on this kind of loan is 69 basis points over the comparable market rate loan. The payments to be made by the borrower under this buydown loan will total $21,419 greater than under the conventional loan. If the payments due under the Buydown loan are discounted at the market-rate interest, 7.75%, the **Net** Present Value of this loan to the lender is $6,980.05, or the approximate equivalent of a 7% loan fee. This is also the premium paid by the borrower, generally for the privilege of qualifying for a loan at a lower starting rate.

This type "Buydown" loan is really a hybrid mortgage combining some features of an ARM (changing payment amounts and changing interest rates) with some features of a Graduated Payment loan (qualifying buyer at a lower starting rate). It differs from the conventional "buydown" in that it raises interest rates later in the schedule in order to qualify the buyer at a rate slightly below market rates earlier in the schedule. The buyer, though initially qualified at a slightly lower rate for a short time, is committed to make payments at an interest rate above market rates for the remainder of the schedule. It differs from an ARM in that the buyer may take no advantage of a decline in rates.

Segment Summary

1. Buydowns are financial arrangements in which the seller assists in the mortgage payments for a specified period of time to make a property more affordable, especially during periods of high interest rates.

2. The effect to the buyer is to reduce the interest rate on the mortgage for the period of the buydown. Thereafter, the interest rate in the note becomes the effective rate to the buyer.

3. Builders frequently employ buydowns and cover the some or all expense of the buydown by small increases in the price of the property.

4. Lenders will require a lump sum payment from the builder/seller. This amount is the Present Value of the future payments the builder/seller is obligated to contribute, discounted at a rate acceptable to both.

5. If the lender discounts the buydown payments by a low interest rate, the cost to the builder/seller increases, and vice versa.

6. Buydown are also available to individual sellers to attract buyers in a competitive market and during times of high interest rates.

IV   The All-Inclusive Deed Of Trust Mortgage

The All-Inclusive Deed of Trust Mortgage (**AITD**), or "Wraparound Mortgage" as it is sometimes called, is a junior[1] lien whose principal (**PV**) includes (or "wraps around") the principal of one or more senior[2] notes. The **PMT**s of an AITD also include the amount of the **PMT** or **PMT**s necessary to service the senior obligations. An AITD can wrap around one, some, or all *previous* notes, including other AITDs, secured by the property. An AITD should never be structured to "wrap" notes which are recorded in a position junior to its own.

The principal use of the **AITD** is to preserve the economic benefit of one or more favorable senior mortgages, most often for the benefit of the seller. Although **AITD**s can also be of value to the borrower, they are not commonly structured primarily for the buyer's benefit.

How They Come About

When a property is sold with an existing mortgage in place, the mortgage may either be "assumed" by the buyer or the property may be transferred to the buyer "subject to" the existing mortgage. Although the terms are sometimes carelessly interchanged, they ought not be, because there is a vast difference between the two. This difference has major legal and economic implications for both seller and buyer, but especially for the buyer.

Consider a property offered for sale for $400,000: The title is encumbered by a first trust deed lien securing a promissory note whose current balance is $150,635. This original note bears interest at the attractive rate of 6% per annum, payable $1,079.91 per month. This loan is all due and payable exactly ten years from now.

Let's further assume that the seller of this property is willing to carry-back part of of the purchase price in the form of a note secured by a lien on the property. He requires a qualified buyer who is able to make a $100,000 down payment. Current mortgages for a property such as this one carry a 12% interest rate.

There are four ways in which the transaction might be structured for sale:

1. The buyer, with $100,000, in hand could find a new mortgage for $300,000 and ignore the seller's carry-back offer. He would, of course, pay the current 12% interest rate on the new mortgage.

---

[1]   "Junior' means that the trust deed securing the promissory note is recorded as a lien on the property *after* one or more prior trust deeds securing one or more earlier promissory notes.

[2]   A note written earlier in time than a succeeding note.

2. The property could be sold "subject to" the balance of the existing mortgage, $150,635. The seller would carry-back the difference as a second trust deed note in the amount of $149,365.
3. The buyer could "assume" the existing mortgage and the seller would carry back the difference as a second trust deed note in the amount of $149,365.
4. The seller could accept the buyer's down payment and carry back an All-Inclusive (second) Deed of Trust mortgage in the amount of $300,000.

Let's compare these capital structures:

	#1 New Mortgage	#2 "Subject To" 1st T.D.	#3 "Assume" 1st T,D.	#4 AITD
Sales Price	$400,000	$400,000	$400,0000	$400,000
New Mortgage	300,000			
Existing Loan		150,635	150,635	
New 2nd T.D.		149,365	149,365	
New AITD				300,000
Buyer's Equity (down payment)	100,000	100,000	100,000	100,000
Total Sales Price	$400,000	$400,000	$400,000	$400,000

As you can see, each arrangement results in the same equity position for the buyer.

There are important differences, however:

1. The New Mortgage option requires the buyer to apply for and secure a new $300,000 mortgage. At closing, the existing first trust deed will be expunged and the new first trust deed will be recorded against the title. The seller will have no further interest in the property.

2. If the property is taken "subject to" the existing mortgage, title will transfer without *any* contact with the present lender. The buyer takes full advantage of the

low 6% interest rate and the fact that the loan has been paid down for a number of years. As a result a greater portion of the buyer's future payments will be devoted to equity buildup.[3]

The buyer will enter into a contract with the seller to make the payments on behalf of the seller on the existing loan. *The seller will remain liable for the* $150,635 loan. In the event of a default by the buyer, the lender will foreclose against the seller, since it is (presumably) unaware of any transfer of title.[4] The seller's second trust deed position may be wiped out unless he is willing to "step up" and cure the default on the first trust deed mortgage and then foreclose under the second which he holds.[5]

3. Under the third option, a formal "assumption," the buyer is contractually obligated to present himself to the existing lender and seek to be placed in the legal shoes of the seller. If the lender approves the assumption of the loan, the seller *may* be relieved of all liability for the loan.[6] Nevertheless, in the event of a default by the buyer on the first trust deed loan, the seller's second trust deed loan is still in jeopardy and must be defended, as above.

4. Under the AITD arrangement, the buyer signs a promissory note for an amount equal to the sales price less his down payment. *This amount includes the amount due on the first trust deed note.* The buyer pays the seller on the amount and at the interest rate specified in the AITD note. The seller removes from the buyer's **PMT** an amount necessary to service the underlying first trust deed note, sends this amount to the holder of the first trust deed note, and pockets the difference.

At close of escrow two trust deeds encumber the property: a first trust deed securing a note whose balance is approximately $150,635 and a junior second deed of trust in the amount of $300,000. This second trust deed, however, legally must specify that it is an AITD and also stipulate the particulars regarding the underlying note which it "wraps around." These stipulations put any person interested in acquiring the property on notice that the property is encumbered by an AITD.

---

[3] More of the total payment is used to reduce the balance of the loan.

[4] A default by the buyer will not necessarily affect the seller's credit rating since he may declare that he was not the owner of the property at the time of the foreclosure.

[5] Trust deeds and mortgages typically give the beneficiary the right to foreclose on the loan if a default occurs in any senior note.

[6] Some lenders will seek to hold the seller as "additionally liable" for the loan. Prudent sellers whose mortgages are assumed arrange to have their sales contract specify, as a condition of the sale, that the assumption of the loan provides for the full release of the seller's liability.

For the purposes of the example, let's assume that the seller offers an 11% interest rate to the buyer. This loan will be scheduled for 30 years, but all due and payable in 10 years.

Seller's Position	Principal	Mo. Payment	Seller's Annual Payments
AITD Face Value	300,000	2,856.97	34,284 Received
1st TD Loan Bal.	150,635	1,079.91	12,959 Paid Out
Net Position	149,365	1,777.06	21,325 Retained

The seller appears to have lent $300,000, but $150,635 of this amount is the bank's funds. His equity in the AITD loan is the difference, $149,365, the same equity he would have had in a note if either the "subject to" or "assume" option had been used to structure this sale.

But the seller, using an AITD, is earning $21,325 on a net equity of $149,365, indicating a true annual interest rate of approximately **14.3%**.

This method of estimating the yield on an AITD is convenient and simple – but not entirely accurate because it ignores the actual payment amount on both loans and the fact that the senior note has a larger proportion of its payment devoted to equity buildup.

Calculating the Yield on an AITD Accurately

First, let's determine the payment amount (**PMT**) and then remaining balance (**FV**) for the AITD note after ten years. We will do this in two steps: first calculating the **PMT** due under the note, and then the remaining balance, the **FV**, after 120 **PMT**s have been made.

	n	i	PV	PMT	FV
	360	0.92	–300,000	?	0
solving				:	
				2,856.97	

Now we can determine the remaining balance after 120 **PMT**s (ten years) have been made. Do this by "writing over" the value in the **n** register:

	n	i	PV	PMT	FV
	120	0.92	–300,000	2856.97	?
solving					:
					276,787.67

The Underlying First Trust Deed

We do not know the *original* amount of the underlying senior note, but we don't need to. We do know that its **Present Value** is now $150,635, that the loan **PMT** is $1,079.91 per month, and that the interest rate, **i**, is 6% per annum. We need to know, however, what the remaining balance of this note will be in ten years (120 months).[7] The keystrokes to accomplish this are:

n	i	<PV>	PMT	FV
120	0.50	(150,635)	1079.91	?

solving

97,089.88

Once again, constructing a T-Bar will help us visualize the AITD cashflows. Note that the payment and the interest rate on the senior note have are specified, not calculated.

	AITD Loan		Senior Loan		Net Position
	(300,000)		(150,635)		(149,365)
1	2,856.97	1	1,079.91	1	1,777.06
:	2,856.97	:	1,079.91	:	1,777.06
:	2,856.97	:	1,079.91	:	1,777.06
:	2,856.97 <–This less this –>	:	1,079.91 equals this –>	:	1,777.06
:	2,856.97	:	1,079.91	:	1,777.06
:	2,856.97	:	1,079.91	:	1,777.06
:	2,856.97	:	1,079.91	:	1,777.06
:	2,856.97	:	1,079.91	:	1,777.06
:	2,856.97	:	1,079.91	:	1,777.06
120	2,856.97 + 276,788	120	1,079.91+ 97,090	120	1,777.06+179698

The T-Bar represented by Net Position is the result of subtracting the Senior Loan T-Bar from The AITD T-Bar. Net Position provides us with the **PV**, the **Pmt**, and the **FV**. It fails only to specify **i**.

---

[7] **Take care** not to structure an AITD note to have a due date longer than the due date on the underlying loan(s). If you do so, the holder of the AITD note would be required to pay off the balloon payment on the underlying senior note without the benefit of a balloon payment on the AITD. He may not have the cash. If the underlying senior note is completely amortized during the term of the AITD, however, then you need not be concerned about this.

But we can calculate the yield:

	n	i	PV	PMT	FV
	120	?	-149,365	1,777.06	179,698
solving		:			
		1.26284			

This yield is the <u>yield per month</u>. The annual yield is 12 times this number, or 15.15% – measurably more than the 14.3% yield we more casually estimated above.

Note that the **FV** of the Net Position T-Bar is greater than the **PV** of the same T-Bar. It says that, in addition to the payments received by the seller over a ten year period of time, he will receive a loan payoff greater than the amount he originally lent. The difference is accounted for by the extra cash earned by the seller in the form of the *equity buildup* in the maturing senior loan. Since the seller remained responsible for the underlying first trust deed loan, he benefited from its reduced balance, although the buyer's cash funded all the payments.

AITDs can be very profitable investments for the holder. But notice too, that the Buyer of the property benefits by obtaining an 11% loan from the seller at a time when the market rate is 12%. The "loser" in this transaction is the lender on the first trust deed mortgage since his loan is continued at a very low interest rate at a time when market rates are much higher. You can readily appreciate why lenders are usually resolute in calling below-market rate loans "due and payable" upon the transfer of the securing property.

Constructing an AITD to Produce a Specified Yield

Suppose that the seller in the above example desires to achieve an 16% *yield* on his net cash position over a ten–year period. What interest rate on the AITD loan would be required to produce this yield?

His net cash position of $149,365 is the **PV** of his loan. Let's amortize this loan over a 30 year schedule and then determine the remaining balance after 10 years.

	n	i	PV	PMT	FV
	360	16÷12	-149,365	?	0
solving				:	
				2008.60	

After ten years, the remaining balance on the net Position T-Bar must be:

	n	i	PV	PMT	FV
	120	16÷12	-149,365	2008.60	?
solving					:
					144,372.88

Knowing the elements of the Net Position T-Bar, and the senior note T-Bar (a given), we can add these two T-Bars together to produce the AITD T-Bar:

Net Position	+	Senior Loan	=	AITD

	(149,365)			(150,635)			(300,000)
1	2,008.60		1	1,079.91		1	3,088.51
:	2,008.60		:	1,079.91		:	3,088.51
:	2,008.60		:	1,079.91		:	3,088.51
:	2,008.60	<-This plus this-> :		1,079.91	equals -> :		3,088.51
:	2,008.60		:	1,079.91		:	3,088.51
:	2,008.60		:	1,079.91		:	3,088.51
:	2,008.60		:	1,079.91		:	3,088.51
:	2,008.60		:	1,079.91		:	3,088.51
:	2,008.60		:	1,079.9		:	3,088.51
120	2,008.60 + 144,373		120	1,079.91 + 97,090		120	3,088.51+241,463

We know everything about the AITD except for **i,** but we can solve for that:

	n	i	PV	PMT	FV
	120	?	–300000	3088.51	241,463
solving		:			
		0.94			

Again, this interest rate is a monthly rate. The annual required rate for the AITD is 0.94% x 12 = 11.29%. Since this rate is still below the market rate of 12%, the buyer may find this an attractive offer, especially in view of the fact that he will typically have no points and loan fees to pay.

AITDs Using Adjustable Interest Rates

There is no reason that the loan in this example could not also be set up as an **ARM**. For example, if the Cost of Funds Index were 9% at this time, the seller-lender could set the initial **AITD** interest rate equal to the COFI index (9%) plus a margin of 2.29% or 11.29%. If interest rates increased, the AITD rate might increase; if rates decline, the AITD rate would decline.[8]

If the underlying senior note is, indeed, an **ARM**, then it behooves the seller/lender to match the timing and term of the **AITD** with the timing and term of the underlying note. If he fails to take this precaution, he may be faced with increased interest rates on the senior note which he cannot recover from the AITD borrower.

Multiple Notes Underlying an AITD

Most AITD notes wrap around only one senior note. But there are times, especially in the sale of certain types of commercial properties,[9] when the AITD wraps a number of prior loans. In these cases, simply insert the required T-Bars for each loan in our diagrams above and follow the same general procedures.

Escrow AITD Payments

There have been a number of instances in which a seller accepts a low down payment from the buyer and carries the balance of the purchase price in the form of an **AITD**, but then never makes the **PMT**s on the senior loans. *Therefore no AITD PMTs should ever be made directly to the seller-holder of the AITD note.* These **PMT**s should be made through an escrow account, or, preferably, the **AITD** note should be collected by a bank or other reputable financial institution which will extract from the **AITD PMT** the **PMT**s necessary to service all the underlying loans. The remaining balance may then be forwarded to the **AITD** note holder.

What About the Deed?

In every discussion of AITDs someone always asks "What About the Deed?"
"When does the buyer get the deed?"

---

8   The alternative to an AITD loan for the seller is to demand cash, then invest his cash with the
     bank at, say, 9%. The bank would lend the buyer the required cash at 12%. AITDs can be an
     excellent investment for empty nesters.
9   Mobile Home Parks, motels and hotels, and small business sales are examples of real estate
     transactions which often involve AITDs which wrap more than one senior note.

The buyer receives a deed to the property at close of the purchase escrow, in exactly the same way he would had he bought all–cash, or financed the acquisition with a new, conventional, bank loan.

Confusion about this probably arises from transactions in which a buyer enters into a **Contract For Deed**, sometimes called a **Land Contract.** Under this arrangement, the buyer (vendee) does not receive legal title to the property until he has made a specified number of payments to the seller (vendor). During this time, the vendor retains legal title, conferring only "possessory" rights to the vendee. These contracts call for the vendee to obtain a loan at some time in the future and to pay off the balance of the Contract held by the vendor. Only at that time does the vendee receive legal title to the property.

AITDs are not Land Contracts; they are *financing* instruments. The buyer receives title to the property at the same time he would have had the financial structure not involved an All-Inclusive Trust Deed.

(There is no rational reason why any buyer should arrange to acquire property using a Land Contract, and no rational reason why a seller should arrange to sell property using a Land Contract. It is an archaism fraught with problems and difficulties.)

CAVEAT

THERE ARE TIMES WHEN THE USE OF AN AITD CAN BE VERY BENEFICIAL TO BOTH BUYER AND SELLER IN A REAL ESTATE TRANSACTION. TODAY, HOWEVER, THE PRESENCE OF DUE-ON-SALE CLAUSES IN ALMOST ALL INSTITUTIONAL LOANS HAS GREATLY REDUCED THE OPPORTUNITY TO USE AITDS IN THE FINANCIAL STRUCTURE. EVEN WHEN THERE IS NO ACCELERATION CLAUSE, OR DUE-ON-SALE CLAUSE, IN A SENIOR NOTE, THE USE OF AN AITD IS NOT A SIMPLE REAL ESTATE LOAN SITUATION. IT IS STRONGLY RECOMMENDED THAT BOTH BUYER AND SELLER CONSULT AN EXPERIENCED REAL ESTATE ATTORNEY FAMILIAR WITH THE MANY PITFALLS THAT AWAIT THE UNWARY IN THE USE OF AITDS TODAY.

Segment Summary

1. All-Inclusive Deed of Trust Mortgages (notes) may represent a useful financing tool under carefully selected circumstances. Both buyer and seller benefits may be found in these mortgage instruments.

2. The presence of a Due-On-Sale Clause in any senior note, however, makes the use an AITD very dangerous unless the approval of the senior lender is obtained.

3. The AITD operates principally for the benefit of the seller. If the prior note(s) contain no Due-On-Sale Clause, it is usually to the Buyer's benefit to take the property "subject to" the existing mortgages.

4. An AITD can "wraparound" one or more senior notes.

5. One of the principal sources of extra yield is the paydown portion of the underlying loan which the lender realizes.

6. AITDs are complex mortgage instruments for which the assistance of an experienced real estate attorney is essential.

V Loan Constants, Ratios and APRs

Before proceeding further, let's look at a few "hand tools" lenders use in formulating loans, computing loan amounts and qualifying borrowers for a loan. in relation to values.

Loan Constants

In Chapter 1 we discussed the calculation of the Present Value of a level annuity for a definite period of time (n) and showed that :

$$\mathbf{PV} = \frac{C}{i}\left(1 - \frac{1}{i(1+i)^n}\right)$$

When **C**, the level cashflow, is equal to $1.00, PV is the Present Value of $1 discounted at rate **i** over **n** periods. When C is something other than $1.00, there is a proportionate relationship between the the PV of $1.00 and the PV of C. This relationship holds true for every separate and distinct combination of **i** and **n**.

For example, when i = .10÷12, and n = 360 and C is $1.00, the PV is equal to 113.95. When C is other than $1.00, the PV is proportionate to C. If PV is $100,000 then

$$\frac{\$1.00}{113.95} = \frac{x}{100000}$$

$$x = \frac{100000}{113.95} = \$877.57$$

We could also say that $\quad x = 100000 * \frac{1}{113.95} = \$877.57$

or, $\quad x = 100000 * \underline{0.0087757} = \$877.57$

Therefore the loan constant (**k**) is the reciprocal of the PV of $1.00 in PMT, discounted at a given rate **i** over **n** periods. In this case, the loan constant for a fully amortized loan at 10% interest over 360 months is **0.0087757** per $1.00 of loan. To make life easier for us, we can express loan konstants in terms of $1,000 of loan, or $8.7757 per $1,000 of loan.[1]

---

[1] Loan amortization tables are still sold in bookstores.

You can see that the loan **k** of this particular loan (with a distinct **i** & **n**) is also the ratio of the loan payment, $877.57, to the principal amount of the loan, $100,000:

$$\text{Loan k} = \frac{877.57}{100000} = .0087757$$

Put in its simplest terms, the "loan constant" is simply the amount of **PMT** required to amortize $1.00 of loan (**PV**) over a given amortization period, **n**, at a selected interest rate **i**. It is also the ratio of the fixed loan payment to the amount of the loan.

The easiest way to calculate a loan **k** is by using the financial calculator or computer. Let's calculate the loan constant for the 30-year fully amortizing loan, **PMT**s made monthly, at an annual interest rate of 10%.

	n	i	PV	PMT	FV
	360	10/12	1	?	0

solving

0.008775716
(expanded to 9 places)[2]

If you own a financial calculator or computer you will rarely have a need to use loan constants since you can key-in the actual loan amount (PV) and obtain the precise PMT for the amount of the loan. But for the record here are the relationships:

(1) **Loan Amt. x Loan k = Loan Payment**

(2) $\frac{\textbf{Loan Payment}}{\textbf{Loan Amount}}$ **= Loan k**

(3) $\frac{\textbf{Loan Payment}}{\textbf{Loan k}}$ **= Loan Amount**

We spend time here with loan konstants, not because they are valuable in this day and age of the calculator and computer, but because they draw attention to the relationship of $1 in PMT to the PV of a loan. We want to use your understanding of this relationship to discuss Graduated Payment Loans , Graduated Payment Leases and Graduated Payment Annuities in the next sections.

---

[2] Press f 9 Key (4,2)

Residential Loan Guidelines

Residential lenders generally screen a prospective home buyer's ability to service the mortgage debt by the use of two ratios applied to monthly household cashflow: the **front-end** and the **back-end** ratios.

The front-end ratio is the ratio of total housing expenses to gross monthly household income. Total housing expenses include the principal and interest payment on the loan, real estate taxes, property insurance and, in applicable cases, home owner fees or other association fees which are required to be paid. If the borrower makes less than a 20% downpayment, mortgage insurance is also generally required. All these costs applicable to housing are counted in determining the front-end ratio.

The most common front-end ratio used by residential lenders is 28%. Therefore a household which enjoys $6,000 in gross income (before deductions and income taxes) would generally be limited to 28% of this amount, or $1,680 per month for the total housing expenses listed above. By subtracting from total housing costs all costs other than the principal and interest payment on the mortgage, the lender determines how many gross dollars remain to service the residential loan. Given a certain interest rate and amortization period, the amount of the residential loan is easily calculated.

For example, using the data above, and estimating "all other housing costs" to be $300 per month, the family with gross household income of $6,000 could qualify for a 8% 30-year loans as follows:

Gross Monthly Household Income	$6,000
28% Front-end ratio	.28
Total housing costs not to exceed	1,680
All other housing costs	300
Amount available to service mortgage	1,380

	n	i	PV	PMT	FV
	360	8÷12	?	1380	0
solving			:		
			−188,071.22		

Therefore this household could support a mortgage of $188,000.

The back-end ratio is similar, except that it includes, in addition to total housing costs, all consumer debt payments. A common back-end ratio is 34%. Therefore in the case of a family with gross household income of $6,000, the total of all housing expenses *and* consumer installment debt may not exceed $2,040 per month. It is easy to see that $100 of consumer debt over the limit of $2,040 reduces the household's mortgage-carrying ability by $13,628. (Substitute $100 for PMT). This shortfall must be made up by added downpayment. Since it is easier to reduce monthly consumer debt installment by $100 than to save $13,628, potential home buyers have a clearly defined strategy before them.

Front and back-end ratios are commonly used but are just as commonly altered by a particular lender for a particular potential borrower. But they do serve as indicators of the cashflows which residential lenders deem to be prudently devoted to periodic (installment) debt.

Loan-to-Value Ratios

Almost all lenders use Loan-to-Value ratios to further insulate themselves against the risk of loss in the event of loan default. Despite the ability of the borrower to service a mortgage of a given size, the residential lender will generally restrict his loan to a percentage of the appraised value of the property. If a residential lender declares that it may not exceed an **LTV** ratio of 80%, it means that:

$$\frac{\text{Amount of Loan}}{\text{Appraised Value of Property}} \leq 0.80$$

Debt Service (Coverage) Ratios

Commercial and investment lenders frequently use a Loan-to-Value ratio as a secondary guideline. Their first preference is the Debt Service Ratio (**DSR**), or Debt Coverage Ratio (**DCR**), as it is sometimes called.

The preference is well justified. The primary source of repayment for a loan placed on income-producing property is its Net Operating Income (NOI): the income the property delivers after operating expenses.[3] This stands in contrast to the single-family residential property in which the primary source of repayment of the loan is the earning power of the homeowner's income – not the property's income. Therefore commercial and investment (C&I) lenders have a vital interest in the **q**uantity, **q**uality and **d**uration[4] of the Net Operating Income.

The **NOI** is the income remaining after payment of operating expense but *before* loan payments. This is why every commercial lender requires an up-to-date operating statement from the prospective borrower, together with copies of all current leases. If the lender

---

[3]   Not a few lenders now require that the borrower also have the capability of making the loan payments in the event the rent derived from the property proves insufficient. These are "recourse" or "credit" lenders.

[4]   "Quantity" refers to the size of the loan; "quality" refers to who is the source of the payments (the tenant); "duration" refers to how long this rent stream is likely to continue.

doesn't care for the way the operating statement looks, he will construct his own and use it to determine a pro-forma **NOI**. He requests an examination of the leases not only to verify present income but also to assess, wherever possible, the financial strength of the tenant.

Once the **NOI** can be verified, the commercial lender will make a judgment regarding the **risk** associated with the income stream by examining the location, the leases and the credit worthiness of the tenants. If, for example, he judges that the risk associated with a residential apartment house of good quality in a healthy market is relatively low, he may require a Debt Service Ratio (DSR), or Debt Coverage Ratio (DCR) of 1.15. Properties which appear to be riskier – for instance, single-purpose, specialized buildings – command higher DSRs. In general, the riskier the property, the higher the DSR. A DSR of 1.15 means that:

$$\frac{\text{Net Operating Income}}{\text{Annual Debt Expense}} = 1.15$$

For example, if the **NOI** of a certain property were $250,000 per year and the lender held to a DSR or DCR of 1.15, we could determine the annual cost of servicing the mortgage as follows:

$$\frac{\$250000}{\text{Annual Debt Expense}} = 1.15$$

Annual Debt Expense = $250,000 ÷ 1.15

Annual Debt Expense = $217,391.30

Since we now know the annual debt expense, we can compute the *monthly* debt expense and ask the lender what interest rate he requires and how long the (amortization) schedule is on a loan to be paid monthly. He replies: "10% and 30 years, all due in 7 (years)."

Now we have all the information to determine the amount of loan this lender *may* lend on this property:

	n	i	PV	PMT	FV
	360	10÷12	?	(217,391.30 ÷ 12)	0
solving			:		
			-2,064,326.41		

Utilizing any of the components we have discussed above, a lender has a number of stratagems to decrease the risk and/or increase the profitability of a loan:

1. He can raise the DSR/DCR factor. A higher factor means less cash allowed for loan servicing, therefore a lower loan amount and a lower loan/value ratio.

2. He can raise interest rates.
3. He can shorten the amortization schedule.
4. He can "pro-forma" the expense statements to lower the NOI.
5. He can call the loan earlier in the schedule. This doesn't influence loan amounts but it does lessen his exposure to changes in long term interest rates and, coincidentally, increases rollover (refinance) fees.

The APR – the Annual Percentage Rate

In Chapter 3 we devoted considerable to attention to the Internal Rate of Return and its calculation from available cashflows. Chapter 3 also explained that IRR, Yield and APR are all one and the same measuring stick under different brand names. A banker's "yield" = automobile dealer's "APR" on car leases = investor's "IRR" on an apartment house.

Actually, bankers talk about "yield" when they discuss their return on a loan, but when they discuss the true cost of the loan to the borrower, they are required by federal law to calculate and disclose the **Annual Percentage Rate (APR)**, which is the true interest cost when all related loan charges are factored in.

This federal law is not limited to real property loans (1-4 residential units), but applies to all kinds of consumer loans. It is not required to be disclosed to commercial borrowers or borrowers on residential properties greater than 4 units.

The **APR** is a very useful number because it permits the informed borrower to compare a myriad of different financial terms offered by different lenders, and to determine which loan offers the lowest total cost of borrowing.

We hasten to add that the least expensive loan is not always the best loan for the consumer because other terms of the loan agreement affect the value of the loan and need to be included in any comparative evaluation. For example, a loan may, by its terms, permit the borrower to transfer the loan to a second party for little or no assignment fee. This kind of loan may take on extra value if rates take a turn to the upside and new money becomes more expensive.

Calculating APRs

Consider, for example, these two loans offered by different lenders:

> Lender A offers a loan of $100,000 at an annual interest rate of 9.375%, payable monthly, over an amortization schedule of 30 years, but all due and payable at the end of 5 years. Lender A will charge 2 points as loan fee.
>
> Lender B offers a loan of $100,000 at an annual interest rate of 9.50%, payable monthly, over an amortization schedule of 30 years, but all due and payable at the end of 5 years. Lender B will charge 1.75 points as loan fee.
>
> Which of these loans is less costly?

Follow these simple steps to determine the true cost of the loan:

1. Set the loan up in the calculator and solve for the monthly payment. This is the amount the borrower contracts to pay each month.
2. Determine the charges[5] and points to be paid (Loan Amount x Points = Fee) and subtract this sum from the **PV**.
3. Enter this net amount into **PV** and solve for **i**, the true interest rate and **APR**.

Using this guide, let's calculate the true interest rate for Lender A's loan:

Key In	Display Shows	Comment
360 [n]	360.00	Enters amort.period
9.375 [g] [i]	0.78	The monthly interest rate
100000 [CHS] [PV]	−100,000.00	Enters PV as a negative
0 [FV]	0.00	Inserts 0 into FV
solving		
[PMT]	831.75	
60 [n] [FV]	96,153.41	The balance at 60 months entered into FV
[RCL] [PV] [CHS]	100,000.00	
[Enter]	100,000.00	Puts 100,000 in Y register

---

[5] Only those charges directly connected with the loan, and not the escrow or other charges, should be used.

2 %	2,000.00	The value of points paid
−	98,000	The net amount after payment of loan points
CHS PV	-98,000.00	Replaces PV as a negative
solving		
i	0.82	Calculates true monthly interest rate
12 x	9.89	The true annual interest, and the APR for Loan A

We can calculate the APR for Loan B in the same way:

360 n	360.00	Enters amort.period
9.5 g i	0.79	The monthly interest rate
100000 CHS PV	−100,000.00	Enters PV as a negative
0 FV	0.00	Inserts 0 into FV
solving		
PMT	840.85	
60 n, FV	96,240.98	The balance at 60 months entered into FV
RCL PV CHS	100,000.00	
Enter	100,000.00	Puts 100000 in Y register
1.75 %	1,750.00	The value of points
−	98,250	The net amount after payment of loan points
CHS PV	-98,250.00	Replaces PV as a negative
solving		
i	0.83	Calculates true monthly interest
12 x	9.95	The true annual interest, The APR for Loan B

As you can see, Loan A is the more economical loan even though it charges higher points than Loan B. This solution is specific for the terms quoted for these particular loans. If, for example, the due date on the loans were shorter than 5 years, the APR would change.

Junk Fees Make a Difference

Lenders augment their yields on loans by charging additional fees to the borrower at the time of loan closing. Some of these fees are legitimate costs incurred by the lender, while others can be of questionable parentage. The more specious charges have come to be known as "junk fees." Some lenders are adept at playing this variation of the "bait and switch" scam with borrowers. At first, the offered interest rate, loan points, and other terms of the loan appear very attractive; but at the end of escrow a whole new set of charges are billed to the buyer.

The practice has been, and still is, widespread. Therefore the informed borrower will also pay attention to the estimate of loan costs and charges which the lender, under federal Regulation Z, is required to deliver to some borrowers[6] within three days of receiving the loan application.

All the fees charged to the borrower are rightfully counted in as "loan costs." These fees include some of the following:

1. Appraisal Fee	$450.00
2. Document Review	150.00
3. Trust Deed Review	175.00
4. Preparation of Note	300.00
5. Review of Note	150.00
6. Recording fees	50.00
7. Tax Notice fees	85.00
8. Lender Messenger fees	60.50

Some lender fees are valid: a property appraisal fee, Tax Notice fees,[7] etc.. But the list of other fees charged by some lenders is often a fairy tale.

All the fees charged in connection with the loan (not escrow service fees) need to be included in a determination of the loan's APR.

The total of the list above is an additional $1,370.50. This amount must be added to the value of the points in determining the actual net amount delivered to the borrower at closing. Therefore in the last example above, the net proceeds available to the borrower would be:

---

[6] In connection with residential loans on 1 to 4 units

[7] Fees to be paid to a service which will notify the lender if the taxes on the property are not paid.

100000 Enter	100,000.00	Face Value of Loan
1.75 %	1,750.00	The value of points
1370.50 +	3,120.50	Total loan charges
-	96,879.50	The net loan amount after payment of <u>all fees</u>
CHS PV	-96,879.5	Replaces PV as a negative
solving		
i	0.86	Calculates true monthly interest
12 x	10.31	The true annual interest, The APR for Loan B, all charges considered

Segment Summary

1. A loan constant is that amount of **PMT** necessary to amortize $1.00 of loan principal over a certain amortization schedule and at a certain interest rate. It is also the quotient obtained by dividing the loan payment by the amount of the loan.

2. Financial calculators have made the use of loan constants all but obsolete.

3. A **Loan-to-Value** ratio refers to the amount of loan divided by the (appraised) value of the residential property.

4. An income-to-debt cost is a variant of this ratio used in commercial and investment lending. This ratio, the **DSR** or **DCR**, substitutes the Net Operating Income (NOI) as the numerator of the ratio, and the annual cost of servicing the debt as the denominator of the fraction.

5. Lenders manipulate **Loan-to-Value** and **Debt Service Ratios** to increase the safety of their loans.

6. High LTV ratio residential loans are likely to be risky loans. Commercial loans carrying high DCRs reflect the lender's risk concern.

7. The **APR** of a loan is the actual interest charged by the lender and paid by the borrower, after including all loan fees and charges.

8. Loans of different interest rates, including different "other loan fees," can be compared by determining their individual **APR**s.

VI The Graduated Payment Mortgage

The Graduated Payment Mortgage is the most interesting of all commonly employed mortgage instruments, not because it is the most frequently used or the most complex, but because it affords the finance professional an excellent insight into those cashflow concepts offering the greatest potential to craft loans, leases, financial plans and other divers financial instruments innovatively to custom-fit problem situations.

In our discussion of loan constants, we defined the loan constant as that amount of payment (**PMT**) necessary to amortize $1.00 of loan principal (**PV**) over a specified amortization schedule (**n**) and at a designated interest rate (**i**).

In addition, we have seen that the **PMT**, for a given amortization schedule and interest rate, is proportional to the amount of the principal (**PV**) to be reduced, so that, given the loan constant, we can multiply any amount of loan principal by the constant in order to determine the necessary **PMT**.

The Discounted Value of the PMTs

There is a second way in which can look at the amortized loan. This view enables us to appreciate that the present values of all the **PMT**s due under the loan, when discounted at the rate **i,** will add up to equal the **PV** of the loan.

To illustrate, calculate the **PV** of a **PMT** in the amount of $877.<u>5715701</u> over a period of 360 months, discounted at the rate of 10% per year on a monthly basis:

	n	i	PV	PMT	FV
	360	.083	?	877.5715701	0
solving			:		
			-100,000		

This loan has a principal value of $100,000 precisely because this sum equals the total **P**resent **V**alue of all future cashflows, discounted at the indicated rate, **i.**

In the fixed-rate amortizing loan, we held the **PMT**s constant; in the **ARM** we varied the **PMT**s according to periodic changes in the interest rate,[1] such that the balance of the loan at any point in its schedule would be reduced to zero by a periodically adjusted **PMT**. The GPM loan, however, is different.

---

[1] A combination of the rate of an underlying base index plus a margin, or spread, for the lender.

The GPM decides beforehand the amount and timing of the periodic changes in the **PMT,** and – given these changes – the amount of principal (**PV**) which the **PMT**s of the loan will amortize.[2] Let's illustrate the GPM by a simple example.

> Suppose that you desire to create a loan instrument which will fully amortize a principal over 10 years with monthly **PMT**s discounted at 9%. The borrower, however, will have a reduced ability to manage a fixed-rate **PMT** during the early years of the loan, and therefore requires a lower initial **PMT**. But the borrower can manage a 5% increase each year for the first five years of the loan on a reasonable initial **PMT** amount.
>
> What <u>initial</u> **PMT** will fully amortize this loan, given five scheduled increases of 5% in the **PMT**s, over a 10-year term?

Unity (1) is a convenient assumption in many math problems, so let's use it here. Let's suppose that the first PMT is $1.00. If we increase the original PMT 5% each year for five years[3] and then hold the PMT steady for the remainder of the ten–year schedule, we can determine the amount of PV which this $1 of PMT, periodically increased as stipulated, will support. Our T-Bar would look like this:

	Month #		(PV) = ?
		1	1.00
		:	:
		12	1.00
$i = .09 \div 12$		13	1.05
		:	:
		24	1.05
		25	1.1025
		:	:
		36	1.1025
		37	1.157625
		:	:
		48	1.157625
		49	1.21550625
		:	:
		60	1.21550625
		61	1.276281563
		:	:
		120	1.276281563

---

2   Over a predetermined schedule and at a predetermined discount rate.

3   There is no reason that the mortgage payment must increase for 5 years, although this is what is commercially available. If you program the increments to continue beyond five years, the initial PMT will be reduced.

This series of cashflows begins with $1.00 PMT. Each 12 periods (months), the PMT is increased 5% for five successive increases. This is one of the formats used in widely available Graduated Payment Mortgages designed by FHA and VA lenders. Since you now know how to discount uneven cash flows these keystrokes should be easy to follow:

Press	Display Shows	Comment
f CLX	0.00	Clears all memory
0 g CFo	0.00	Set n counter to zero
1 g CFj	1.00	Enters first cashflow
12 g Nj	12.00	Enters number of times cashflow occurs
1.05 g CFo	1.05	Enters second cashflow
12 g Nj	12.00	Enters number of times cashflow occurs
1.1025	1.10^4	Enters third cashflow
12 g Nj	12.00	Enters number of times cashflow occurs
1.157625	1.16	Enters third cashflow
12 g Nj	12.00	Enters number of times cashflow occurs
1.2155065	1.22	Enters fourth cashflow
12 g Nj	12.00	Enters number of times cashflow occurs
1.276281563	1.28	Enters last cashflow
60 g Nj	60.00	Enters number of times cashflow occurs
9 g i	0.75	Enters discount rate/mo.
RCL n	6.00	Confirms six different cashflows have been entered
solving		
f NPV (1,3)	92.04	92.04369870, actually. the PV of this series of cashflows

We have determined that $1.00 of initial monthly **PMT**, increased 5% per year for five increases, will support a **P V** of $92.04369870 amortized over ten years at a 9% annual interest/discount rate.

---

[4] Assumes your calculator is set to show two places

If we want to amortize $25,000 of principal under these same terms, the beginning **PMT** would be proportionate:

$$\frac{\$1.00}{\$92.04....} = \frac{x}{\$25,000} .$$

$$x = \frac{\$25,000}{\$92.04...} = \$271.61.. \quad (\$271.6101195)$$

Determining the Payments

Now that we know the first year's **PMT**, $271.61, we can easily calculate the **PMT**s due under the entire schedule by increasing the initial **PMT** of $271.61 by 5% per year for *five increases*:

Months	Payment per Month
1 - 12	$271.61
13 - 24	285.19
25 - 36	299.45
37 - 48	314.42
49 - 60	330.14
61 - 120	346.65

GPM Loan Factors

Notice that the initial **PMT** of $271.61 is equal, in our example, to $25000 ÷ 92.04, which is the same as multiplying $25,000 by the reciprocal of 92.04.[5] The reciprocal of 92.04 is 1/92.04, or 0.010865.

This "factor," 0.010865, is the *kind* supplied by FHA and VA to real estate professionals to enable them to determine the amount of initial **PMT** for a Graduated Payment Mortgage of a particular amortization schedule and interest rate.[6] They need only multiply the principal amount of the new mortgage times the GPL factor, for the appropriate term and interest rate, in order to determine the first payment under the GPM. These factors are **GPM constants**.

---

5   The reciprocal of a number is equal to 1 ÷ by that number. The reciprocal of 10 is 1/10, or .10

6   In this case we used a very short amortization period for the convenience of the example. Therefore this factor will not apply to loans of a longer amortization period.

Annual Percentage Increase Can Vary

In this case we increased the annual **PMT** amounts 5% per year, but we could just as easily have increased them 2.5% per year, or 6%, or 7.5% per year.... or any percentage we might have chosen.

But since most residential loans are resold in the secondary market, managing an infinite variety of GPM loans, all with different percentage steps in the **PMT**s, would be an infinite nightmare to loan servicing administrators. Therefore Federal Housing Authority (FHA) and Veteran's Administration (VA) loans limit the annual percent increases in the **PMT**s to three basic choices: 2.5%, 5.0% and 7.5% annual increases. If the annual percent increase is low, the beginning **PMT** will be higher. If the annual percent increase is high, the initial **PMT** will be lower.

You can test the validity of our structured **GPM** loan by constructing a ten-year amortization schedule to determine whether this structure of increasing **PMT**s will indeed amortize the loan to zero in ten years.

Some Practical Observations

Notice that the first **PMT** in our schedule is significantly below the fixed-rate, constant **PMT** amount that would be needed to amortize $25,000 over 10 years at 9% annual interest.[7] The final **PMT** amount is also measurably greater than what the fixed-rate, constant **PMT** amount would be.

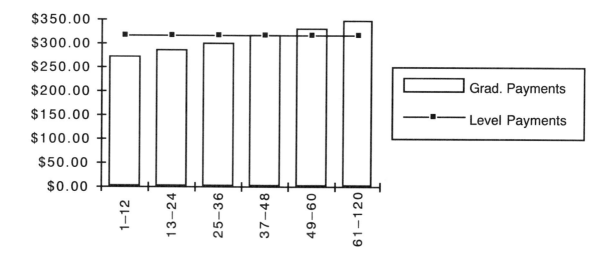

---

7   What would this fixed-payment amount be, please?

This means that **GPM** mortgages are best suited to those borrowers (both residential and commercial) who can reliably anticipate the increases in the funds needed to service the debt.

GPM loans also allow the borrower to qualify for a larger loan since qualification of the buyer to make the **PMT**s is usually based on the ability to make the first year's **PMT**. As individual borrowers advance along in age, however, their increases in income generally begin to moderate and eventually income usually declines. Therefore it would be entirely inappropriate to place a couple about to retire in a residence utilizing a 7.5% increasing **GPM**. In just a few years, the increasing annual **PMT**s under the **GPM** schedule would likely outstrip their housing budget. So great care must be taken by the professional not to arrange such a financial structure for those whose ability to meet future scheduled payments is problematical.

A second point worth noting is that longer scheduled (25-30 years) **GPM** loans fail to amortize in their early years. Therefore the borrower accumulates unpaid interest which is added to principal.

Consider, for example that a $100,000 loan, bearing annual interest at 9%, with monthly **PMT**s, and amortized over 30 years, would be fully amortized by a fixed monthly **PMT** of $839.20. The same loan, constructed as a **GPM** with payments increasing 7.5% in the second, third, fourth, fifth and sixth years, would require an initial monthly **PMT** of only $583.78. This loan, however, would fail to amortize in the early years:

PMT	Beginning Balance	Payment	Interest 9%	Equity (Paydown)	Remaining Balance
(1)	100,000.00	583.78	750.00	-166.22	100,**166.22**
(2)	100,166.22	583.78	751.25	-167.47	100,**333.69**

This "negative amortization" builds more quickly with loans whose **PMT**s have steeper annual increments. For this reason, it is quite common to see GPM loans develop balances during the early life of the loan which are greater than the original balance. If a property subject to a 25-30 year **GPM** loan is to be sold during the first 5-6 years of the loan, the payoff required in escrow will be greater than the original loan amount, thereby reducing perceived equity. This may come as a shock to some sellers.

Negative amortization is generally not a problem in the case of GPM loans amortized over short periods since these loans incorporate in their **PMT** large amounts of equity/paydown sums which can easily cover the interest due.

GPM-ARMs

We have not covered the combination of an **ARM** and a **GPM**, but **GPM-ARM** loans are offered. They are arranged exactly as would be a **GPM** loan except that the interest rate adjusts periodically according to the underlying Index, forcing an adjustment in the remaining **PMT**s. These loans are difficult to program on the HP-12C because the entire loan must be "recast" with every change in the interest rate. Their calculation is best done on a computer, not a calculator, and therefore we will not attempt them here.

Some Commercial Applications

There are times when a valuable tenant seeks relief from payments due under a longer-term lease because of, perhaps, a temporary industry setback, or a general recession. The lessor may wish to accommodate the tenant but does not wish to reduce the present value of the lease. The concepts behind the Graduated Payment Mortgage can be translated to serve a Graduate Payment <u>Lease</u> under which a series of **PMT**s under the lease will result in a Net Present Value for the new lease not less than the **NPV** of the original lease.

Consider this situation.

> ABC Inc. leases a large industrial building under a 20-year lease. The current rent is $10,000 per month. The original lease calls for a 25% increase in rent every five years, and has 15 years to term. At the beginning of the 6th year, the CFO of ABC Inc. approaches the lessor for some other rent schedule which can soften the required rental increase at hand. The lessor agrees and comes to you for help in modifying the lease PMTs in such a way that the NPV of the lease will not be diminished.
>
> What can be done?

First, we can calculate the NPV of the existing rental schedule as follows:

Months Remaining		? NPV
	1-60	12,500
	61-120	15,625
	121-180	19,531

Since this is a triple-net lease,[8] and the tenant has excellent future business prospects, the lessor is content to realize a 10% return (discount rate) on his money. Therefore we will

---

[8] In common parlance, a lease in which the tenant pays all expenses of property operation including taxes, maintenance and insurance. Sometimes called a "pure" net lease. Terminology here is confusing.

discount this cashflow by 10% annually, computed monthly, to arrive at the **NPV** of the present schedule of lease **PMT**s.

To allow for the fact that the first lease **PMT** is to be made in advance, we will store the first **PMT** in **CFo**. The keystrokes are:

Key In	Display Shows
f CLX	0.00
12500 g CFo	12,500.00
12500 g CFj	12,500.00
59 g Nj	59.00
15625 g CFj	15,625.00
60 g Nj	60.00
19531 g CFj	19,531.00
60 g Nj	60.00
10 g i	0.83
solving	
f NPV (1.3)	1,386,311.11

We stored the first **PMT** of $12,500 (in **CFo**) from the cashflow because the rent is paid in advance and the calculator does not respond to a change in **BEG** (1,7) or **END** (1,8) when working with uneven cashflows. When we solved for **NPV**, the calculator added (netted) the Present Value of the subsequent cashflows to the amount stored in **CFo**.

We now know that whatever the new arrangement may be, it must preserve the lessor's **NPV** of $1,386,311.

Further consultation with ABC Inc. indicates that they would be agreeable to a lease which increases 6% yearly, if the beginning rent were sufficiently below the $12,500 they now face. Therefore we can construct a new lease whose payments increase annually rather than every five years. We will use the concept of unity to represent the first initial monthly **PMT** and also discount this cashflow by 10%, payable monthly:

<u>Key In</u>	<u>Display Shows</u>	<u>Comments</u>
f CLX	0.00	
1 g CFo	1.00	
1 g CFj	1.00	
11 g Nj	11.00	
1.06 g CFj	1.06	the first annual increase
12 g Nj	12.00	
1.1236 g CFj	1.12	the second annual increase
12 g Nj	12.0	
1.1910 g CFj	1.19	the third annual increase
12 g NJ		
etc., etc.		
:		
2.2609 g CFj	2.26	the fourteenth annual increase
12 g Nj	12.00	
10 g i	0.83	
solving		
f NPV (1.3)	130.89	

Now we can establish a ratio between the **PMTs** and the **NPVs**:

$$\frac{1}{130.89} = \frac{x}{1386311.11}$$

$$x = \frac{1386311.11}{130.89}$$

$$x = 10,591.42$$

The lease payments would then become:

<u>Months</u>	<u>$ Rent per Month</u>	<u>Months</u>	<u>$ Rent per Month</u>
1 - 12	10,591	97 - 108	16,880
13 - 24	11,227	109 - 120	17,893
25 - 36	11,900	121 - 132	18,967
37 - 48	12,614	133 - 144	20,105
49 - 60	13,371	145 - 156	21,311
61 - 72	14,173	157 - 168	22,590
73 - 84	15,023	169 - 180	23,945
85 - 96	15,925		

As was true for the mortgage, the initial payments under this (more) graduated lease arrangement are lower than what had been originally scheduled, thereby satisfying the tenant's need. But the **PMT**s are also scheduled to preserve the lessor's (present) value of the lease. Note that the rent paid by the tenant toward the end of the lease will be greater than that which was originally scheduled. Therefore the Graduated Payment Lease does increase somewhat the lessor's risk that the tenant may default before the higher **PMT**s are made. But this consideration needs to be balanced against the other advantages to the lessor.

Financial Planning Applications of GPM Concept

Consider the following situation:

> The Browns desire to establish an college education fund for their daughter who will be entering the university in 10 years. They estimate that they will need $80,000 in today's dollars at that time. Inflation is estimated to average 4% per year.
>
> If funds on deposit are projected to earn 7% per year after tax, compounded monthly, what monthly amount must be set aside at the beginning of each month to accumulate that sum?

This appears to be a relatively simple problem to solve:

First, let's calculate the effective monthly interest rate when the nominal rate is 7% p.a. and the inflation rate is 4% p.a.:

$$\text{Effective rate} = \frac{1+\text{nominal rate}^9}{1+\text{inflation rate}} - 1 = \frac{12.07}{12.04} - 1 = .002492 = 0.2492\%$$

Using this effective rate we can calculate the monthly investment required to acquire a FV of $80,000:[10]

---

[9] Note that the expression $(1 + .07/12) \div (1+.04/12) = 12.07/12.04$

[10] This can be treated as a future value since we have already converted it to constant dollars by using the effective rate.

Set to BEG

	n	i	PV	PMT	FV
	120	.2492	0	?	80,000
solving				:	
				−571.35	

This estimate represents a constant, level payment each month of $571.35 for a total of 120 months. This solution, however, would not be acceptable to many couples who could not afford this initial monthly sum. Many more families, however, could afford a plan which called for smaller initial payments and periodic annual increases (paralleling their expected earning curve). This application of the cashflow concept behind the Graduate Payment Mortgage may mean the difference between a workable plan and no plan at all for the Browns.

Notice that we could also accumulate this constant-dollar FV by investing a lump sum today at the effective rate:

Set to BEG

	n	i	PV	PMT	FV
	120	.2492	?	0	80,000
solving					
	−59,346.62				

You now know the equivalent PV of the investment which the Brown's need to make to attain their financial goal. Now you need to determine what monthly PMT, increased each year, will have the same PV.

Following consultation, the Brown's agree that they would be comfortable with a monthly payment which increased 5% each year for the next ten years. "But," they ask – "what will be the amount required to initiate the plan?"

First, you need to determine what **PV** will be supported by the monthly payment of $1 made at the beginning of each month, and increased on a yearly basis by 5%.

Month	Pmt Req'd	Month	Pmt Req'd
1-12	1.00	61-72	1.27628
12-24	1.05	73-84	1.34010
25-36	1.1025	85-96	1.40710
37-48	1.15763	97-108	1.47746
49-60	1.21551	109-120	1.55133

When this cashflow is discounted at the <u>effective</u> monthly rate (to allow for inflation), the resulting PV is $128.7668. Therefore, since $1.00 in initial PMT will support a total PV of $128.7668, you need only ask what proportionate PMT would be required to support a PV of $59,346.62?

$$\frac{\$1.00}{\$128.7668} = \frac{x}{\$59346.62}$$

$$x = \$460.88$$

This initial amount is almost 20% below the amount which would be required by a level PMT. The full schedule would be:

Month	Pmt Req'd	Month	Pmt Req'd
1-12	460.88	61-72	588.22
12-24	483.93	73-84	617.63
25-36	580.13	85-96	648.51
37-48	533.53	97-108	680.94
49-60	560.21	109-120	714.98

The risk in this plan is that the Brown's may "default" on the plan in later years as the monthly PMT increases. Therefore you may wish to plan the annual increase conservatively. Using a lower annual percent increase raises the initial PMT, but it also results in a lower PMT toward the end of the schedule.

This plan is also very sensitive to the rate at which invested funds grow. An increase in yield of only 1% will lower the initial PMT more than 9%. As you can see, there is a balance to be struck between the need to ensure the growth of the fund and the risk the Browns may be willing to take in order to lower their initial PMT.

This concept of graduated PMTs to achieve a stated PV can be adapted for many types of funds and plans. It can result in a financial plan much better tailored to the individual needs of the client, and therefore be much more likely to be successful..

Segment Summary

1. Construction of Graduated Payment financial plans depends on the fact that the Present Value of a cashflow is equal to the sum total of all the individual **PMTs** which can be expected under the schedule, discounted at a rate acceptable to the receiver of the cashflow. PMTs need not be equal.

2. Real estate professionals who make use of **GPMs** may help qualify buyers for a home mortgage greater than that for which they could qualify under a standard **ARM** or fixed-payment mortgage.

3. Greater annual percentage increases in the **PMT** schedule enable buyers to qualify for a larger mortgage, but subject them to higher monthly payments later on. Smaller annual percentage rates ease the rate at which the initial payment will increase and are therefore less risky. Special care should be taken to ensure that the clients are confident that they will be able to meet the increasing monthly payments required to service the plan or the mortgage.

4. Long-term amortizing **GPM**ortgages result in a negatively progressing loan balance over the first 5 years of the loan.

5. The concept of the **GPM** need not be confined to mortgages but can be applied by financial advisors and planners to special circumstances such as education funds, retirement plans, and other investment programs requiring periodic investments over a number of years. The benefit of using this concept is that many more individuals and families will be able to participate in a graduated payment plan than in a fixed plan of comparable Present Value.

VII The Participation Mortgage

A participation mortgage is one in which a lender lends money to a project and receives, in addition to a negotiated rate of interest, a share in either the net operating income from the property, or a share in the proceeds upon sale, or, most commonly, a share in both.

Most lenders who do not wish to enter into a joint-venture[1] partnership with the developer want to avoid taking an ownership interest in the property. Under the terms of a participation loan the lender can share in the profitability of the project as additional consideration for making a loan without necessarily incurring the additional risks of a partner. Under the terms of a participation loan, the lender becomes entitled to an agreed upon share of operating income and a share of the reversionary value as additional interest on sale or exchange.[2]

The circumstances under which a participation loan may be arranged are many and varied. Oftentimes when interest rates are quite high, the developer may be willing to convey a share of net operating income and sale proceeds in the property in exchange for a below-market rate loan whose interest rate will be low enough to enable the property to service the debt and return a cashflow to the developer. The lender makes up for this lower-than-market-rate loan by collecting a share of net income and a "kicker"[3] at the time of sale or exchange. At other times, a project may be perceived to carry an above-average risk for which the lender seeks to be additionally rewarded.

Consider a situation in which a developer has completed a new retail center which required a $9,000,000 construction loan. The center has been built when interest rates are high. The construction lender will not provide funds for longer than the time required to attain an occupancy rate of 95%, but in no case longer than 3 years. The developer finds a permanent-loan lender willing to make a 7-year loan[4] in the amount of $9,000,000, sufficient to "take out, " or retire, the construction loan at the end of the initial three years.

The permanent lender agrees to fund $9,000,000 at closing at a 9.5% interest-only rate, plus 50% of the cashflow after servicing the loan. According to the agreement, the developer must sell[5] the property at the end of 7 years, at which time the lender is also entitled to 50% of the net sale proceeds, after reasonable expenses of sale.

---

[1] A joint venture is a partnership entered into to accomplish one specific project.

[2] As part of the agreement, a predetermined sale date is established between the owner/developer and the lender.

[3] A share of the reversionary income.

[4] Scheduled (amortized) over a longer period, however.

[5] The developer may also refinance the property with a new lender. The participating lender's share would be determined by using as a sale price its appraised value at that time.

A pro-forma[6] constructed for seven years indicates that the center will have the following Net Operating Income, debt service and lender's share of the cashflow over the holding period:

Year	1	2	3	4	5	6	7
Loan Balance	9,000,000	9,000,000	9,000,000	9,000,000	9,000,000	9,000,000	9,000,000
Gr. Income	1,250,000	1,312,500	1,378,125	1,447,031	1,519,383	1,595,352	1,675,120
Expenses	375,000	393,750	413,438	434,109	455,815	478,606	502,536
N.O.I.	875,000	918,750	964,688	1,012,922	1,063,568	1,116,746	1,172,584
Debt Service	855,000	855,000	855,000	855,000	855,000	855,000	855,000
Cashflow	20,000	63,750	109,688	157,922	208,568	261,746	317,584
50% Share	10,000	31,875	54,844	78,961	104,284	130,873	158,792
Lender's Total	865,000	886,875	909,844	933,961	959,284	985,873	1,013,792

The Reversion Value & Lender's Share

Assume also that the property is sold (or appraised) at the end of year 7 for $13,800,000. The lender is entitled to 50% of the net proceeds after expenses of the sale. If the net sales proceeds were $13,400,000, the lender would receive an additional $2,200,000 (50% of (13,400,000 −9,000,000)).

With these data a T-Bar can be constructed to depict the lender's cashflows:

Year	Interest	50% Share of NOI	Loan Balance	50% Reversion	Totals
	9,000,000				9,000,000
1	855,000 +	10,000			865,000
2	855,000 +	31,875			886,875
3	855,000 +	54,844			909,844
4	855,000 +	78,961			933,961
5	855,000 +	104,284			959,284
6	855,000 +	130,873			985,873
7	855,000 +	158,792	+ 9,000,000 +	2,200,000	12,213,792

---

6 A series of prospective annual operating statements linked together by assumptions about future operations

The T-Bar represented by <u>Totals</u> provides all the data necessary to calculate the lender's yield on its funds:

Press	Display Shows	Comment
f CLX	**0.00**	**Clears all memories**[7]
9000000 **CHS g CFo**	**-9,000,000.00**	**Enters CFo**
865000 **g CFj**	**865,000.00**	**First PMT**
8886875 **g CFj**	**886,875.00**	**Second PMT**
909844 **g CFj**	**909,844.00**	**hird PMT**
933961 **g CFj**	**933,961.00**	**Fourth PMT**
959284 **g CFj**	**959,284.00**	**Fifth PMT**
985873 **g CFj**	**985,873.00**	**Sixth PMT**
12213792 **g CFj**	**12,213,792.00**	**Last PMT**

solving

f IRR	**12.65**	**The lender's yield**

Although the lender's share may seem to exact a high price for its participation, without it the project may never be built. In addition, the lender incurs significant risk for which it is entitled to be rewarded.

This technique may be used to estimate either the lender's anticipated yield on funds, or the other side of the same coin, the developer's true cost of a participation loan.

Segment Summary

1. Participation loans deliver a portion of the income from a property to the lender as additional interest in the form of a share of cashflows.

2. The added cashflow can be in the form of a share of net operating income, a share of reversionary income, or both – whatever is required for a successful financial structure.

2. Most participation loans are constructed during times of high interest rates when the subject property cannot service the debt on a required new mortgage. Delaying a major project can erode all future profits in the form of holding costs.

3. Each segment of the agreement can be represented in the form of a T-Bar in which the cashflows to the lender are plotted out over time.

4. Thereafter, calculating the yield of a participation mortgage is no different than any other cashflow with uneven payments.

---

[7] Except Programmable memory

Chapter 6
Valuing
Cashflows
from *Real Estate*

It has been said that an investment in real property is an investment in cashflows. The same could be said for making any investment where cash is advanced in the reasonable expectation of receiving back the invested cash, together with a profit.

Yet many investments offered to investors use the most specious methods to evaluate the return. For example, limited partnerships are frequently offered using the following type format to calculate anticipated returns:

Original Investment $25,000.00
Returns:

        First Year....................................$500.00
        Second Year...............................1,000.00
        Third Year.............................. 10,500.00
        Fourth Year 12,000.00
        Fifth Year............................... 15,000.00

               Total Return $39,000.00

$$\text{Return on Investment} = \frac{\$39000}{25000} = 156\%$$

This approach to measuring investment returns is analogous to the example given in Chapter 1 in which a buyer offers to pay you $1,000,000 for your home whose present value is only $250,000 but doesn't bother to specify *when* you will receive the cash. Both proposals ask the investor to ignore the time-value of money. In Chapter 3, we explained in some detail how the true time-value rate of return on an investment could be calculated using the Internal Rate of Return method.

If the IRR method is applied to this example, we find that the true yield on this investment is 11.8% – a far cry from the 156% represented.

The investor who requires a 12% annual return on invested funds may prefer to use the Net Present Value Method described in Chapter 2. If the NPV method is applied to this same cashflow, one finds that the NPV of the investment is –$145.06, meaning that this investment would fail to deliver a 12% annual rate of return on invested funds.

Both the IRR and NPV methods of measuring cashflows utilize discounting techniques which respect the time value of money. But there are other methods of valuing investments which deserve comment.

Capitalization Rates

In Chapter 1 we discussed the method of determining the Present Value of an even cashflow which continues in perpetuity. You will recall that the Present Value of such an annuity is represented by the formula:

$$\textbf{Present Value} = \frac{C}{i}$$

where **C** is the even cashflow and **i** is the capitalization rate.

Understanding this, it is a small step to understand that the Capitalization Method of Determining Market Value is really a method of determining the Present Value of an investment by discounting all the anticipated cashflows by a rate acceptable to the investor. Then, by changing our terminology a bit we, have:

$$\textbf{Fair Market Value (PV)} = \frac{\textbf{Net Operating Income}}{\textbf{Capitalization Rate}}$$

Most experienced investors understand the relationships of the capitalization rate, the discount rate and the *Present* or *Fair Market* Value:

1. Fair Market Value	x Capitalization Rate	= Net Operating Income
2. Net Operating Income	÷ Capitalization Rate	= Fair Market Value
3. Net Operating Income	÷ Fair Market Value	= Capitalization Rate

Therefore a property having a Fair Market Value of $1,000,000 and producing Net Operating Income of $100,000 will be determined to have an overall[1] capitalization rate of:

$$\frac{\$100000}{\$1000000} = .10 = 10\% \quad \text{(Formula \#3 above)}$$

The second relationship, #2, is the relationship real estate appraisers use to establish Fair Market Value using the **Income Approach to Value**. The appraiser determines the Net Operating Income of the property by reviewing the rental income and operating expenses[2] and then *selecting* an appropriate overall capitalization rate. He arrives at an estimate of Fair Market Value by dividing the NOI by the selected "cap" rate:

$$\frac{\text{Net Operating Income}}{\text{Capitalization Rate}} = \frac{\$100000}{0.10} = \$1,000,000 = \text{FMV}$$

Where Capitalization Rates Come From

Real estate capitalization rates come from different sources. One such source is the market itself. The appraiser who uses the *Income Approach to Value* will search the marketplace for a *similar* property, of a *similar* age, in a *similar* condition, of a *similar* size, in a *similar* location. He needs then to determine the recent sales price of the property and its net operating income. If you suspect this to be a very difficult task, you are absolutely correct. It is!

In fact, very few investment properties are so similar to the property under review that the appraiser can make a direct extrapolation from one property to another. Nevertheless the appraiser will collect data on recent sales and then attempt to determine the net operating income for each of the sold properties.

With each set of Fair Market Values and Net Operating Incomes the appraiser can calculate the overall capitalization rate of each property sold. If an adjustment is to be made because of property *dis*similarities, the adjustment is made to the capitalization rate selected. These adjustments are "judgment calls" by the appraiser. An increase in the capitalization rate lowers the Fair Market Value of the subject property, while a decrease raises the Fair Market Value.

---

[1] "Overall" because it measures the return on both the investor's equity and the lender's debt.

[2] Effective (collected) income minus operating expenses = Net Operating Income (NOI).

Let's take an example. Suppose a similar property were found which had recently sold for $750,000. Careful inquiry revealed that the property was producing net operating income at the rate of $75,000 per year. The capitalization rate is readily determined:

$$\frac{\$75000}{\$750000} = .10 = \text{Capitalization Rate}$$

Capitalization rates are most often derived from current and recent market data. It has already been shown that, given a capitalization rate, we can estimate the Fair Market Value of a property if we can determine its NOI:

$$\frac{\text{Net Operating Income}}{\text{Capitalization Rate}} = \text{Fair Market Value}$$

$$\frac{\$75,000}{.10} = \$750,000$$

The Fair Market Value varies inversely to the capitalization rate. Notice that as the cap rate increases, small changes in the rate result in large differences in Value:

$$\frac{\$75,000}{.07} = \$1,074,285 \qquad \frac{\$75,000}{.08} = \$937,599$$

$$\frac{\$75,000}{.09} = \$833,333 \qquad \frac{\$75,000}{.10} = \$750,000$$

Why Capitalization Rates Change

If you would like to know what causes capitalization rates to change, you have to be willing to dissect one to find out what's inside: You would find that a capitalization rate consists of three <u>sub-rates.</u> The Capitalization Rate is the summation of these three sub-rates:

1. A rate of return **of** the cash made available
2. A safe rate of return **on** the cash made available, and
3 A rate to reflect the **risk** that one or both these events will never happen.

Capitalization rates do *not* include adjustments for inflation.

The Rate of Return ON Invested Capital

If you ask your neighbor to identify the safest investment, he or she may well cite securities (bills, notes and bonds) issued by the U.S. Treasury. "After all," they may say, "if the U.S. Government can't pay its obligations, what good is its money?"

That may be true, but it doesn't mean that an investment in U.S. Treasury securities is risk-free. For example, a standard U.S. Treasury ten-year bond with a face value of $1,000 not only pays periodic interest over ten years but will also repay the principal ($1,000) at the end of the ten years. The government typically makes no adjustment in its pay-off of $1,000 to reflect any inflation which has occurred over the intervening ten years.[3]

If, however, the government has coined so much money that the $1,000 received at maturity will buy only 200 loaves of bread rather than the 300 loaves it could buy when you first lent the money to Uncle Sam,[4] then you will have lost the purchasing power, or *value*, of your money during the holding period. The risk in holding standard U.S. Securities is inflation.

U.S. Government bonds may indeed be among the safest domestic investments, but they are decidedly not risk-free. If you were to subtract from the coupon rate of return on U.S. Government 30-year bonds in any year over the last 30-40 years, the inflation rate for the same year, you may be surprised to find that the difference has been remarkably consistent – between two and three percent per year, although these rates in the mid-1990s are now trending toward the 3-4% range.

This has been the *safest* rate, the *basic* interest rate charged for the use of money. During those years in which investors perceived added risk from future inflation, they required an additional percentage to be added to the safe rate resulting in higher when-issued coupon rates for newly issued bonds. When investors perceived the risk of inflation to be low, they reduced their demands, and the total coupon rate for U.S. Treasuries drifted downward toward the basic, safest rate. Therefore the rate on U.S. securities, at any particular time, reflects a combination of the safe rate for the use of money and a rate levied for perceived (inflationary) risk. It bears repeating that capitalization rates do not include rates reflecting the risk of inflation.

---

[3] The U.S. government began issuing bonds in 1997 whose FVs are adjusted for inflation. In relieving the investor's concern about inflation, the government hopes to lower the true cost of borrowing. The idea is not new and has received a tepid response both here and in other countries.

[4] Reflecting an inflation rate of about 4% compounded annually.

The Rate of Return OF the Capital

The second sub-rate we would find is a rate which would account for the return *of* the capital invested. Interest rates do not provide for the recovery *of* the capital in an investment. If the investment is a depreciable asset, such as a building on a parcel of land, the building has an economic life beyond which it will no longer produce income. Therefore the capital cost of a depreciating asset[5] must be recovered by the investor over its remaining economic life.[6]

A new apartment building which is estimated to last 50 years requires the recovery of 2% of its cost each year (100% ÷ 50) in order to effect a return *of* its capital cost. An older building with only 25 years remaining economic life must return its capital cost in half the time, or at twice the rate: 4% per year (100% ÷ 25 years). All things considered, this is essentially why older buildings sell at capitalization rates measurably higher than newer buildings. Land, of course, does not wear out but may nevertheless decline in value. Allowance for this is made in the risk rate.

The Risk Rate

The third sub-rate involved in the overall capitalization rate is an allowance for *risk*. The more reliable the flow of income from the investment is judged to be, the less is added to compensate the investor for risk. Consequently a building leased to a strong credit tenant[7] will have a smaller risk factor built into the rate than a building occupied by short-term tenants of lesser credit worthiness. This fact emphasizes the economic value of a strong tenant, on a strong lease, for a long term. A good tenant adds substantially to the value of the property by justifying a lower capitalization rate, which, in turn, results in a higher investment value.

Specialized buildings (bank buildings, gasoline filling stations, theaters, fast food stores, etc.) command higher cap rates because their very specialization limits their adaptability to a new use. Potential investors view the specialized configuration as added risk in the form of potentially longer periods of vacancy in the event of a termination by the present tenant, and therefore they add to the risk rate required to purchase them.

---

5   Don't confuse this kind of economic depreciation with the kind associated with tax law. Here we are referring to real loss of value due to aging of the assets, in contrast to a tax-orient depreciation deduction from income which may have nothing to do with the actual remaining economic life of the asset.

6   The length of time an improvement on the land can be expected to generate income.

7   A tenant whose financial statement offers a high degree of assurance that the rent will be paid for the term of the lease contract, whether or not the tenant continues to occupy the property.

When added together, these three sub-rates result in the *overall* capitalization rate. For example:

Return *on* Investment........ 3.5%
Return *of* Investment......... 2.5
Risk Rate 3.5
Overall Cap. Rate............. 9.5%

Required Return Rates and Risk Are Subjective Issues

While the first of these sub-rates (the safe rate) may be somewhat objective, the second and third rates are decidedly subjective.

One investor may view a certain property as having a longer remaining economic life, or having a stronger likelihood of remaining leased because of a favorable location. A second investor may be more critical of the quality of the building's construction and less certain of its marketability over time. Accordingly, the first investor will accept a lower cap rate (yield) than the first, and will pay more for the property than the second investor.

This is most apparent in the market for lower-priced properties where many more investors compete. The beginning investor, especially, is prone to overpay for properties by accepting very low cap rates. As a beginner, he may not know the factors which make up the cap rate; nevertheless, he is still accepting a lower return rate *on* his capital, and/or he assesses the *risk* associated with the property to be much less than do others.

Band of Investments Approach to Cap Rates

In addition to the Market Data and Sub-rate Summation methods of selecting Capitalization rates, a third method is an approach which relates the investor's risk to those incurred by other entities which have a concurrent financial interest in the property.

Consider this capital structure which combines ownership (equity) and debt interests in a recently acquired office building:

Total Value $1 Million

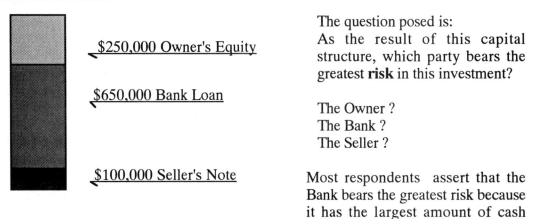

$250,000 Owner's Equity

$650,000 Bank Loan

$100,000 Seller's Note

The question posed is:
As the result of this capital structure, which party bears the greatest **risk** in this investment?

The Owner ?
The Bank ?
The Seller ?

Most respondents assert that the Bank bears the greatest risk because it has the largest amount of cash invested; others say the recent Seller who holds a second trust deed, because a foreclosure by the Bank would erase the Seller's position.

In truth, the greatest risk of loss is borne by the Owner since the property could decline in value as much as $250,000, eliminating all the Owner's equity, without reducing either the Bank's or the second trust deed holder's security interest in the property.

A well established precept of investment is that *returns run with risk.* Those participants in an investment who bear greater risk are entitled to a greater reward. If the Bank charges an 8.5% interest rate on its share of the cash advanced, some observers would hold that the second trust deed holder is entitled to a 10% rate of return. If this is so, to what return is the Owner entitled if he carries the greatest risk of loss? Many would opine that he is entitled, by comparison, to at least a 12%, or greater, return.

Therefore each investment position would require the following amounts of net operating cash to meet its particular yield requirements. The total of these sums is the amount of annual net income the property must produce, which also happens to be its **Net Operating Income:**

Risk Position	Cash at Risk	Required Rate	Cash Required
# 1. Owner	$250,000	12%	$30,000
# 2. Seller	100,000	10	10,000
# 3. Bank	650,000	8.5	55,250

Total Capitalization $1,000,000   **N.O.I.** Required $95,250

But a Net Operating Income of $95,250 flowing from a property valued at $ 1 million indicates an overall capitalization rate of:

$$\frac{\$95,250}{\$1,000,000} = .09525 = \textbf{9.525\%}$$

Overall Capitalization Rates, therefore, can be determined from Comparative Market Data, by the Summation of sub-rates, and by the Band of Investment method. Of the three, the most commonly used method is the Comparative Market Data approach.

Strengths and Weaknesses of Cap Rates

As an index of Fair Market Value, the capitalization rate is certainly easy to understand and easy to apply. Its weaknesses, however, may be less evident.

For most investors, the capitalization method of determining market value is relatively quite simple. But many of these same investors do not appreciate that this method is based on two important assumptions: 1) the net operating income (cashflow) from the property will never change; and 2) the cashflow will go on forever (in perpetuity). Neither of these assumptions is valid.

Some investors, who would never buy a widget business on the strength of next year's projected income *alone,* balk at any method of arriving at real property values which involve estimating future income. Real estate ownership *is* a business, and, like a widget business, demands the very best effort to assess its present health, the market in which it operates today, the market in which it is likely to operate tomorrow, and the strengths and weaknesses of the product (the property) in the light of present and foreseeable competition. The informed investor does not buy real property on the strength of cap rates alone.

A second objection to reliance on capitalization rates *gathered from market data* is that they are always *retro*spective in nature. They tell where the market has been, not where it may be headed. But income property (as does any investment) derives its value from the present worth of *future* benefits, not from the value of bygone benefits. To emphasize this point, capitalization rates are most properly applied to the following year's Net Operating Income.[8] By using last year's cap rates, an investor can overpay in a declining market or miss opportunities in a rising market.

The last weakness pertains to the difficulty of finding truly comparable properties and then accurately uncovering their Net Operating Incomes. While it is common to see appraisals comparing income properties that are not in the same location, not of the same quality, not on the same side of town, and not of the same age, the Market Data approach to selecting

---

8   The Income Approach to Value depends on the "Principle of Anticipation" (of income).

capitalization rates to determine fair market value remains the most frequently used determinant of value for the average investor.

Market Value vs. Investment Value of Property

A note of caution may be appropriate here because there can be an important difference between the *market value* of an income property and its *investment value.*

Appraisers define the Fair Market Value of a property as the highest price which *an informed , willing and knowledgeable* buyer, *not acting under duress,* will pay to an *informed,willing and knowledgeable* seller, who is also *free from duress.*

There are eight conditions in this definition, most of which are not met in a great number of income property transactions, especially those involving new, inexperienced or ill-advised buyers dealing in lower-priced properties where competition is keen. Quite often, a large number of *uninformed but willing* buyers pursue properties offered for sale by equally *uninformed but willing* sellers, and a market is created by their transactions at price levels which simply do not make good financial/investment sense.
This is frequently the case with the beginning investor with a relatively modest amount of capital. This investor often competes with a greater number of potential buyers, some of whom are very willing to pay a price for property which precludes any reasonable chance of a satisfactory return. Many of these competitors have neither acquisition standards nor return requirements, and therefore play roles as "loose financial cannons" on the investment deck.

There is no simple "solution" to the market influence of competitors willing to overpay for investment property. Perhaps the best offense is for the informed investor to know beforehand the financial profile of the property which will best suit his or her particular investment criteria and move quickly when such a property is found. If no such property seems to be available which fits these specifications, the investor must either change his or her investment standards, or look elsewhere (alter the investment strategy).

Cash-on-Cash & Gross Rent Multipliers

Two other single-period investment yardsticks are in popular use: **Cash-on-Cash**, and the **Gross Rent Multiplier.**

The latter index, the Gross Rent Multiplier (**GRM**), is simply the quotient resulting from the division of a property's Fair Market Value by its Gross Scheduled Income:[9]

---

[9] Sometimes described as Gross Potential Income

$$\frac{\text{Fair Market Value}}{\text{Annual Gross Scheduled Income}} = \text{Gross Rent Multiplier}[10]$$

If it can be ascertained that a property which recently sold for $1 million had a Gross Scheduled Income (**GSI**) of $125,000, then its "gross multiplier" would be:

$$\frac{\$1000000}{\$125000} = 8.0 \text{, the } \textbf{GRM}$$

Therefore, a nearby property of similar characteristics, sporting a Gross Scheduled Income of $150,000, could be expected to have a market value of:

$$\$150,000 \text{ x } 8.0 = \$1,200,000$$

The GRM is very widely used in the marketing of smaller multi-family residential units, probably because operating expenses submitted by owners of these units are notoriously unreliable.[11] Any estimate of Net Operating Income based on understated or under-reported expenses consequently will be overstated, resulting in overstatement of market value.

The GRM is best used as a screening tool, since it measures nothing below the level of *Scheduled* rental income. It certainly provides no indication of a property's operating income due to vacancy or credit losses, no gauge of operating expenses, nor of future cashflows. But it is precisely future cashflows for which the informed investor is paying.

The **Cash-on-Cash** index is a useful, *single-period* measurement of value because it looks beyond vacancy, beyond operating expenses and beyond net operating income to income remaining after mortgage payments. It is the relationship of the *Spendable Income* (income after debt service, but before taxes)[12] to the Cash *initially* invested in the property, or:

$$\frac{\text{Cash After Debt Service}}{\text{Cash Initially Invested in the Property}}$$

It, too, may be faulted in that it does not encourage a look at the potential for future income. But it does give a rather good indication of the cash return the investor can expect in relation to his total cash investment *at the end of the first period of ownership*. Since it measures cash after operating expenses *and* after the costs of servicing the debt, it is also a reflection of the mortgageability of the property and its potential leverage.

---

[10] The Gross Rent Multiplier can be expressed either as an annual or monthly figure.

[11] Frequently as the result of poor record keeping and poor management; sometimes as the result of dishonesty

[12] Cash-on-Cash after taxes is also, but less frequently, measured.

Investors who rely upon the Cash-on-Cash index operate on the implicit assumption that if the property can perform to a reasonable standard in its first year of operation, it should, in the absence of any obvious or foreseeable problems, continue to perform well. Sometimes it does, sometimes it does not.

This useful and valuable index is often misused by promoters who forecast future (spendable) cashflows and then compare these future cashflows to the first year's cash investment. This is a serious analytical mistake, similar to comparing $1 to be received in Year 50 to $1 invested today: the process ignores the time value of money. It has the same inborn-error-of-metabolism found in the example cited earlier in which a promoter is willing to pay $1,000,000 for a property worth only $250,000,[13] but neglects to tell the seller *when* the price is to be paid.

Distinguishing Cash-on-Cash, ROI, ROE & IRR

These four indices are often confused, and more frequently mis-used. The first, Cash-on-Cash, is a measure of the rate of pre-tax cash returned on initially invested capital and is commonly understood to be limited to the first year of ownership.

For example, $100,000 in pre-tax spendable income from a property in which the investor placed $1,200,000 *equity* would indicate a Cash-on-Cash return of 8.3%.
The **R**eturn on **I**nvestment (ROI) is a measure of the total return on *total* investment (equity + debt).

The **R**eturn on **E**quity (ROE) is a *single*-period measure of return on currently invested equity. It is sometimes referred to as the *Equity Capitalization Rate.* Note that the ROE is a single-period index of performance, whereas the Internal Rate of Return, which also measures return on invested equity, is a multi-period index involving *all* the cashflows from each year's operations *plus* the reversion value of the investment.

The Return on Net Equity lines at or near the very bottom of Spreadsheets SS-2, 3, 4, 5 and 6 in the following chapter measure return on invested capital *for each year* of the holding period. The IRR measures the return over the entire holding period. For example, the ROE for Year 3 measures the net Yield on Equity *during* the third year of ownership, whereas the IRR for Year 3 measures the Yield on Equity beginning in year 1 *through* the third year of ownership.

---

[13] "If it sounds too good to be true, it usually is."

Why the Buildup of Equity Needs To Be Monitored

Investments in real estate differ from investments in mutual funds or stock/bond programs in which dividends can easily be re-invested in additional shares. Dividends from equities or payments from bond funds can be added to principal and earn additional cash dividends. This is an attractive advantage to mutual funds. The financial result is the compounding of the dividends at a rate equal to future dividend or distribution rates. All the distributed cash from the investment is always working.

Individual ownership of real estate, however, provides no practical opportunity for continued reinvestment (in real estate) of spendable income.[14] The annual cashflow from an individually owned real estate investment is generally too small to constitute a down payment on a similar investment. Therefore the cash is typically withdrawn from the investment for other uses.[15]

But as the net operating income of the property increases so does its market value (given a constant capitalization rate). The increase in market value is proportionate to the increase in Net Operating Income, but because of the multiplying effect of leverage, results in a disproportionate increase in owner equity. For example, a $1 increase in NOI capitalized at 10% results in $10 added to market value, *all of which accrues to owner equity*. This appreciation in value, however, tends to lie fallow in the property until it can be retrieved and reinvested either by a sale, exchange or re-finance of the property.

Annual paydown on mortgage debt also adds to owner's equity. As a result the owner's pre-tax Return on Invested Equity (ROE) for any one year becomes:

$$\text{Return on Equity} = \frac{\text{Net Income After R.E. Taxes and Total Debt Service}}{\text{Initial Investment} + \text{Appreciation} + \text{Loan Paydown}}$$

This ratio may be calculated using both pre-tax and after tax cashflows and is a prime index of investment performance. It does not measure, however, total return on investment since it omits income from other periods as well as the reversion value of the investment. We can use the IRR for this purpose.

Now let's turn to the measurement of future benefits.

---

[14] Real Estate Investment Trusts (REITs) provide an opportunity for dividends to be periodically reinvested.

[15] A number of investors use this increasing amount of spendable income to improve their standard of living, so that they become unable to refinance the property without suffering a reduction of spendable income.

Discounted Cash Flow Analysis (DCF)

The astute investor will recognize that, in an attempt to arrive at current investment value, direct capitalization of a property's current income assumes that the income will not change. Ever. Common sense tells us that it will. And that the cashflow will go on forever. And it won't.

Therefore, if a property's net operating income will not remain forever constant, the investor is faced with important questions: Why will it change; By how much will it change; When will it change; and How can I value these different cashflows over the time I expect to receive them?

In an attempt to answer these questions, the investor is forced to look to the circumstances and events likely to affect the property's *future* financial operations, to evaluate them, and to assess their impact on future cashflows. This is a much more demanding task than overall capitalization of next year's income, comparable to fundamental analysis of stocks and bonds. But the rewards are invariably worth the effort.

This approach to estimating and measuring cashflows – and converting these estimates to a Present Value by discounting their future receipt by a required return rate – is known as Discounted Cash Flow (**DCF**) analysis. DCF is a decidedly *prospective* approach to valuing an investment opportunity.

The method of discounting future cashflows has previously been covered in Chapter 1 and Chapter 2. Since most cashflows associated with income producing investments will be Uneven Cashflows, the material and methods outlined in Chapter 2 are especially relevant and may merit a quick review by the reader. There are however, certain special considerations which need to be addressed in arriving at income property value using DCF.

Pre-tax or After-tax?

One important consideration is whether or not an investment should be evaluated on a pre-tax or after-tax basis. This is a relatively simple problem: any real estate valuation made with respect to an individual investor should always be made on an after-tax basis, since tax benefits are a significant source of the investor's overall return. Stocks and bonds carry no tax benefits, other than the deductibility of interest on margin loans.[16] The deductibility of real estate Passive Losses, produced by depreciation, amortization of loan fees and the deductibility of interest , are significant sources of cashflows from real estate, and part of the future benefits for which the investor pays.

---

[16] Loans made to acquire stocks and bonds and which are collateralized by the securities bought.

Determining Pre-tax & After-tax Cashflows

There is an important difference between an income property's Pre-tax cashflow and its After-tax cashflow. The determination of both the Pre-tax and After-tax income begins with the Net Operating Income:

> Rent
> **Less** Operating Expenses
> **Equals** Net Operating Income (NOI)

If the property is encumbered by one of more loans, the annual cost of servicing these loans must be deducted from the Net Operating Income. The result is the **Spendable Income:**

Determining Cashflow Before Taxes

Scheduled Annual Rent (Gross Scheduled Income)
Less Vacancy & Credit Loss Allowance
Equals Gross Operating Income (GOI)
Less Annual Operating Expenses
Equals Net Operating Income

Less Annual Debt Service[17]
Equals Pre-tax Annual Cashflow   (Spendable Income)

The income on which taxes are to be paid, however, is calculated differently, but begins with the same Net Operating Income number:

Determining Taxable Income & Cashflow After Taxes

Net Operating Income (as determined above)
Less Annual Amortized Loan Points
Less Annual Depreciation Allowance
Less Annual Interest on Loans[18]
Equals Annual Taxable Income (or Taxable Loss if the result is a negative)

The **After-tax Cashflow**, therefore, is equal to:

Cashflow Before Tax
Less tax due on Taxable Income
Equals After-tax Cashflow

---

17   "Debt Service" consists of the periodic interest plus the amount devoted per period toward the reduction of the loan balance

18   In determining taxable income only the interest is deductible, not the paydown amount

This is a very important number to the investor, since he is most interested in how his investment fares *after* payment of taxes.

This **After-tax Cashflow** number is the **PMT** to be received by the owner each year, every year, of his ownership. Since these After-tax cashflows, or **PMTs**, are likely to vary from year to year, they represent **PMTs** in an Unequal Cashflow problem. An example may help to illustrate these important points, and at the same time demonstrate how these numbers can very easily be transferred to a computer spreadsheet:

> Consider a 60–unit apartment house which is expected to generate $378,947 in Gross Scheduled Income[19] in the coming year. Five percent of this income is expected to be lost due to vacancies and credit problems. Its operating expenses are estimated to be $144,000 per year of which $27,000 will be property taxes.
>
> A $1,620,000 loan is available which will cost (first year) $161,595 in interest and $9,005 in loan reduction, for a total payment of $170,600. The fee to obtain this loan is 1.5 points, or 1.5% of the loan amount. Under these assumptions, what will be its first-year Pre-tax cashflow and After-tax cashflow?

Refer to spreadsheet SS-1 for the references which follow.

The Net Operating Income is easily calculated. Refer to Spreadsheet SS-1 and examine Lines 30 through 40. These Lines, under column **E**, tabulate the Gross Scheduled Rent, estimate of vacancy loss, deductible operating expenses, and arrive at the NOI.

Once the NOI has been determined, we can descend through Lines 42 and 43 of the spreadsheet to determine the Cashflow Before Tax. The calculations to determine the Taxable Income begin on Line 46 and end on Line 52.

Let's place the Pre-tax Cashflow and Taxable Income side-by-side for comparison:

Pre-tax Cashflow		**Taxable Cashflow**
$ 216,000	Net Operating Income	$216,000
0	Less Amort. of **Points**	-810[20]
0	Less **Depreciation**	**-60,218**
–161,595	Less **Interest** on Loan	–161,595
–9,005	Loan **Paydown**	0
$45,400		-$6,623

---

[19] The potential rents from a property calculated as though it were 100% occupied.

[20] Loan amount x 1.5% divided by 30 years

	A	B	C	D	E	F	G	H	I	J
1	**Real Estate Investment Analysis**									
2	**Property Identification**		**Example:**		**60 Residential Apartment Units**					
3	**Date of Analysis**		**Today**							
4										
5										
6										
7	Total Acquisition Cost				2,160,000					
8	Tax Rate for Area				1.25%					
9	Allocation to Improvement				80.00%					
10	Client's Incremental Tax Bracket (Fed Only)				36.00%					
11	Capital Gains Tax Rate (Fed Only)				28.00%					
12	Capitalization Rate on Acquisition				10.00%					
13	Capitalization Rate on Disposition				10.50%					
14	Loan Points Paid on First TD				1.5					
15	Cash Investment, Including Points				564,300					
16										
17	**Loan Information**									
18				Year	1	2	3	4	5	6
19	**First Trust Deed Loan**									
20	Beginning Balance of Loan				1,620,000	1,610,995	1,601,047	1,590,057	1,577,916	1,564,504
21	Interest Rate				10.00%	10.00%	10.00%	10.00%	10.00%	10.00%
22	Monthly Amortization Period				360	348	336	324	312	300
23	Annual Payment				170,600	170,600	170,600	170,600	170,600	170,600
24	Year End Balance of Loan				1,610,995	1,601,047	1,590,057	1,577,916	1,564,504	1,549,688
25	Interest Paid				161,595	160,652	159,610	158,459	157,188	155,784
26	Debt Service Ratio (Line 40 ÷ Line 23)				1.27	1.33	1.40	1.47	1.54	1.62
27	Beginning Leverage (Loan-to-Value = Line 20 ÷ E7)				75.0%					
28										
29	**Income**									
30	Gross Scheduled Income				378,947	397,895	417,789	438,679	460,613	483,644
31	Other Income				0	0	0	0	0	0
32	Total Gross Scheduled (Effective) Income				378,947	397,895	417,789	438,679	460,613	483,644
33	Less Reserve For Vacancy & Credit Losses				18,947	19,895	20,889	21,934	23,031	24,182
34	Gross Operating (Effective) Income				360,000	378,000	396,900	416,745	437,582	459,461
35										
36	**Operating Expenses**									
37	Taxes at COE				27,000	27,540	28,091	28,653	29,226	29,810
38	Other Operating Expenses				117,000	123,660	130,669	138,045	145,807	153,974
39	Total Operating Expenses				144,000	151,200	158,760	166,698	175,033	183,785
40	**Net Operating Income (Line 34 – Line 39)**				216,000	226,800	238,140	250,047	262,549	275,677
41										
42	Less Debt Service (From Line 23)				170,600	170,600	170,600	170,600	170,600	
43	**Cash Flow Before Taxes (Line 40- Line 42)**				45,400	56,200	67,540	79,447	91,949	
44										
45	**Taxable Income**									
46	Net Operating Income (Line 34 — Line 39)				216,000	226,800	238,140	250,047	262,549	
47	Amortization of points				810	810	810	810	810	
48	Depreciation Allowance				60,218	62,836	62,836	62,836	60,218	
49	Total Depreciation & Amortization				61,028	63,646	63,646	63,646	61,028	
50	Interest on Loan				161,595	160,652	159,610	158,459	157,188	
51	Total Deductibles				222,623	224,298	223,256	222,106	218,216	
52	**Taxable Income or –Loss (Line 46 - Line 51)**				-6,623	2,502	14,884	27,941	44,333	
53	Owner's Incremental Tax Bracket				36.0%	36.0%	36.0%	36.0%	36.0%	
54	Taxes Paid or (Saved)				-2,384	901	5,358	10,059	15,960	
55	**Total Cash Flow After Tax (Line 43 - Line 54)**				47,784	55,299	62,182	69,388	75,989	

Spreadsheet SS-1

	A	B	C	D	E	F	G	H	I	J
56										
57	**Cash/Cash Before Tax (Line 43 ÷ cell E-15)**				8.05%					
58	**Cash/Cash AfterTax (Line 55 ÷ cell E-15)**				8.47%					
59	**Adjusted Basis at Sale**									
60	Original Basis				2,160,000	2,160,000	2,160,000	2,160,000	2,160,000	
61	Plus Costs of Final Sale (from below)		5.00%		108,000	113,400	119,070	125,024	131,275	
62	Less Depreciation Taken				60,218	123,055	185,891	248,727	308,945	
63	Plus Unamortized Loan Points				23,490	22,680	21,870	21,060	20,250	
64	Adjusted Basis at Sale				2,231,272	2,173,025	2,115,049	2,057,356	2,002,579	
65										
66	**Estimated Tax Due on Sale**									
67	Sales Price, End of Year				2,160,000	2,268,000	2,381,400	2,500,470	2,625,494	
68	Less Adjusted basis				2,231,272	2,173,025	2,115,049	2,057,356	2,002,579	
69	Capital Gain (Loss)				-71,272	94,975	266,351	443,114	622,914	
70	Long Term Capital Gains Tax (Fed Only)				-19,956	26,593	74,578	124,072	174,416	
71										
72	**Estimate of Net Proceeds After Tax**									
73	Sales price				2,160,000	2,268,000	2,381,400	2,500,470	2,625,494	
74	Less Costs of Sale				108,000	113,400	119,070	125,024	131,275	
75	Less Mortgage Balance				1,610,995	1,601,047	1,590,057	1,577,916	1,564,504	
76	Net Proceeds Before Tax				441,005	553,553	672,273	797,531	929,715	
77	Less Capital Gains Tax for Owner				-19,956	26,593	74,578	124,072	174,416	
78	Net Proceeds > Mortgage, Sales Cost,Taxes				460,961	526,961	597,695	673,459	755,299	
79										
80										
81	Computation Worksheet For Internal Rate of Return									
82			Year		1	2	3	4	5	6
83	Initial Investment		1	-564,300	508,746					
84			2	-564,300	47,784	582,260				
85			3	-564,300	47,784	55,299	659,877			
86			4	-564,300	47,784	55,299	62,182	742,847		
87			5	-564,300	47,784	55,299	62,182	69,388	831,288	
88										
89										
90			IRR Calculation		-9.8%	5.9%	11.4%	14.1%	15.6%	

Spreadsheet SS-1

In the paragraph above we separated the Debt Service, which appears on Line 42 of the spreadsheet, into its Interest and Paydown components.

Note that the entire loan payment (Interest + Paydown) is deducted in calculating Pre-tax cashflow, but only the interest component of the loan payment is an allowable deduction in arriving at Taxable Income. Points are not included in current Pre-tax Cashflow since they were paid at the time of loan origination. Now they are being gradually recaptured (amortized) as periodic deductions from Taxable Income over the life of the loan.

The *major* difference between the two columns is that the annual Depreciation allowance is deductible from NOI in arriving at Taxable Income. It is not deducted under the Cashflow column since *depreciation is a non-cash expense*.[21] Note that Pre-tax Cashflow is positive $45,400 while Taxable Income is negative (-$6,623) at the end of the first year of ownership.

In actual practice this taxable loss would be transferred to the owner's tax return as an ordinary[22] income deduction. It is impossible to say what savings would accrue to the owner as the result of this taxable "loss" deduction without first knowing the owner's incremental tax bracket, i.e. the tax rate which would apply to the owner's *next* dollar of income or loss, and therefore to this deduction.

For example, if the owner were in the 36% (federal) incremental tax bracket,[23] the taxable loss of $6,623 would result in a negative tax, or tax savings. Lines 53 and 54 calculate what this tax would be if the incremental bracket were 36%:

Taxable Income (Loss)	−$6,623
Incremental Rate	x 0.36
Tax (or Savings)	−$2,384

Now that we know the tax to be paid, we can easily estimate the After-tax cashflow:

Pre-tax Cashflow	$45,400
Less tax due	−(−2,384)[24]
Equals After-tax Cashflow	$47,784

---

21 Accountants are used to preparing net operating statements for tax purposes and therefore frequently deduct depreciation, interest and amortization from income to arrive at taxable income. If this net income figure is used to arrive at market value, the property will be seriously undervalued.

22 Profits and losses realized as the result of <u>operating</u> real estate are ordinary income, taxed at ordinary rates. The applicable rate is determined by the owner's overall taxable income level.

23 Meaning that he would pay 36¢ on each dollar of additional income

24 The subtraction of a minus number results in an addition.

Since we now know both the Pre-tax and After-tax cashflows, we can measure the Cash-on-Cash Returns by dividing each value by the amount of cash invested in the property (Line 15). The results are shown on Lines 57 & 58. These are the indices discussed earlier in this chapter.

This After-tax Cashflow number is an important number to the investor since it represents the After-tax annual **PMT** to be received as part of his total ownership cashflow. In terms of our T-Bar, this **PMT** will be:

EOY		?
1	47,784
2	PMT
3	PMT
4	PMT
5	PMT + FV

As you can see, this T-Bar needs to be developed to include the estimated After-tax **PMT**s (cashflows) for each successive year during the holding period and the amount of the reversionary income at the end of the holding period. These estimates of cashflows in successive years require the development of a **Pro-forma**.

Developing a Pro-forma

A Pro-forma is simply two or more Annual Operating Statements linked together over the holding period by a series of **Assumptions**. These assumptions constitute the basis for specific *forecasts* made with regard to future rents, expenses, debt costs, taxable income, and therefore the After-tax cashflows, or **PMTs**, which the owner may reasonable expect over the holding period. They are analogous to the assumptions which a stock analyst would make about a particular issue or industry.

There is a great advantage to understanding how these cashflows are derived, because – once understood – the pro-forma can be re-configured to represent any situation which a particular investment situation presents. Commercially available pre-packaged, investment analysis computer programs do no more, but cost far more, and in the end are much less flexible, than your own self-generated spreadsheets.

The model Pro-forma (SS–1) depicts one possible operating scenario for this property over a 5-year holding period.

While it is not within the scope of this text to review the methods of anticipating all the variables for all the different classes of income property which could be reasonably considered, the following comments may be helpful to the beginning investor:

- The reasonableness of the assumptions as they pertain to income and expenses is the underpinning of a valid and useful pro-forma. *Any property* can be made to "look good" on paper if the investor is willing to accept optimistic assumptions which produce rosy projections for future rent and expenses.[25]

- The major and most reliable source of information about present and projected income is a reading of <u>each lease</u> currently in effect on the property. Do not assume that all leases, each covering different spaces in the same building, are the same. Leases are negotiable instruments, and a careful reading of each lease will reveal those differences which have been negotiated by each tenant which will affect the <u>quantity</u> and <u>duration</u> of the cashflow from that tenant.

- In those cases where the income is not derived from longer-term leases, or where leases-in-place are short-lived, the trend of current market rent for similar space in the same locality may be the best indicator of future income potential.

- Whenever and wherever possible, verify not only rent to be paid but also any offsets (deductions) from rent, or rent concessions due a tenant as the result of an agreement, or by virtue of services performed by the tenant. *Discovery* is by means of reading each lease. *Verification* is by means of an *Estoppel Certificate*[26]. If some of the rent concessions available to the tenant, as negotiated by the prior owner, will take effect during a period of future ownership, these concessions will decrease collected (effective) income for the future owner.

- Discount heavily income from extraneous sources, such as laundry-room income associated with multi-family apartment properties, or on-site vending machine income. There is no contractual obligation for the tenant to use these facilities and therefore rent from them should be treated as income from a business, and discounted at a higher rate.

- View very cautiously estimates of expenses proffered by the present owner. Oftentimes expenses are significantly <u>under</u>-stated to improve NOI, and therefore indicated market value. Sometimes an Expense Statement from the current owner <u>over</u>-estimates total operating expenses because the current owner includes certain "operating" expenses which he has been deducting on his tax returns but which are not required in the operation of the property. For example, the cost of operating a personal vehicle not essential to the operation of the property is extraneous, and would probably be denied on audit.

---

[25] Ink will print anything you want.

[26] Estoppel Certificates ask the tenant to verify the terms of the current lease and subsequently bar the tenant who verifies the accuracy of the current lease from later claiming offsets to rent due or other rent concessions or deductions which have not been declared at the time the Estoppel Certificate is obtained.

- Obtain your own estimates of property and liability insurance. The prior owner may have been carrying insurance at too low a rate to replace the improvement in the event of total destruction. In other instances, the insurance premium paid by the current owner is the result of a blanket insurance policy[27] on a number of owned properties with reduced rates not available to a new owner.
- Construct your own operating expense estimates based on current local and industry averages, using data available from lenders, appraisers, property managers, utility companies and informed brokers experienced in the type investment you are considering.
- Verify new taxes to be paid. Taxes paid by the seller may be based on lowered assessed values not available to a new owner. Obtain current tax rates for the area in which the property is located and use these rates to estimate future taxes.
- Conduct a careful walk-through of the property not only in the initial period of acquisition, but also immediately prior to closing to verify actual tenancy, condition and occupancy. Inspect *every* unit.
- Verify terms, conditions and assumability of all loans to remain on the property at closing by securing and reading a copy of each note secured by the property.
- Check with the local building department for the planned construction of any competitive type properties in the market area, or other kinds of development, which could affect the subject property. Ask the planning department what it "knows" about the property. What you may learn may surprise you.
- Check at the local engineering department of the city or county to ascertain whether the property lies on or near a geological fault, or on unstable ground.
- Determine the likely presence or absence of environmentally hazardous materials which may be on, in, or under the property. The cost of removing some toxic contaminants may exceed the purchase price of the property.

As the result of these inquiries, some judgment needs to be made regarding the progress of future rents, vacancy rates, operating expenses, capital repairs, debt servicing costs and the continuing tax status of the owner. The result, in SS-1, is a series of 5 juxtaposed, annual operating statements (estimates) interconnected by means of the underlying assumptions linking one period to the next. The "bottom line" will be estimates of the After-tax cash (**PMTs**) flowing from the operation (not the disposition) of the property over the holding period.

In both the Lotus 1-2-3® and Excel® programs, "Notes" can be made for any referenced cell. These Note holders are convenient places to store not only the assumptions used, but also any other helpful information regarding the value itself, or the circumstances used to generate it.

Do not expect that your estimates of future operations will be entirely accurate. Pro-formas constructed for income property will vary in the same way as will an operating pro-forma for a widget business. One does not abandon the planning process of a business because

[27] A policy issued by one insurer covering a number of properties owned by the same entity.

the original plan didn't work out as first estimated. Experience can be gained by recording the assumptions made for each important line of the pro-forma. Later, perhaps in a few years, it becomes highly instructive to go back to the original pro-forma to examine the assumptions made vs. the facts as they actually developed.

A Word About Real Property Depreciation Allowance

Changes in tax law have made the determination of deductible allowances for the wear and tear on the improvement a relatively easy task.

Since the value of the underlying land is non-depreciable, the real property investor must first make an **allocation** of the value of the property attributable to the land and, separately, to the improvements, or structures. *Only the value of the improvements is depreciable.*

All surveying, engineering, inspection fees, escrow fees, legal fees, brokerage fees (if paid by the buyer), and any other legitimate cost of acquiring the property (excluding loan costs), are includable in "acquisition cost" before the process of allocation.

Unfortunately there are no guidelines to assist the investor in selecting a percentage of the acquisition cost attributable to *existing* depreciable improvements. In the case of new construction, the value of the land and the cost of constructing the improvements are matters of recent record. But in the case of existing improvements, judgment must be the guide.

The safest procedure is to arrange for a formal appraisal of the property by a well-qualified appraiser. But this is an expensive solution not always followed by most private investors.[28] The local tax assessor will make his own judgment of the relative value of land and improvement but, although it could be of some support, his allocation may not be acceptable to the I.R.S. on audit. If the I.R.S. will not accept the tax assessor's allocation, a formal appraisal by a competent and experienced appraiser is probably the only way to mount a challenge to the allocation by the I.R.S.

On the model Pro-forma, SS-1, an estimate of improvement value has been made at 80% of total Acquisition Value (property price plus acquisition costs), and entered in cell E-9. The first year's depreciation allowance (cost recovery allowance) will be based[29] on the product of the Acquisition Value (cell E-7) times the percent Allocation To Improvement (cell E-9). This value is the basis on which the appropriate depreciation allowance is entered in cell E-62. Note that the cost of loan points is not included in the depreciable basis

---

28 The lender may require an appraisal to make a new loan, but this appraisal may not allocate land and improvement value. The lender's appraisal is made for loan purposes and not to establish market value.

29 The first year's depreciation (cost recover) allowance is modified by the Half-Month Convention.

of the property (they are amortized separately) but it is included in the total of the investor's *initial investment*, which will be used to measure return rates.

Choosing the Correct Depreciation Schedule

The theoretical purpose of the annual allowance for depreciation (cost recovery) of the improvement is to permit the owner to set aside a sum to compensate for the wearing out of his income-producing asset. The rate at which the investor could recovery the cost of the improvement was once open to a number of options.[30] Tax law revisions in 1986 and later years, however, set specific time periods over which the cost of real property improvements must be recovered: [31]

> Residential real property................27.5 years
> Non-residential real property...........39.0 years

These "economic lives" are applicable regardless of the actual age of the property. A 60 year-old apartment house *must* be depreciated over not less than 27.5 years, even though its true remaining economic life may be only a few more years. A 50 year-old industrial building *must* be depreciated by a new owner over 39.0 years. These depreciable lives begin anew for each new owner beginning on the day he places the property in service.[32]

In the case of property composed of both residential dwelling units and non-residential units, the shorter period (27.5 years) may be used only if the total gross rental[33] from the residential units is equal to or greater than 80% of the total gross rental income from the entire property in the taxable year. This becomes significant when dealing with new, mixed-use property which is composed of both residential and non-residential space. "Gross rental income" here means collected, or effective, or Gross Operating Income. If collected residential income is less than 80% of total collected income, the longer 39-year schedule must be used until the 80% level is reached.

---

[30]   Such as the 125%, 150% and 200% Declining Balance methods, and the Sum-of-the-Years-Digits method.

[31]   As of 1997

[32]   "Placed in Service" means offered for rent, not necessarily rented.

[33]   In this case, "total gross rental income" means rent actually collected during the tax year (GOI), and not scheduled rent (GSI).

Here's how the Annual Depreciation Amount of the model residential property (SS-1) was determined:

Total Acquisition Cost	$2,160,000
Allocation to Improvement.	80%
Depreciable Basis	1,728,000
Depreciable Life	27.5 years

$$\text{Allowance per year} \quad = \quad \frac{\$1728000}{27.5} \quad = \quad \$62{,}836*$$

> * All rental real estate is subject to a **"mid-month convention"** which limits the depreciation deduction in the first month of operation to one-half month's depreciation allowance. If a real property is acquired at any time during the month of January, for example, it would be entitled to only one-half month's depreciation for the month of January, <u>regardless of the day during the month</u> the property were placed in service. Therefore, such a property would receive only 11.5/12 of the full year's allowance. The same mid-month convention applies, in exactly the same way, for the month of the sale or disposition of the property. In the example above, the first year's depreciation allowance would be $60,218. This same depreciation number would be applicable in the year of the sale.
>
> If the property were to be sold in a month other than January, the applicable depreciation allowance would be equal to the depreciation allowance per month times the number of months in the taxable year *less* 1/2 month's depreciation allowance.

In those cases in which a property is acquired my means other than construction or cash purchase, the Acquisition Basis[34] of the property may be quite different from its market value. In the case of property acquired by gift, by exchange, by foreclosure or by inheritance, a competent tax advisor should be consulted.

---

34 *Basis* pertains the cost of a property for the purpose of determining taxable gains and losses. Cost refers to what one must pay for the property, and may have little or nothing to due with *Basis*

How Loan Points are Handled

Line 47 of SS-1 provides for an annual deduction from Taxable Income for the amortization of loan points. Points[35] paid on loans should be excluded from the Depreciable Basis since these must be deducted separately and ratably over the life of the mortgage.[36] For example, if the investor paid 1.5 points for the first trust deed loan, this expense must be recovered over the life of the loan. If the property is transferred, or the loan paid–off, before the entire cost of the points has been fully recovered, the un-amortized (unrecovered) portion of the points is <u>added to</u> the Adjusted Basis of the property at the time of sale. Our Pro-forma adds these un-amortized loan points to the Basis on Line 63 in calculating the Adjusted Basis at the time of sale.

When a property is refinanced the unrecovered loan points are deducted from that year's taxable income. Points associated with the new loan are recovered over the life of the new loan.

Determining the Original Basis

With respect to existing properties acquired by purchase, the Original Basis, Line 60, is something more than the contract price; it includes, as well, all the necessary and legitimate costs of placing title to the property in the investors hands. Adjustments to the Original Basis are made during the holding period as the result of depreciation allowances taken, capital additions made to the property, and also as the result of any partial sales. Since these rules are complicated, professional advice should be obtained.

If personal property is included in the sale, these items should be excluded from the total and depreciated under more favorable rules pertaining to shorter recovery periods for personal property. These rules are contained in S. 167 and S.168 of the Internal Revenue Code.

The Adjusted Basis at Time of Disposition

As you can see on Spreadsheet SS-1, the Adjusted Basis starts with the Original Basis, which in this case is equal to the total Acquisition Cost in cell E-7. To this value are *added* the costs of final sale (cell E-61) and the un-amortized loan points (cell E-63). Total depreciation taken over the holding period (cell E-62) is subtracted from this total to produce the **Adjusted Basis** at Sale.

---

[35] A Point = 1%. A Basis Point = 1/100 of 1%

[36] This is true for all loans except for the loan obtained for the acquisition of a personal residence.

If capital improvements are made during the holding period, this section of SS-1 can be "opened up" and the depreciation allowance added in the appropriate year.[37] If a partial sale of the property had also occurred during the holding period, the amount of the partial sale would be added to the Basis, since a tax would already have been paid on the value of the partial interest sold.

The Reversion Value of the Investment Property

The result of a sale of the property is the return, or **reversion**, to the owner of his **net** equity in the property. The net reversion value of the property is equivalent to the Future Value of the property and occupies the same place on the analysis T-Bar as it did in Chapter 2. If we are to determine the reversion value of the property, it should be on an After-tax basis, since the computation of the annual cashflows (**PMT**s) was also done on an After-tax basis.

Estimating the Final Gross Sales Price

There are a number of ways in which the final gross sales price of the property can be estimated at the end of the holding period. Since income-producing property derives its value from the net income it produces, the easiest method is to capitalize the net operating income which is projected for the property in the first full year <u>following</u> the sale date.

The capitalization rate chosen is a matter of judgment, but many conservative investors use a capitalization rate somewhat higher than the cap rate at which the property was acquired. In the case of SS-1, 1/2 point was added to the capitalization rate and entered on Line 13 as "Capitalization Rate on Disposition."

Because the final sales price is more properly determined using the NOI in the year following the sale,[38] it is necessary to extend the pro-forma for the 6th year through the NOI line, Line 40. Data below this line are irrelevant and therefore are omitted.

---

[37] If a capital improvement is added, the depreciation allowance on Line 48 would also be increased.

[38] If it is inappropriate to determine the reversion value by the capitalization method, then the reversion value must be determined by discount the anticipated remaining cashflows which would accrue to the next owner. In some cases the value of the improvement will decline to zero, while the value of the land may either decline or increase in value.

The owner's net equity is the result of the following deductions from final sales price:

Final Sales Price, say,	$2,625,494
Less Transaction fees @ 5.0%[39]	131,275
Equals Net Sales Price	$2,494,219
Less Capital Gains Tax	?
Less Mortgage Balance	?
Equals Owner's Net Equity	?

Let's estimate what the Capital Gains tax and remaining mortgage balance will be at the time of disposition.

The Capital Gains and Capital Gains Tax

A capital gain (or loss) is currently defined as a gain (or loss) arising from the disposition of a capital asset. Gains from real estate held for investment, or for use in a trade or business, are taxed as is a capital asset: gains from property held one year or less are taxed as short term capital gains at *ordinary* income rates; gains from property held more than one year are taxed as *long-term* capital gains. Losses from the disposition of **real** property are fully deductible regardless of the holding period. Losses from the sale of stocks and bonds are deducted as ordinary income if disposed of within one year: long term losses on these investments are currently deductible only to the extent of 50% of the loss. Losses from the disposition of a personal residence are not at all deductible under current tax law.

The federal government experiments frequently with the long-term capital gains tax rate. Prior to 1986 all capital gains were entitled to a 60% capital gains exclusion. The remaining amount, 40%, was added to the taxpayer's ordinary income and taxed at ordinary rates. Since the maximum ordinary rate at that time was 50%, the non-excluded portion of the capital gain, 40%, resulted in a net tax of 20% (40% x 50%). The 1986 law eliminated the long term capital gains exclusion and taxed capital gains at the "reduced" rate of 28%. The effective rate was therefore increased from 20% to 28%, a 40% increase in taxes.

Since that time, maximum *ordinary* federal income tax rates have increased from 28% to 39.6%.[40] The Long Term Capital Gains (LTCG) rate, however, has held at 28%. The investor needs to remain current with these tax rate changes because a substantial portion of the total yield from investment in real estate is derived from the net reversion amounts.

---

[39] Commissions, and some closing costs, are fully negotiable.

[40] The Alternate Minimum Tax is not considered here.

Estimating the Capital Gain at Sale Time

The diagram which follows illustrates the source of the capital gains on depreciable property held for a number of years. Part of the gain is attributable to appreciation in the property. Part of the capital gains is attributed to depreciation, since in each year that a depreciation allowance was taken as a deduction from taxable income, the Original Basis was lowered. At the end of the holding period, the final *Adjusted* Basis in the property is equal to the Original Basis less the total accumulated depreciation deducted over the holding period.

Graphically, the distance between the <u>Net</u> Sales Price and the Adjusted Basis at the time of disposition represents the Long Term Capital Gain.[41]

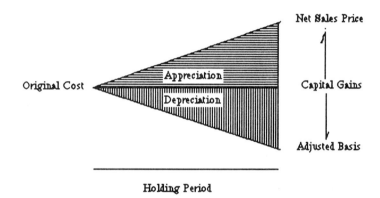

Note that the Sales Price is net of (after) the costs of sale and that the Depreciation allowances, taken in the past as deductions from Taxable Income, are now "recaptured" – which is to say, taxed – but taxed, not at the ordinary rate, but at the lower capital gains rate.

The tax is applied, therefore, to the total of the gains attributable to appreciation *plus* the total of the depreciation allowances taken over the holding period.

Since we know the amount of the depreciation taken over five years (allowing for the mid-month convention), we can calculate the Adjusted Basis of the property at the time of disposition. These calculations are represented on Lines 60-64, Column I, of SS-1:

> Original Basis $2,160,000
> **Plus** Costs of Sale ....+131,275[42]
> **Less** Accumulated Depreciation.............–308,945
> **Plus** Unrecovered Loan Points .... +20,250
>
> Adjusted Basis at Sale Time................$2,002,580

---

41   We assume the property has been held more than one year.

42   The Costs of Sale may be added to the Adjusted Basis or subtracted from the Gross Sales Price. We have chosen to add these costs to Basis.

The Capital Gains is the difference between the Sales Price and the Adjusted Basis:

Sales Price (I-73) $2,625,494
Less Adjusted Basis (I-63)................. 2,002,580
Indicated (Realized) Gain (I-69)............. $622,914[43]

The federal tax on the Gain is equal to the recognized gain times the current LTCG tax rate :

Recognized Gain $622,914
Times LTCG Tax Rate   x 0.28
Equals Capital Gains Tax.................. $174,416

Estimate of Net Proceeds After-tax

The balance of the mortgage is easily calculated following the procedures outlined in Chapter 5, Amortizing Mortgages. The final net cash proceeds can be estimated (Lines 72-78 on SS-1):

Final Sales Price, say, ... 2,625,494
Less Transaction fees @ 5.0%[44].............131,275
Equals Net Sales Price.....................$2,494,219
Less Mortgage Balance 1,564,504
Less Federal Capital Gains Tax.................174,416

Equals Owner's Net Equity = $755,299 = Reversion = F V

Finally, we have determined the projected Future Value of this investment to the investor after five years of ownership. The spreadsheet SS-1 provides the After-tax cashflows for each year of ownership enabling us to complete our 5-year T-Bar. The amount of the Initial Cash Investment (cell E-15) is equal to the down payment required plus the cost of the loan (points).

```
        0 |
          |_____
E-O-Y   1 |  47,784
        2 |  55,299          (Line 55 of SS-1)
        3 |  62,182
        4 |  69,388
        5 |  75,985   + 755,299   (Cell I-55 + I-78)
```

---

[43] Gains become *recognized* rather than simply *realized* when they become subject to current taxation.

[44] Commissions are fully negotiable.

All this work has been done to complete this T-Bar and to answer the four most significant questions which an informed investor should ask:

1. *How much* cash must I invest ?   3. *How much* cash can I expect to receive back ?
2. *When* must I advance this cash ?   4. *When* am I to receive it ?

Since we now know the amount of the returning cashflows *and their timing*, the investor has the option of:

> 1) Asking the calculator (or computer), given a discount rate, to determine a **Present Value** for this cashflow series, or
> 2) Calculating the yield by supplying the amount of the initial investment and asking the calculator to solve for the **Internal Rate of Return**, or
> 3) Determining the Net Present Value (**NPV**) of the investment by supplying the amount of the initial investment *and* a desired discount rate.

Let's consider each of these solutions separately.

Option 1 requires that we provide a discount rate, which raises the question "How should a discount rate be chosen? "

Selecting an Appropriate Discount Rate

The discount rate should be equal to the capitalization rate *plus* an estimated rate of inflation over the holding period. This assumes that the initial capitalization rate by which the property was acquired contains allowances for: 1) a satisfactory safe rate ON the investment, 2) a satisfactory rate of return OF the investment, and 3) a satisfactory risk rate allowance. The overall capitalization rate <u>does not</u> provide an allowance for inflation.

To demonstrate that the discount rate is equal to the capitalization rate + an allowance for inflation, consider this situation.

> Your investment property returns $100 000 per year in NOI,
> which will increase an estimated 5% annually as the result
> of anticipated inflation. You hold the property 5 years and
> sell at the end of the fifth year, using a 10% capitalization
> rate applied to the sixth year's income to determine the sales
> price. The annual NOIs are:

Year 1	Year 2	Year 3	Year 4	Year 5	Year 6
$100,000	$105,000	$110,250	$115,762	$121,551	$127,628

If the present value of the property were determined by capitalizing the Year 1 income, the value would be:

$$\frac{\$100000}{0.10} = \$1,000,000$$

If the value of the property is determined by discounting future income, we need to determine the reversion amount of the sale at the end of year 5, by capitalizing the 6th year's estimated income:

$$\text{Reversion} = \frac{\$127628}{0.10} = \$1,276,280$$

The T– Bar would be:

		(PV ?)
EOY	1	100,000
	2	105,000
i = 15%	3	110,250
	4	115,762
	5	121,551 + FV of $1,276,280

Applying the methods for discounting uneven cashflows (Chapter 2), the Present Value is determined to be $1,000,000. Therefore an appropriate discount rate may be determined by adding to the capitalization rate (10%) the inflation rate (5%) anticipated over the holding period.

Applying this discount rate to the T–Bar for the apartment house, we can determine the Present Value of the Investment:

		(PV ?)
EOY	1	47,784
	2	55,299
i = 15%	3	62,182
	4	69,388
	5	75,989 + FV of $755,299

Using the same discount technique, we find the the Present Value of the cashflows from this investment, discounted at 15% per year,[45] is $577,220, which is a number greater than the required up-front cash investment. Since a $1,620,000 loan is available for the model property, the investor desiring a 15% yield on *his* invested cash could afford to pay *as much as* $2,197,220 ($577,220 + 1,620,000) and still realize his yield objective.

---

[45] Note that this particular discount rate consists of a capitalization rate plus an allowance for inflation. If the discount rate is derived from overall market capitalization rates, be mindful that it will include someone's estimate of future inflation. If the discount rate is constructed by summing up the sub-rates, an allowance for inflation must be added.

In order to employ Option 2, above, we need to provide the total initial investment amount of \$564,300 (Cell E–15 on the SS-1). We are now asking the calculator (or computer) to determine the yield on the cash invested (the IRR):

		(564,300) (cell E-15)
EOY	1	47,784
	2	55,299
i = ?%	3	62,182
	4	69,388
	5	75,989 + FV of \$755,299

The IRR, or Yield, for this cashflow is 15.6%. In order to solve for the Net Present Value, Option 3, the investor would supply *both* the initial cash investment *and* the desired yield as a discount rate:

		NPV = $\sum$PV – 564,300
EOY	1	47,784
	2	55,299
i = 15 %	3	62,182
	4	69,388
	5	75,989 + FV of \$755,299

The Net Present Value is \$577,220 - 564,300 = \$12,920. Since the **NPV** is positive, this investment would exceed the requirement of an investor seeking a 15% yield.

These three functions, Present Value, Net Present Value and Internal Rate of Return, are available on Lotus 1-2-3® and Excel.® In order to calculate the IRR on a spreadsheet, however, all the values of the T-Bar must be in a <u>continuous</u> array, starting with the amount of the initial investment (cell E-15) and continuing through each year's operating income and the reversion value. This can be done by constructing a matrix which represents these values in an uninterrupted, lineal format. This matrix is depicted on SS-1 on Lines 83-87 The value of cell E-83 is the sum of the After-tax cashflow, cell E-55, and the reversionary amount, cell E-78). The IRR function on Line 90 reads each Line (83-87) from left to right. Note that the initial cash investment is a negative number in keeping with the sign convention which requires that at least one element be a negative number.

Chapter Summary

1. The acquisition of income producing property can be considered title to the future cashflows which can reasonably be produced by the property.

2. Cashflows derived from improved property consist of the annual, After-tax proceeds from operations and from the After-tax reversionary income derived from the disposition of the property at the end of the holding period.

3. Property may be valued using single-period indices such as the overall capitalization rate, gross rent multiplier and the cash–on–cash methods.

4. Multiple-period indices of performance, such as the Internal Rate of Return, Net Present Value and Present Value methods of valuation, require the investor to address in some detail the probable performance of the property and the resulting changes in cashflow for a number of years into the future.

5. The computer spreadsheet is the easiest way to perform Discounted Cashflow Analysis since values can be changed and new results obtained almost instantly.

6. An understanding of the underlying principles of investment analysis and DCF enables the investor or his advisor to devise spreadsheets capable of representing both the commonplace and unusual investment situations.

Cashflow analysis is a particularly useful tool to the investor who faces the question of what to do with the owned investment. The owner's options are limited to four:

Chapter 7
Sell, Hold, Trade or Refinance ?

- **Continue to Hold**
- **Sell**
- **Trade (Exchange) If Possible**
- **Refinance**

Unfortunately, current tax code does not permit the owner of stocks, bonds or notes to carry out a tax-deferred exchange, so our discussion here is limited to real property.

Each of the options above can be expressed in terms of the cashflows it will produce. These cashflows can then be compared over similar holding periods. In order to compare these alternatives, let's construct an example retail property which an investor has already owned for exactly five years:

It was initially acquired at a total cost of $1,500,000 (excluding points) and financed with a new first trust deed note in the amount of $1,100,000, payable $9,610.66 monthly, including interest at the rate of 9.5% per year. The property is being depreciated under the recovery schedule available at the time of acquisition (1986-93 rules), 31.5 years. Two points were paid for the loan and these are being recovered on a 25-year amortization schedule. The Net Operating Income of the property during the year following acquisition was $145,000. NOI and expenses have both grown at an annually compounded rate of 4.5%. Present NOI_5 is $172,915. Taxes are separate since they are estimated to increase only 2% per year.

The Decision to Sell or to Hold

There are many personal reasons why an investor may wish to sell income-producing property, but really only two valid *financial* reasons related to property performance:

1. The property does not now, nor is it expected to, fulfill the owner's financial objectives, and/or
2. A better investment opportunity presents itself which requires a sale.

The financial spreadsheet, SS-2, depicts the cashflows from the Retail Center over the *past five years* and indicates the amount of net after-tax equity, $560,421 (in Cell I-72), which can be expected from an outright sale today. Spreadsheet SS-2 extends this ownership for an additional 10 years, and shows the Internal Rate of Return (Line 94) for each year of the holding period.[1] The IRRs calculated on Spreadsheet SS-2 are based on the original acquisition and depict the rate of return on *capital remaining in the investment* for each year of the holding period, *beginning with the year of the original acquisition.*

Spreadsheet SS-2 answers the question "What will be the IRR if this property is held from year 0 through year 15," but it does not answer the question "What part of the return will be attributable to holding the property for future years 6 through year 10?" This is precisely the problem posed by a "Sell or Hold?" question: what is the present value of *future* benefits? In order to appreciate the difference, consider the concept of the **Investment Base.**

Chapter 3 established that the Internal Rate of Return measures the return on invested capital *remaining* in the property. We need to determine, therefore, how much capital remains invested in the property at the end of year 5. If the property is to be held for an additional 5 years, we can consider that the owner's capital invested in the property at the beginning of year 6 to be equal to the net cash the owner would have realized had he sold the property, paid off the mortgage, the expenses of the sale, and his taxes at the end of year 5.[2] This amount is the **Investment Base.**

The amount of after-tax cash remaining in the property at the end of Year 5 is shown in Cell I-72 of SS-2: $560,421. This is the amount of after-tax, net proceeds that the owner could reasonably expect to pocket on sale. Therefore it is the amount he has invested in the property at that time, his investment base. All other values in the operation of the property from year 6 through year 10 as depicted on SS-3 will remain the same.

---

[1] This spreadsheet calculates the IRR for each year of the holding period, assuming that the property will be sold at the end of each year.

[2] Some specialists will characterize the decision to hold a property as the financial equivalent of buying the property from yourself for the amount of the net after-tax cash remaining in the investment.

Real Estate Investment Analysis

Property Identification	Example: Retail Center Purchased 5 years ago
Date of Analysis	Today
Prepared For	Introduction To Cashflow Analysis

SPREADSHEET SS-2

Parameters

Acquisition Value	1,500,000
Tax Rate for Area	1.20%
Allocation to Improvement	75.00%
Client's Incremental Tax Bracket (Fed Only)	36.00%
Capital Gains Tax Rate (Fed Only)	28.00%
Capitalization Rate on Acquisition	9.67%
Capitalization Rate on Disposition	10.17%
Loan Points Paid on First TD	2.0
Cash Investment, Including Points	422,000

Loan Information

	First 5 Yrs. of Ownership					Next 5 Years					Period of Refinance or Trade					
Year	1	2	3	4	5	6	7	8	9	10	11	12	13	14	15	16
First Trust Deed Loan																
Beginning Balance of Loan	1,100,000	1,088,688	1,076,253	1,062,584	1,047,559	1,031,042	1,012,886	992,928	970,989	946,873	920,364	891,223	859,190	823,978	785,272	742,724
Interest Rate	9.50%	9.50%	9.50%	9.50%	9.50%	9.50%	9.50%	9.50%	9.50%	9.50%	9.50%	9.50%	9.50%	9.50%	9.50%	9.50%
Monthly Amortization Period	300	288	276	264	252	240	228	216	204	192	180	168	156	144	132	120
Annual Payment	115,328	115,328	115,328	115,328	115,328	115,328	115,328	115,328	115,328	115,328	115,328	115,328	115,328	115,328	115,328	115,328
Year End Balance of Loan	1,088,688	1,076,253	1,062,584	1,047,559	1,031,042	1,012,886	992,928	970,989	946,873	920,364	891,223	859,190	823,978	785,272	742,724	695,953
Interest Paid	104,016	102,893	101,659	100,302	98,811	97,172	95,370	93,389	91,212	88,818	86,187	83,295	80,116	76,621	72,780	68,557
Debt Service Ratio	1.26	1.31	1.37	1.43	1.50	1.57	1.64	1.71	1.79	1.87	1.95	2.04	2.13	2.23	2.33	2.43
Beginning Leverage	73.3%															
Debt Coverage Ratio	1.26															
Income																
Gross Scheduled Income	234,818	245,385	256,427	267,966	280,025	292,626	305,794	319,555	333,935	348,962	364,665	381,075	398,223	416,143	434,870	454,439
Other Income	0	0	0	0	0	0	0	0	0	0	0	0	0	0	0	0
Total Gross Scheduled Income	234,818	245,385	256,427	267,966	280,025	292,626	305,794	319,555	333,935	348,962	364,665	381,075	398,223	416,143	434,870	454,439
Reserve For Vacancy & Credit Losses (5.00%)	11,741	12,269	12,821	13,398	14,001	14,631	15,290	15,978	16,697	17,448	18,233	19,054	19,911	20,807	21,743	22,722
Gross Operating (Effective) Income	223,077	233,115	243,606	254,568	266,023	277,994	290,504	303,577	317,238	331,514	346,432	362,021	378,312	395,336	413,126	431,717
Operating Expenses																
Taxes at COE	18,000	18,360	18,727	19,102	19,484	19,873	20,271	20,676	21,090	21,512	21,942	22,381	22,828	23,285	23,751	24,226
Other Operating Expenses	60,077	63,230	66,535	69,997	73,624	77,425	81,406	85,576	89,943	94,518	99,309	104,327	109,581	115,083	120,844	126,875
Total Operating Expenses	78,077	81,590	85,262	89,099	93,108	97,298	101,676	106,252	111,033	116,030	121,251	126,707	132,409	138,368	144,594	151,101
Net Operating Income	145,000	151,525	158,344	165,469	172,915	180,696	188,828	197,325	206,205	215,484	225,181	235,314	245,903	256,968	268,532	280,616
Less Debt Service	115,328	115,328	115,328	115,328	115,328	115,328	115,328	115,328	115,328	115,328	115,328	115,328	115,328	115,328	115,328	115,328
Cash Flow Before Taxes	29,672	36,197	43,016	50,141	57,587	65,368	73,500	81,997	90,877	100,156	109,853	119,986	130,575	141,640	153,204	
Taxable Income																
Net Operating Income	145,000	151,525	158,344	165,469	172,915	180,696	188,828	197,325	206,205	215,484	225,181	235,314	245,903	256,968	268,532	280,616
Amortization of points	880	880	880	880	880	880	880	880	880	14,080	736	736	736	736	736	736
Depreciation Allowance	34,226	35,714	35,714	35,714	34,226	35,714	35,714	35,714	34,226	35,714	35,714	35,714	34,226	35,714	35,714	35,714
Total Depreciation & Amortization	35,106	36,594	36,594	36,594	35,106	36,594	36,594	36,594	35,106	49,794	36,451	36,451	34,962	36,451	36,451	36,451
Interest on Loan	104,016	102,893	101,659	100,302	98,811	97,172	95,370	93,389	91,212	88,818	86,187	83,295	80,116	76,621	72,780	68,557
Total Deductibles	139,122	139,487	138,253	136,897	133,917	133,766	131,964	129,984	126,318	138,613	122,638	119,746	115,079	113,072	109,230	105,008
Taxable Income or –Loss	5,878	12,038	20,090	28,572	38,998	46,930	56,863	67,341	79,887	76,871	102,543	115,568	130,824	143,896	159,302	175,608
Owner's Incremental Tax Bracket	36.0%	36.0%	36.0%	36.0%	36.0%	36.0%	36.0%	36.0%	36.0%	36.0%	36.0%	36.0%	36.0%	36.0%	36.0%	36.0%

	A	B	C	D	E	F	G	H	I	J	K	L	M	N	O	P	Q	R	S	T
50	Taxes Paid or (Saved)				2,116	4,334	7,233	10,286	14,039	16,895	20,471	24,243	28,759	27,674	36,915	41,604	47,097	51,803	57,349	
51	Total Cash Flow After Tax				27,556	31,864	35,783	39,855	43,548	48,474	53,029	57,754	62,117	72,482	72,937	78,381	83,478	89,838	95,855	
52	Net Proceeds from Refinance														-18,407					
53	Cash/Cash Before Tax				7.0%															
54	Cash/Cash AfterTax				6.53%															
55	Adjusted Basis at Sale			Year	1	2	3	4	5	6	7	8	9	10	11	12	13	14	15	
56	Original Basis				1,500,000	1,500,000	1,500,000	1,500,000	1,500,000	1,500,000	1,500,000	1,500,000	1,500,000	1,500,000	1,500,000	1,500,000	1,500,000	1,500,000	1,500,000	
57	Plus Costs of Final Sale (from below)		5.00%		74,520	77,874	81,378	85,040	88,867	92,866	97,045	101,412	105,976	110,745	115,728	120,936	126,378	132,065	138,008	
58	Less Depreciation Taken				34,226	69,940	105,655	141,369	175,595	211,310	247,024	282,738	316,964	352,679	388,393	424,107	458,333	494,048	529,762	
59	Plus Unamortized Loan Points				21,120	20,240	19,360	18,480	17,600	16,720	15,840	14,960	14,080	13,200	17,671	16,935	16,198	15,462	14,726	
60	Adjusted Basis at Sale				1,561,414	1,528,173	1,495,083	1,462,151	1,430,872	1,398,277	1,365,861	1,333,634	1,303,091	1,271,266	1,245,006	1,213,763	1,184,243	1,153,479	1,122,972	
61	Estimated Tax Due on Sale																			
62	Sales Price, End of Year				1,490,410	1,557,478	1,627,565	1,700,805	1,777,341	1,857,322	1,940,901	2,028,242	2,119,513	2,214,891	2,314,561	2,418,716	2,527,558	2,641,298	2,760,157	
63	Less Adjusted basis				1,561,414	1,528,173	1,495,083	1,462,151	1,430,872	1,398,277	1,365,861	1,333,634	1,303,091	1,271,266	1,245,006	1,213,763	1,184,243	1,153,479	1,122,972	
64	Capital Gain (Loss)				-71,004	29,305	132,481	238,654	346,470	459,045	575,040	694,608	816,421	943,625	1,069,555	1,204,953	1,343,315	1,487,819	1,637,185	
65	Long Term Capital Gains Tax (Fed Only)				-19,881	8,205	37,095	66,823	97,011	128,533	161,011	194,490	228,598	264,215	299,475	337,387	376,128	416,589	458,412	
66	Estimate of Net Proceeds After Tax																			
67	Sales price				1,490,410	1,557,478	1,627,565	1,700,805	1,777,341	1,857,322	1,940,901	2,028,242	2,119,513	2,214,891	2,314,561	2,418,716	2,527,558	2,641,298	2,760,157	
68	Less Costs of Sale				74,520	77,874	81,378	85,040	88,867	92,866	97,045	101,412	105,976	110,745	115,728	120,936	126,378	132,065	138,008	
69	Less Mortgage Balance				1,088,688	1,076,253	1,062,584	1,047,559	1,031,042	1,012,886	992,928	970,989	946,873	920,364	891,223	859,190	823,978	785,272	742,724	
70	Net Proceeds Before Tax				327,201	403,351	483,602	568,206	657,432	751,570	850,928	955,841	1,066,664	1,183,783	1,307,610	1,438,590	1,577,202	1,723,962	1,879,425	
71	Less Capital Gains Tax for Owner				-19,881	8,205	37,095	66,823	97,011	128,533	161,011	194,490	228,598	264,215	299,475	337,387	376,128	416,589	458,412	
72	Net Proceeds > Mortgage, Sales Cost, Taxes				347,083	395,146	446,508	501,383	560,421	623,037	689,917	761,350	838,066	919,568	1,008,135	1,101,203	1,201,074	1,307,372	1,421,014	
73																				
74																				
75	Computation Worksheet For Internal Rate of Return																			
76			Year		1	2	3	4	5	6	7	8	9	10	11	12	13	14	15	
77			1	-422,000	374,639															
78			2	-422,000	27,556	427,009														
79			3	-422,000	27,556	31,864	482,291													
80			4	-422,000	27,556	31,864	35,783	541,238												
81			5	-422,000	27,556	31,864	35,783	39,855	603,969											
82			6	-422,000	27,556	31,864	35,783	39,855	43,548	671,511										
83			7	-422,000	27,556	31,864	35,783	39,855	43,548	48,474	742,946									
84			8	-422,000	27,556	31,864	35,783	39,855	43,548	48,474	53,029	819,104								
85			9	-422,000	27,556	31,864	35,783	39,855	43,548	48,474	53,029	57,754	900,183							
86			10	-422,000	27,556	31,864	35,783	39,855	43,548	48,474	53,029	57,754	62,117	992,050						
87			11	-422,000	27,556	31,864	35,783	39,855	43,548	48,474	53,029	57,754	62,117	67,730	1,062,665					
88			12	-422,000	27,556	31,864	35,783	39,855	43,548	48,474	53,029	57,754	62,117	67,730	72,876	1,179,585				
89			13	-422,000	27,556	31,864	35,783	39,855	43,548	48,474	53,029	57,754	62,117	67,730	72,876	97,426	1,284,552			
90			14	-422,000	27,556	31,864	35,783	39,855	43,548	48,474	53,029	57,754	62,117	67,730	72,876	97,426	103,291	1,397,210		
91			15	-422,000	27,556	31,864	35,783	39,855	43,548	48,474	53,029	57,754	62,117	67,730	72,876	97,426	103,291	110,495	1,516,869	
92																				
93																				
94		IRR Calculation			-11.2%	3.9%	9.2%	11.8%	13.3%	14.2%	14.7%	15.1%	15.4%	15.6%	15.5%	15.7%	15.9%	16.0%	16.1%	
95	SS-2	Loan-to-Value			73.0%	69.1%	65.3%	61.6%	58.0%	54.5%	51.2%	47.9%	44.7%	41.6%	38.5%	35.5%	32.6%	29.7%	26.9%	
96		Pre-tax Return on Invested Equity (ROI)			-10.72%	24.28%	23.88%	23.52%	23.26%	22.84%	22.53%	22.24%	22.01%	21.68%	21.58%	21.13%	20.93%	20.64%	20.41%	

#	A	B	C	D	E	F	G	H	I	J
1	Real Estate Investment Analysis									
2	Property Identification		Retail Center		Financial Consequence of Holding Years 6-10					
3	Date of Analysis		Today							
4	Prepared For		Introduction to Cashflow Analysis							
5										
6	Original Cost				1,500,000					
7	Tax Rate for Area				1.20%					
8	Allocation to Improvement				75.00%					
9	Client's Incremental Tax Bracket (Fed Only)				36.00%					
10	Capital Gains Tax Rate (Fed Only)				28.00%					
11	Capitalization Rate on Acquisition				9.67%					
12	Capitalization Rate on Disposition				10.17%					
13	Unrecovered (unamortized) Loan Points Paid on First TD				17,600					
14	Investment Base				560,421					
15										
16	Loan Information									
17				Year	6	7	8	9	10	11
18	First Trust Deed Loan									
19	Beginning Balance of Loan				1,031,042	1,012,886	992,928	970,989	946,873	920,364
20	Interest Rate				9.50%	9.50%	9.50%	9.50%	9.50%	9.50%
21	Monthly Amortization Period				240	228	216	204	192	180
22	Annual Payment				115,328	115,328	115,328	115,328	115,328	115,328
23	Year End Balance of Loan				1,012,886	992,928	970,989	946,873	920,364	891,223
24	Interest Paid				97,172	95,370	93,389	91,212	88,818	86,187
25	Debt Service Ratio				1.57	1.64	1.71	1.79	1.87	1.95
26	Percentage Leveraged (Loan-to-Value)				55.5%					
27	Debt Coverage Ratio				1.57					
28	Income									
29	Gross Scheduled Income				242,173	305,793	319,554	333,934	348,961	364,664
30	Other Income				0	0	0	0	0	0
31	Total Gross Scheduled Income				242,173	305,793	319,554	333,934	348,961	364,664
32	Reserve For Vacancy & Credit Losses				12,109	15,290	15,978	16,697	17,448	18,233
33	Gross Operating (Effective) Income				277,994	290,504	303,576	317,237	331,513	346,431
34	Operating Expenses									
35	Taxes at COE				19,873	20,270	20,676	21,089	21,511	21,941
36	Other Operating Expenses				77,425	81,406	85,576	89,944	94,518	99,309
37	Total Operating Expenses				97,298	101,676	106,252	111,033	116,029	121,251
38	Net Operating Income				180,696	188,827	197,325	206,204	215,483	225,180
39	Less Debt Service				115,328	115,328	115,328	115,328	115,328	115,328
40	Cash Flow Before Taxes				65,368	73,499	81,997	90,876	100,155	
41	Taxable Income									
42	Net Operating Income				180,696	188,827	197,325	206,204	215,483	
43	Amortization of points				880	880	880	880	880	
44	Depreciation Allowance				35,714	35,714	35,714	35,714	34,226	
45	Total Depreciation & Amortization				36,594	36,594	36,594	36,594	35,106	
46	Interest on Loan				97,172	95,370	93,389	91,212	88,818	
47	Total Deductibles				133,766	131,964	129,984	127,806	123,925	
48	Taxable Income or –Loss				46,930	56,863	67,341	78,398	91,559	
49	Owner's Incremental Tax Bracket				36.0%	36.0%	36.0%	36.0%	36.0%	36.0%

	A	B	C	D	E	F	G	H	I	J
50	Taxes Paid or (Saved)				16,895	20,471	24,243	28,223	32,961	
51	Total Cash Flow After Tax				48,473	53,029	57,754	62,653	67,194	
52										
53	Cash/Cash Before Tax				11.7%					
54	Cash/Cash AfterTax				8.65%					
55	Adjusted Basis at Sale									
56	Original Basis				1,500,000	1,500,000	1,500,000	1,500,000	1,500,000	
57	Plus Costs of Final Sale (from below)		5.00%		92,866	97,045	101,412	105,975	110,744	
58	Less Depreciation Taken				211,309	247,024	282,738	318,452	352,678	
59	Plus Unamortized Loan Points				16,720	15,840	14,960	14,080	13,200	
60	Adjusteu Basis at Sale				1,398,277	1,365,861	1,333,634	1,301,603	1,271,266	
61	Estimated Tax Due on Sale									
62	Sales Price, End of Year				1,857,318	1,940,897	2,028,238	2,119,508	2,214,886	
63	Less Adjusted basis				1,398,277	1,365,861	1,333,634	1,301,603	1,271,266	
64	Capital Gain (Loss)				459,041	575,036	694,604	817,905	943,620	
65	Long Term Capital Gains Tax (Fed Only)				128,532	161,010	194,489	229,013	264,214	
66	Estimate of Net Proceeds After Tax									
67	Sales price				1,857,318	1,940,897	2,028,238	2,119,508	2,214,886	
68	Less Costs of Sale				92,866	97,045	101,412	105,975	110,744	
69	Less Mortgage Balance				1,012,886	992,928	970,989	946,873	920,364	
70	Net Proceeds Before Tax				751,566	850,924	955,836	1,066,660	1,183,778	
71	Less Capital Gains Tax for Owner				128,532	161,010	194,489	229,013	264,214	
72	Net Proceeds > Mortgage, Sales Cost, Taxes				623,034	689,914	761,347	837,646	919,565	
73										
74										
75	Computation Worksheet For Internal Rate of Return									
76	Year				6	7	8	9	10	11
77	Initial Investment		1	-560,421	671,508					
78			2	-560,421	48,473	742,943				
79			3	-560,421	48,473	53,029	819,101			
80			4	-560,421	48,473	53,029	57,754	900,299		
81			5	-560,421	48,473	53,029	57,754	62,653	986,759	
82										
83										
84	IRR Calculation				19.8%	19.5%	19.3%	19.1%	18.8%	
85	Loan-to-Value				54.5%	51.2%	47.9%	44.7%	41.6%	
86										
87										
88										
89										
90										
91										
92										
93										
94										
95	SS-3									

SPREADSHEET SS-4

Real Estate Investment Analysis		
Property Identification	Example:	Refinance Retail Center EOY 10
Date of Analysis	Today	
Prepared For	Introduction To Cashflow Analysis	

Acquisition Value	1,500,000
Tax Rate for Area	1.20%
Allocation to Improvement	75.00%
Client's Incremental Tax Bracket (Fed Only)	36.00%
Capital Gains Tax Rate (Fed Only)	28.00%
Capitalization Rate on Acquisition	9.67%
Capitalization Rate on Disposition	10.17%
Loan Points Paid on First TD	2.0
Cash Investment, Including Points	422,000

Loan Information

Year	1	2	3	4	5	6	7	8	9	10	11	12	13	14	15	16
First Trust Deed Loan												Refinanced this period				
Beginning Balance of Loan	1,100,000	1,088,688	1,076,253	1,062,584	1,047,559	1,031,042	1,012,886	992,928	970,989	946,873	1,707,611	1,690,050	1,670,747	1,649,528	1,626,202	1,600,562
Interest Rate	9.50%	9.50%	9.50%	9.50%	9.50%	9.50%	9.50%	9.50%	9.50%	9.50%	9.50%	9.50%	9.50%	9.50%	9.50%	9.50%
Monthly Amortization Period	300	288	276	264	252	240	228	216	204	192	300	288	276	264	252	240
Annual Payment	115,328	115,328	115,328	115,328	115,328	115,328	115,328	115,328	115,328	115,328	179,032	179,032	179,032	179,032	179,032	179,032
Year End Balance of Loan	1,088,688	1,076,253	1,062,584	1,047,559	1,031,042	1,012,886	992,928	970,989	946,873	920,364	1,690,050	1,670,747	1,649,528	1,626,202	1,600,562	1,572,377
Interest Paid	104,016	102,893	101,659	100,302	98,811	97,172	95,370	93,389	91,212	88,818	161,471	159,729	157,813	155,707	153,392	150,847
Debt Service Ratio	1.26	1.31	1.37	1.43	1.50	1.57	1.64	1.71	1.79	1.87	1.26	1.31	1.37	1.44	1.50	1.57

Income

	1	2	3	4	5	6	7	8	9	10	11	12	13	14	15	16
Gross Scheduled Income	234,818	245,385	256,427	267,966	280,025	292,626	305,794	319,555	333,935	348,962	364,665	381,075	398,223	416,143	434,870	454,439
Other Income	0	0	0	0	0	0	0	0	0	0	0	0	0	0	0	0
Total Gross Scheduled Income	234,818	245,385	256,427	267,966	280,025	292,626	305,794	319,555	333,935	348,962	364,665	381,075	398,223	416,143	434,870	454,439
Reserve For Vacancy & Credit Losses (5.00%)	11,741	12,269	12,821	13,398	14,001	14,631	15,290	15,978	16,697	17,448	18,233	19,054	19,911	20,807	21,743	22,722
Gross Operating (Effective) Income	223,077	233,115	243,606	254,568	266,023	277,994	290,504	303,577	317,238	331,514	346,432	362,021	378,312	395,336	413,126	431,717

Operating Expenses

	1	2	3	4	5	6	7	8	9	10	11	12	13	14	15	16
Taxes at COE	18,000	18,360	18,727	19,102	19,484	19,873	20,271	20,676	21,090	21,512	21,942	22,381	22,828	23,285	23,751	24,226
Other Operating Expenses	60,077	63,230	66,535	69,997	73,624	77,425	81,406	85,576	89,943	94,518	99,309	104,327	109,581	115,083	120,844	126,875
Total Operating Expenses	78,077	81,590	85,262	89,099	93,108	97,298	101,676	106,252	111,033	116,030	121,251	126,707	132,409	138,368	144,594	151,101
Net Operating Income	145,000	151,525	158,344	165,469	172,915	180,696	188,828	197,325	206,205	215,484	225,181	235,314	245,903	256,968	268,532	280,616
Less Debt Service	115,328	115,328	115,328	115,328	115,328	115,328	115,328	115,328	115,328	115,328	179,032	179,032	179,032	179,032	179,032	179,032
Cash Flow Before Taxes	29,672	36,197	43,016	50,141	57,587	65,368	73,500	81,997	90,877	100,156	46,148	56,282	66,871	77,936	89,500	

Taxable Income

	1	2	3	4	5	6	7	8	9	10	11	12	13	14	15	16
Net Operating Income	145,000	151,525	158,344	165,469	172,915	180,696	188,828	197,325	206,205	215,484	225,181	235,314	245,903	256,968	268,532	
Amortization of points	880	880	880	880	880	880	880	880	880	14,080	1,366	1,366	1,366	1,366	1,366	
Depreciation Allowance	34,226	35,714	35,714	35,714	35,714	35,714	35,714	35,714	35,714	35,714	35,714	35,714	35,714	35,714	34,226	
Total Depreciation & Amortization	35,106	36,594	36,594	36,594	36,594	36,594	36,594	36,594	36,594	49,794	37,080	37,080	37,080	37,080	35,592	
Interest on Loan	104,016	102,893	101,659	100,302	98,811	97,172	95,370	93,389	91,212	88,818	161,471	159,729	157,813	155,707	153,392	
Total Deductibles	139,122	139,487	138,253	136,897	135,405	133,766	131,964	129,984	127,806	138,613	198,552	196,809	194,893	192,787	188,984	
Taxable Income or –Loss	5,878	12,038	20,090	28,572	37,510	46,930	56,863	67,341	78,398	76,871	26,629	38,505	51,010	64,181	79,548	
Owner's Incremental Tax Bracket	36.0%	36.0%	36.0%	36.0%	36.0%	36.0%	36.0%	36.0%	36.0%	36.0%	36.0%	36.0%	36.0%	36.0%	36.0%	36.0%

#	Label	C	D	E	F	G	H	I	J	K	L	M	N	O	P	Q	R	S	T
50	Taxes Paid or (Saved)			2,116	4,334	7,233	10,286	13,503	16,895	20,471	24,243	28,223	27,674	9,586	13,862	18,363	23,105	28,637	
51	Total Cash Flow After Tax			27,556	31,864	35,783	39,855	44,084	48,474	53,029	57,754	62,653	72,482	36,562	42,420	48,507	54,831	60,863	
52	Net Proceeds from Refinance													787,247					
53	Cash/Cash Before Tax			7.0%															
54	Cash/Cash AfterTax			6.53%															
55	Adjusted Basis at Sale	Year		1	2	3	4	5	6	7	8	9	10	11	12	13	14	15	
56	Original Basis			1,500,000	1,500,000	1,500,000	1,500,000	1,500,000	1,500,000	1,500,000	1,500,000	1,500,000	1,500,000	1,500,000	1,500,000	1,500,000	1,500,000	1,500,000	
57	Plus Costs of Final Sale (from below)	5.00%		74,520	77,874	81,378	85,040	88,867	92,866	97,045	101,412	105,976	110,745	115,728	120,936	126,378	132,065	138,008	
58	Less Depreciation Taken			34,226	69,940	105,655	141,369	177,083	212,798	248,512	284,226	319,940	355,655	391,369	427,083	462,798	498,512	532,738	
59	Plus Unamortized Loan Points			21,120	20,240	19,360	18,480	17,600	16,720	15,840	14,960	14,080	0	32,786	31,420	30,054	28,688	27,322	
60	Adjusted Basis at Sale			1,561,414	1,528,173	1,495,083	1,462,151	1,429,384	1,396,788	1,364,373	1,332,146	1,300,115	1,255,090	1,257,145	1,225,273	1,193,634	1,162,241	1,132,592	
61	Estimated Tax Due on Sale																		
62	Sales Price, End of Year			1,490,410	1,557,478	1,627,565	1,700,805	1,777,341	1,857,322	1,940,901	2,028,242	2,119,513	2,214,891	2,314,561	2,418,716	2,527,558	2,641,298	2,760,157	
63	Less Adjusted basis			1,561,414	1,528,173	1,495,083	1,462,151	1,429,384	1,396,788	1,364,373	1,332,146	1,300,115	1,255,090	1,257,145	1,225,273	1,193,634	1,162,241	1,132,592	
64	Capital Gain (Loss)			-71,004	29,305	132,481	238,654	347,958	460,533	576,528	696,096	819,398	959,801	1,057,416	1,193,444	1,333,924	1,479,058	1,627,565	
65	Long Term Capital Gains Tax (Fed Only)			-19,881	8,205	37,095	66,823	97,428	128,949	161,428	194,907	229,431	268,744	296,076	334,164	373,499	414,136	455,718	
66	Estimate of Net Proceeds After Tax																		
67	Sales price			1,490,410	1,557,478	1,627,565	1,700,805	1,777,341	1,857,322	1,940,901	2,028,242	2,119,513	2,214,891	2,314,561	2,418,716	2,527,558	2,641,298	2,760,157	
68	Less Costs of Sale			74,520	77,874	81,378	85,040	88,867	92,866	97,045	101,412	105,976	110,745	115,728	120,936	126,378	132,065	138,008	
69	Less Mortgage Balance			1,088,688	1,076,253	1,062,584	1,047,559	1,031,042	1,012,886	992,928	970,989	946,873	920,364	1,690,050	1,670,747	1,649,528	1,626,202	1,600,562	
70	Net Proceeds Before Tax			327,201	403,351	483,602	568,206	657,432	751,570	850,928	955,841	1,066,664	1,183,783	508,782	627,033	751,653	883,031	1,021,587	
71	Less Capital Gains Tax for Owner			-19,881	8,205	37,095	66,823	97,428	128,949	161,428	194,907	229,431	268,744	296,076	334,164	373,499	414,136	455,718	
72	Net Proceeds > Mortgage, Sales Cost,Taxes			347,083	395,146	446,508	501,383	560,004	622,620	689,500	760,934	837,233	915,038	212,706	292,869	378,154	468,895	565,868	
73																			
74	Computation Worksheet For Internal Rate of Return																		
75		Year		1	2	3	4	5	6	7	8	9	10	11	12	13	14	15	
76		1	-422,000	374,639															
77		2	-422,000	27,556	427,009														
78		3	-422,000	27,556	31,864	482,291													
79		4	-422,000	27,556	31,864	35,783	541,238												
80		5	-422,000	27,556	31,864	35,783	39,855	604,088											
81		6	-422,000	27,556	31,864	35,783	39,855	44,084	671,094										
82		7	-422,000	27,556	31,864	35,783	39,855	44,084	48,474	742,529									
83		8	-422,000	27,556	31,864	35,783	39,855	44,084	48,474	53,029	818,688								
84		9	-422,000	27,556	31,864	35,783	39,855	44,084	48,474	53,029	57,754	899,886							
85		10	-422,000	27,556	31,864	35,783	39,855	44,084	48,474	53,029	57,754	62,117	987,521						
86		11	-422,000	27,556	31,864	35,783	39,855	44,084	48,474	53,029	57,754	62,117	67,730	1,036,516					
87		12	-422,000	27,556	31,864	35,783	39,855	44,084	48,474	53,029	57,754	62,117	67,730	878,530	335,289				
88		13	-422,000	27,556	31,864	35,783	39,855	44,084	48,474	53,029	57,754	62,117	67,730	878,530	97,426	426,661			
89		14	-422,000	27,556	31,864	35,783	39,855	44,084	48,474	53,029	57,754	62,117	67,730	878,530	97,426	103,291	523,726		
90		15	-422,000	27,556	31,864	35,783	39,855	44,084	48,474	53,029	57,754	62,117	67,730	878,530	97,426	103,291	110,495	626,731	
91																			
92	IRR Calculation			-11.2%	3.9%	9.2%	11.8%	13.3%	14.2%	14.7%	15.1%	15.4%	15.6%	15.4%	16.2%	16.9%	17.4%	17.8%	
93	Loan-to-Value			73.3%	73.0%	69.1%	65.3%	61.6%	58.0%	54.5%	51.2%	47.9%	44.7%	77.1%	73.0%	69.1%	65.3%	61.6%	
94	Annual Return on Invested Net Equity (ROI)			-11.2%	23.0%	22.1%	21.2%	20.5%	19.8%	19.3%	18.7%	18.3%	18.0%	-72.8%	57.6%	45.7%	38.5%	33.7%	
95																			
96	SS-4																		

	A	B	C	D	E	F	G	H	I	J	K	L	M	N	O	P	Q	R	S	T
1	Real Estate Investment Analysis																			
2	Property Identification		Example: Reinvestment of Loan Proceeds from Retail Center Refinance																	
3	Date of Analysis		Today																	
4	Prepared For			Introduction To Cashflow Analysis								SPREADSHEET SS-5								
5																				
6	Acquisition Value				2,795,026															
7	Tax Rate for Area				1.20%															
8	Allocation to Improvement				75.00%															
9	Client's Incremental Tax Bracket (Fed Only)				36.00%															
10	Capital Gains Tax Rate (Fed Only)				28.00%															
11	Capitalization Rate on Acquisition				9.67%															
12	Capitalization Rate on Disposition				10.17%															
13	Loan Points Paid on First TD				2.0															
14	Cash Investment, Including Points				787,247															
15																				
16	Loan Information																			
17				Year											11	12	13	14	15	16
18	First Trust Deed Loan																			
19	Beginning Balance of Loan														2,048,754	2,027,685	2,004,525	1,979,067	1,951,082	1,920,319
20	Interest Rate														9.50%	9.50%	9.50%	9.50%	9.50%	9.50%
21	Monthly Amortization Period														300	288	276	264	252	240
22	Annual Payment														214,799	214,799	214,799	214,799	214,799	214,799
23	Year End Balance of Loan														2,027,685	2,004,525	1,979,067	1,951,082	1,920,319	1,886,504
24	Interest Paid														193,730	191,639	189,340	186,814	184,036	180,983
25	Debt Service Ratio														1.26	1.31	1.37	1.44	1.50	1.57
26																				
27																				
28	Income																			
29	Gross Scheduled Income														437,548	457,237	477,813	499,315	521,784	545,264
30	Other Income														0	0	0	0	0	0
31	Total Gross Scheduled Income														437,548	457,237	477,813	499,315	521,784	545,264
32	Reserve For Vacancy & Credit Losses		5.00%												21,877	22,862	23,891	24,966	26,089	27,263
33	Gross Operating (Effective) Income														415,670	434,375	453,922	474,349	495,695	518,001
34	Operating Expenses																			
35	Taxes at COE														33,540	34,211	34,895	35,593	36,305	37,031
36	Other Operating Expenses														111,944	117,820	123,977	130,429	137,188	144,269
37	Total Operating Expenses														145,485	152,031	158,873	166,022	173,493	181,300
38	Net Operating Income														270,186	282,344	295,049	308,327	322,201	336,700
39	Less Debt Service														214,799	214,799	214,799	214,799	214,799	
40	Cash Flow Before Taxes														55,387	67,545	80,251	93,528	107,403	
41	Taxable Income																			
42	Net Operating Income														270,186	282,344	295,049	308,327	322,201	
43	Amortization of points														1,639	1,639	1,639	1,639	1,639	
44	Depreciation Allowance														63,775	66,548	66,548	66,548	63,775	
45	Total Depreciation & Amortization														65,414	68,187	68,187	68,187	65,414	
46	Interest on Loan														193,730	191,639	189,340	186,814	184,036	
47	Total Deductibles														259,144	259,826	257,528	255,001	249,451	
48	Taxable Income or –Loss														11,041	22,518	37,522	53,326	72,751	
49	Owner's Incremental Tax Bracket														36.0%	36.0%	36.0%	36.0%	36.0%	36.0%
50	Taxes Paid or (Saved)														3,975	8,106	13,508	19,197	26,190	

#	Label	C	D	E	F	G	H	I	O	P	Q	R	S
51	Total Cash Flow After Tax								51,412	59,439	66,743	74,331	81,212
52	Net Proceeds from Refinance												
53	Cash/Cash Before Tax								7.0%				
54	Cash/Cash AfterTax								6.53%				
55	Adjusted Basis at Sale		Year						1	2	3	4	5
56	Original Basis								2,795,026	2,795,026	2,795,026	2,795,026	2,795,026
57	Plus Costs of Final Sale (from below)	5.00%							138,858	145,106	151,636	158,460	165,591
58	Less Depreciation Taken								63,775	130,324	196,872	263,420	327,196
59	Plus Unamortized Loan Points								22,946	21,307	19,668	18,029	16,390
60	Adjusted Basis at Sale								2,893,054	2,831,116	2,769,458	2,708,095	2,649,811
61	Estimated Tax Due on Sale												
62	Sales Price, End of Year								2,777,156	2,902,128	3,032,724	3,169,196	3,311,810
63	Less Adjusted basis								2,893,054	2,831,116	2,769,458	2,708,095	2,649,811
64	Capital Gain (Loss)								-115,898	71,012	263,265	461,102	661,999
65	Long Term Capital Gains Tax (Fed Only)								-32,452	19,883	73,714	129,108	185,360
66	Estimate of Net Proceeds After Tax												
67	Sales price								2,777,156	2,902,128	3,032,724	3,169,196	3,311,810
68	Less Costs of Sale								138,858	145,106	151,636	158,460	165,591
69	Less Mortgage Balance								2,027,685	2,004,525	1,979,067	1,951,082	1,920,319
70	Net Proceeds Before Tax								610,613	752,496	902,021	1,059,655	1,225,900
71	Less Capital Gains Tax for Owner								-32,452	19,883	73,714	129,108	185,360
72	Net Proceeds > Mortgage, Sales Cost, Taxes								643,065	732,613	828,306	930,546	1,040,541
73													
74	Computation Worksheet For Internal Rate of Return												
75	Year			1	2	3	4	5					
76	1		-787,247	694,477									
77	2		-787,247	51,412	792,052								
78	3		-787,247	51,412	59,439	895,049							
79	4		-787,247	51,412	59,439	66,743	1,004,877						
80	5		-787,247	51,412	59,439	66,743	74,331	1,121,753					
81													
82	IRR Calculation			-11.8%	3.6%	9.1%	11.7%	13.2%					
83	Leverage			0.733	69.87%	66.10%	62.45%	58.91%					
84	Annual Return on Net Equity (ROI)			-11.3%	24.4%	24.0%	23.6%	23.4%					

SS-5

#	Label		E	F	G	H	I	J
1	**Real Estate Investment Analysis**							
2	Property Identification	Example: Exchange of Retail Center into Anchored Shopping Center						
3	Date of Analysis	Today						
4	Prepared For	Introduction to Cashflow Analysis	SPREADSHEET SS-6					
5								
6	Original Cost		4,202,879 (See page 2)					
7	Tax Rate for Area		1.20%					
8	Allocation to Improvement		75.00%					
9	Client's Incremental Tax Bracket (Fed Only)		36.00%					
10	Capital Gains Tax Rate (Fed Only)		28.00%					
11	Capitalization Rate on Acquisition		9.67%					
12	Capitalization Rate on Disposition		10.17%					
13	Loan Points Paid		2.0%					
14	Investment Base		980,348	(Cell N-72 from SS-2 plus loan points)				
15								
16	**Loan Information**							
17		Year	11	12	13	14	15	16
18	**First Trust Deed Loan**							
19	Beginning Balance of Loan		3,080,710	3,049,029	3,014,203	2,975,922	2,933,840	2,887,583
20	Interest Rate		9.50%	9.50%	9.50%	9.50%	9.50%	9.50%
21	Monthly Amortization Period		300	288	276	264	252	240
22	Annual Payment		322,993	322,993	322,993	322,993	322,993	322,993
23	Year End Balance of Loan		3,049,029	3,014,203	2,975,922	2,933,840	2,887,583	2,836,734
24	Interest Paid		291,312	288,167	284,711	280,912	276,735	272,144
25	Debt Service Ratio		1.26	1.31	1.37	1.44	1.50	1.57
26								
27								
28	**Income**							
29	Gross Scheduled Income		657,942	687,550	718,489	750,821	784,608	819,916
30	Other Income		0	0	0	0	0	0
31	Total Gross Scheduled Income		657,942	687,550	718,489	750,821	784,608	819,916
32	Reserve For Vacancy & Credit Losses		32,897	34,377	35,924	37,541	39,230	40,996
33	Gross Operating (Effective) Income		625,045	653,172	682,565	713,280	745,378	778,920
34	**Operating Expenses**							
35	Taxes at COE		50,435	51,443	52,472	53,522	54,592	55,684
36	Other Operating Expenses		168,331	177,167	186,426	196,127	206,290	216,938
37	Total Operating Expenses		218,766	228,610	238,898	249,648	260,882	272,622
38	Net Operating Income		406,279	424,562	443,667	463,632	484,496	506,298
39	Less Debt Service		322,993	322,993	322,993	322,993	322,993	
40	Cash Flow Before Taxes		83,287	101,569	120,674	140,639	161,503	
41	**Taxable Income**							
42	Net Operating Income		406,279	424,562	443,667	463,632	484,496	
43	Amortization of points		2,465	2,465	2,465	2,465	2,465	
44	Depreciation Allowance		60,012	62,621	62,621	62,621	60,012	
45	Total Depreciation & Amortization		62,476	65,085	65,085	65,085	62,476	
46	Interest on Loan		291,312	288,167	284,711	280,912	276,735	
47	Total Deductibles		353,788	353,253	349,796	345,997	339,211	
48	Taxable Income or –Loss		52,492	71,309	93,871	117,635	145,284	
49	Owner's Incremental Tax Bracket		36.0%	36.0%	36.0%	36.0%	36.0%	36.0%
50	Taxes Paid or (Saved)		18,897	25,671	33,794	42,349	52,302	

#	A	B	C	D	E	F	G	H	I	J
51	Total Cash Flow After Tax				64,390	75,898	86,881	98,291	109,201	
52	Cash/Cash Before Tax				8.5%					
53	Cash/Cash AfterTax				6.57%					
54	**Adjusted Basis at Sale**									
55	Substituted Basis		5.00%		3,256,278	3,256,278	3,256,278	3,256,278	3,256,278	
56	Plus Costs of Final Sale (from below)				208,801	218,197	228,016	238,277	248,999	
57	Less Depreciation Taken				60,012	122,632	185,253	247,874	307,885	
58	Plus Unamortized Loan Points				59,150	56,685	54,220	51,756	49,291	
59	Adjusted Basis at Sale				3,464,217	3,408,528	3,353,261	3,298,437	3,246,683	
60	**Estimated Tax Due on Sale**									
61	Sales Price, End of Year				4,176,018	4,363,939	4,560,317	4,765,531	4,979,980	
62	Less Adjusted basis				3,464,217	3,408,528	3,353,261	3,298,437	3,246,683	
63	Capital Gain (Loss)				711,801	955,411	1,207,055	1,467,094	1,733,297	
64	Long Term Capital Gains Tax (Fed Only)				199,304	267,515	337,975	410,786	485,323	
65										
66	**Estimate of Net Proceeds After Tax**									
67	Sales price				4,176,018	4,363,939	4,560,317	4,765,531	4,979,980	
68	Less Costs of Sale				208,801	218,197	228,016	238,277	248,999	
69	Less Mortgage Balance				3,049,029	3,014,203	2,975,922	2,933,840	2,887,583	
70	Net Proceeds Before Tax				918,189	1,131,539	1,356,379	1,593,414	1,843,398	
71	Less Capital Gains Tax for Owner				199,304	267,515	337,975	410,786	485,323	
72	Net Proceeds > Mortgage, Sales Cost, Taxes				718,884	864,024	1,018,404	1,182,627	1,358,075	
73										
74	Computation Worksheet For Internal Rate of Return									
75				Year	11	12	13	14	15	
76	Initial Investment		1	-980,348	783,274					
77			2	-980,348	64,390	939,921				
78			3	-980,348	64,390	75,898	1,105,285			
79			4	-980,348	64,390	75,898	86,881	1,280,918		
80			5	-980,348	64,390	75,898	86,881	98,291	1,467,275	
81										
82	IRR Calculation				-20.1%	1.3%	8.8%	12.4%	14.4%	
83	Leverage				73.3%	69.9%	66.1%	62.4%	58.9%	
84	Annual Return on Net Equity (ROI)				-20.1%	30.7%	27.9%	25.8%	24.1%	
85										
86	**Calculation of Acquis. Price**				**Calculation of Substitued Basis**					
87	Cash Available = $1,183,783					Acquisition Cost, replacement		4,202,879		
88	AP = Loan + (1183783 - .02 * Loan)					Less Unrecognized Gain from Retail Center		946,601	Cell N-64, SS-2	
89	AP= .98 * Loan + 1,183,783					Substituted Basis		3,256,278		
90	and,					Allocation to Improvement		75%	From Cell E-9, this SS.	
91	Loan /AP = 73.30%					Depreciable Basis		2,442,209		
92	Loan = .733 * AP									
93	Therefore,									
94	AP = .98 *.733 *AP + 1,183,783				Cash Available	1,183,783				
95	AP= 0.71834 * AP + 1,183,783				Less Loan Points	61,614				
96	.28166*AP = 1,183,783				Net Cash	1,122,169				
97	AP = $4,202,879				Plus Loan Proceeds	3,080,710				
98	Loan = AP * .733 = $3,080,710				Acquisition Price	4,202,879	SS-6			

The results of the cashflow analysis show, in SS-3, Line 84, that the IRR_{6-10} will range from 18.8% to 19.8%, significantly greater than the 14.2% to 15.6% IRR sequence on SS-2 for the same years. This difference is accounted for by the fact that holding the property for an additional 5 years does not require an additional investment in loan points, incurs no additional acquisition costs, and that an increasing segment of the annual debt service is going to reduction of the loan principal, increasing the owner's equity.

The results also suggest that maintaining an investment in the Retail Center for an additional 5 years offers the potential of a minimum 18.8% return on net capital. remaining in the investment. If the investor seeks to sell the Retail Center and acquire a "better" investment, the "better" investment should indicate a return of 18.8% or more over a 5 year hold.

This method of "buying back" your own property using the **Investment Base** as the downpayment is of great aid in answering the question "Should I Sell or Hold?" The investor can decide whether the *next* holding period will deliver acceptable returns on net invested equity, or whether a new investment is more attractive than his current holding. This is a convenient point to note that many properties with excellent future prospects are sold because of past problems. The decision to transfer equity must always be made with regard to future earnings, and not on past earnings or losses.

Effect of Low Depreciation on Holding Period

In the early 1980's, Cost Recovery rules permitted the investor to choose fairly liberal depreciation schedules which "front-loaded" the investment with heavy deductions from taxable income. These deductions were so high that many income properties did not show a positive Taxable Income for many years. These losses[3] were translated to the owner's otherwise taxable income, partially or completely sheltering this income from taxation. But these deductions waned rapidly,[4] exposing annual operating income to high ordinary income tax rates. Therefore many owners became motivated to sell or exchange their properties after only 5-7 years of ownership in order to reestablish higher depreciation deductions which could continue to shelter ordinary income.

The rather stringent cost recovery schedules which investors are now required to use spread current depreciation deductions evenly over 27.5 or 39 years. Depletion of depreciation benefits, therefore, is now an uncommon reason for a sale and most income producing properties now show positive Taxable Income after only 1-2 years of ownership.

---

[3] These losses are now characterized as "Passive Losses" deductible (for most investors) only from Passive Gains.

[4] Schedules such as 125%, 150% and 200% of straight line amounts were commonly used.

The Decision To Refinance

Experienced investors know that a good investment property is hard to find. Quality property, well-managed and in a good location is a fine asset – and one which ought not to be disposed of simply because the investor's rate of return on invested equity has fallen below a targeted level. One attractive alternative available to the investor is to refinance the property and with the net proceeds, acquire other quality property.

Refinancing not only lowers the total equity remaining in the original property, thereby improving its rate of return, but also provides *tax-free cash* for investment in a second property. All this is accomplished without many of the costs required by an outright sale. An important correlative benefit is the retention of a quality property which is performing well and can be expected to continue to perform well.

Spreadsheets SS-4 depict the cashflows resulting from the refinance of the Retail Center at the end of year 10 and continued operations through year 15. The reinvestment of the net[5] loan proceeds in a similar property is depicted by Spreadsheets SS-5 over the ensuing 5-year holding period. (Spreadsheets SS-2 depicts how the original Retail Center would fare if the investment were held through the 15th year *without* refinancing.)

The $753,737 (SS-4, Cell O52) made available as the result of the refinance is invested in a new center under the same terms and conditions as the original center in order to limit variables. This amount, less the required loan fees, will now control a property whose comparable value would be $2,795,026 (Cell E-6 of SS-5), encumbered by a loan of $2,048,254. The loan to value ratio for the newly acquired property is kept at 73.3%.

In both the "hold" and "refinance" scenarios, the properties are sold at the end of the 15th year in order to compare the net, after-tax cashflows from each strategy, which are:

      (1) Holding original w/o refinance (SS-2) $1,421,014

      (2) Holding original w refinance SS-4.................565,868
      (3) New property from refi proceeds SS-5........ <u>1,040,541</u>
                 Total (2)+(3) $1,606,409

The net, after-tax cashflows, over a period of 5 years, from refinancing and reinvesting are $185,395 (13%) higher than from a "do nothing" strategy, emphasizing the financial reward for monitoring the rate of return on invested capital and taking appropriate actions when this rate begins to falter.

---

5 The amount remaining after having paid off the original loan.

The Decision To Exchange (Trade)

Real estate investments still enjoy the exchange privilege, a privilege not presently accorded to dealer property (inventory), stocks, bonds, promissory notes, partnership interests, certificates of trust, or "choses in action." [6]

While exchange regulations have become quite complex, the basic premise of the qualified exchange is simply stated in the Internal Revenue Code (S. 1031):

> "No gain or loss shall be recognized on the exchange of property held for productive use in a trade or business or for investment if such property is exchanged solely for property of like kind which is to be held either for productive use in a trade or business or for investment."

While it is not within the scope of this text to cover the regulations pertaining to exchanges under S.1031, it is a dependable general guideline that if the value of the replacement property equals or exceeds the value of the relinquished property, *and* the amount of the mortgage on the new property equals or exceeds the mortgage on the relinquished property, then there will be no immediate recognition of gain.

The advantage of exchanging, as opposed to selling, the real property is that the capital gains tax on the relinquished property, which would ordinarily be recognized in the year of the sale, is deferred until the sale of the replacement property. If the replacement property is also later exchanged, rather than sold, the tax on accumulated gains on all prior properties is deferred until the last replacement property is sold. It is easy to see therefore, that this deferred tax, in the hands of the investor, can be reinvested, leveraged, and used to control property of greater and greater value. Exchanging is a very valuable tool for the investor seeking to build the value of a real estate portfolio.

Exchanging Results in Loss Of Depreciable Basis

The disadvantage of exchanging is that any unrecognized gain carried over from the relinquished property must be deducted from the cost of the acquired property, thereby reducing annual depreciation allowances and exposing more of the replacement property's operating income to taxation at ordinary rates. This disadvantage is most often minimized because the replacement property typically has a market value substantially higher than the relinquished property, and the higher depreciable basis more than offsets that lost because of the deduction cited above.

To illustrate, let's exchange the Retail Center at the end of year 10 (Spreadsheet SS-2) for a multi-family residential property, and examine the effect on the resulting cashflows.

---

6 Claims or debts which may be recovered through legal action.

Cell N-70 of this spreadsheet indicates that $1,183,783 would be available for reinvestment if payment of the federal capital gains tax were deferred. While this is the amount of cash available for the replacement property, it is not the Investment Base which was defined earlier. The Investment Base is equal to Net Proceeds *less the tax which would have been payable had the property been sold.* The Investment Base would also include any cash expenditures added to the pre–tax net proceeds, including the costs of acquisition of the replacement property. In this example we assume no additional cash is available, and that the miscellaneous costs of acquisition, other than loan points, are included in the Acquisition Cost (Cell E–6 of Spreadsheet SS-6).

Calculating the Basis of the Replacement Property

S. 1031 specifies that as the result of an exchange the current Basis of the relinquished property is *substituted* as the Basis of the replacement property. But the receipt of "boot" or the addition of cash to the exchange complicates the determination of the replacement property's tax Basis.

The most uncomplicated method of identifying the Substituted Basis of the replacement property is to subtract from its total Acquisition Cost the unrecognized gain carried over from the relinquished property.

Cell N-64 of Spreadsheet SS-2 indicates that the realized capital gain for the Retail Center at the end of year 10 is $943,625. It is this amount which must be subtracted from the Acquisition Cost of the replacement property (before allocation of land and improvement).

If we assume that the cash available from the relinquished property, $1,183,783, will serve as a 26.7% (110%-73.3%)[7] downpayment on the replacement property, and pay 2 points for the new loan, the value of the replacement property would be $4,202,879.

Before allocating this value between non-depreciable land and depreciable improvement, we must subtract *from* the Acquisition Cost of the replacement property the unrecognized gain from the retail property:

Acquisition Cost, replacement	$4,202,879
Less Unrecognized Gain carryover	–943,625
Substituted Basis, replacement	$3,259,254

Now we are ready to allocate between land and improvement:

Substituted Basis, replacement	$3,259,254
Allocated to Improvement	75%
Depreciable Basis, replacement	$2,444,440

---

[7] In order to compare properties using the same Loan-To-Value ratio.

If the Retail Center had been sold and the capital gains tax paid, the amount remaining for investment in a new property would have been $919,568 (Cell N-72, SS-2). In that case, this lower downpayment would control a new property whose value would be $3,444,075. The Depreciable Basis of the *purchased* property would be $2,583,056 (75% of $3,444,075). Therefore while the penalty for exchanging property is the loss of depreciable basis, most exchanges involve a replacement property of sufficiently higher value that the loss of depreciable basis is very tolerable.

Adjustments When Some Gain is Recognized

Many otherwise qualified exchanges result in some recognition of realized gain. Under the rules of S.1031, any unlike[8] property received in the exchange is considered "boot." The receipt of boot exposes the exchangor to tax on the value of the boot, up to the limit of the realized gain in the relinquished property.[9] In other words, gain is recognized to the value of the boot received, and a tax becomes due on the amount of the recognized gain.

For example, let us assume that the owner of the Retail Center disposed of the center through an exchange which resulted in his receipt of $100,000 in cash.[10] This cash would be considered boot and taxable (up to the limit of his total gain) in the year of the sale.

Realized Gain[11] from relinquished prop.	$943,625
Less recognized gain	−100,000
Unrecognized gain	$843,625

Then,

Acquisition Cost, replacement	$4,202,879
Less unrecognized gain	843,625
Substituted Basis	$3,359,254
Allocation to Improvement	75%
Depreciable Basis, replacement	$2,519,440

The exchangor would pay the tax only on the amount of the recognized gain, $100,000. The remaining unrecognized gain, $843,625, would be carried over[12] into the replacement property and taxed at the time of its eventual sale. Payment of tax on part of the gain results in a higher depreciable basis in the replacement property, as compared to a transaction in which no boot is received.

---

[8] Like-kind property means real property for real property (or personal property for personal property). The receipt of personal property in a real property exchange results in "boot."

[9] But never more than the tax which would have been paid had the property been sold.

[10] Cash is unlike property since it is personal property received in an exchange involving real property.

[11] Also "Indicated Gain."

[12] In the form of a lower Adjusted Basis

Cashflows From the Replacement Property

Spreadsheet SS-6 assumes that no boot was received in the exchange transaction and depicts the cashflows from the replacement property over a 5–year holding period.

The important changes which must be made to the cashflows in Spreadsheet SS–6 include these:

1. **The Investment Base** is used in Cell E-14 rather than the actual cash rolled over from the relinquished property.
2. The Depreciable Basis is not the product of Cell E-6 times Cell A-9, but rather Cell H-91, which is the result of the computation of the Substituted Basis.
3. Annual Depreciation Allowances (Cost Recovery) beginning on Line 44 are determined using the value in Cell H-91. This value reflects the reduced depreciable basis.
4. Line 55 is now the Substituted Basis (from H-88) rather than the Original Basis.

These changes also result in changes in the computation of the IRR (Line 82) and, in particular, the capital gains tax due on sale. The capital gains tax now represents the tax on *both* the unrecognized gain from the Retail Center and the tax on the capital gain from the replacement property accrued over its holding period. This total gain may be recognized by a sale, or again postponed by means of a qualified exchange.

The IRR for year 1 is –20.1%. This large negative is due to the fact that the spreadsheet assumes a sale at the end of each year. If the property were to be sold at the end of year 1 the deductions from owner's equity would not only be the costs of the sale, but also the capital gains tax from the Retail Center. Nevertheless, this IRR figure improves rapidly and reflects an IRR at the end of year 5 of 14.4%.

We can summarize these different Sell or Hold, Trade or Refinance options in the following way:

Investment Strategy	Net Wealth EOY 15
Hold for 15 years	$1,421,014
Hold 10 Yrs.; Refinance Hold 5 Yrs.	1,606,409
Hold 10 Yrs.; Exchange. Hold 5 Yrs	1,358,075

These comparison are not offered as absolutes since we have held many important variables constant that would otherwise vary considerably. For example, leasing commissions have not been included, nor has any consideration for a reduction in sales costs been made as the value of the property sold increases. The comparisons are for the purpose of demonstrating the *methodology* by which various investment decisions can be subjected to cashflow analysis. Undoubtedly, different results would be obtained under actual circumstances.

Nevertheless, the comparison highlights the high cost of acquiring and selling real estate, and emphasizes that real estate is indeed an investment whose profitability is seriously eroded by frequent relocations of equity. When inflation adds considerable value to the owner's equity, properties can be bought and sold after shorter holding periods. But when inflation is quite low, or during periods of deflation, the high cost of transferring property equity favors longer holding periods.

Although the Retail Center was exchanged at the end of year 5, the property could not be made available for exchange without the payment of sales costs on the relinquished property, and acquisition costs, including points, on the replacement property. Had the replacement property been held longer than 5 years, the benefits of exchanging may have become more apparent.

Chapter Summary

1. For the investor who already owns a real property investment, four investment alternatives are available: 1) to continue to hold the property; 2) to refinance the property and with the proceeds acquire other quality property; 3) or to exchange the property for a replacement property, 4) or to simply sell the property outright.

2. Each of these decision alternatives can be subjected to cashflow analysis to depict the most probable outcomes and the effect on the ROI and IRR.

3. In the examples used here, employing rigid operating assumptions, a strategy to refinance and hold a quality property, while acquiring a new property, offers significant advantages over a simple hold or a tax-deferred exchange.

4. The *methodology* of such a comparison is the major point here, not the outcome.

Chapter 8
Effect of Leverage on Investment Cashflows

Leverage is an important investment tool which can have a profound effect on cashflows from an investment.[1]

Leverage can be defined simply as the use of other people's money to control the investment. When a great deal of other people's money is used to acquire the investment, we describe the investment as being "highly leveraged." The advantage of financial leverage arises from two facts:

1. Money borrowed at a rate lower than the rate at which the investment earns income results in added cashflow to the owner.
2. Any increase in investment value belongs entirely to the owner of the investment.

Neutral, Positive and Negative Leverage

We know from previous discussion that the rate at which a real property of a given market value throws off Net Operating Income (NOI) is its capitalization rate. The property produces this NOI regardless of how much or how little of someone else's money may be invested in it. Therefore a property acquired at a capitalization rate of 10% will cast off $10.00 for each $100.00 invested in it, regardless of who makes the investment.

---

[1] When securities are the investment, leveraging is knows as "trading on margin."

But if $50.00 of invested capital is acquired through the use of lender's funds, and the lender charges 10% for the use of these funds, then the owner pays a rate for the use of money equal to the rate at which the borrowed funds earn income. This is a situation of **neutral leverage**.

If, however, the lender requires 11% for the use of $50 ($5.50 interest), then the owner must take this extra 50¢ from his share of the NOI. The borrower loses 50¢ (1%) on every $50 he borrows at 11%. This is a situation of **negative leverage.**

When the lender requires only 9% for the use of $50 in capital ($4.50 interest), the owner adds 50¢ to his cashflow. This is a situation of **positive leverage**.

Therefore positive leverage occurs at any time the capitalization rate on the property exceeds the interest rate on borrowed funds. Negative leverage occurs at any time the interest rate on borrowed funds exceeds the capitalization rate on the property. Neutral leverage occurs when the capitalization rate is equal to the interest rate on borrowed funds, in which case the investor neither makes nor loses money on these borrowed funds.

Appreciation and Leverage

If it were not for appreciation, it would make little financial sense at all to borrow any money when prevailing interest rates exceed prevailing capitalization

Give Me a Place To Stand and I Will Move the World

rates. But the market value of a property is somewhat independent of its capital structure.[2] The market value is tied to rents, and when these rents are increasing, as in periods of inflation, market value also increases. When it does, *the entire amount of the increase accrues to the equity owner*. This is the fact which justifies negative leverage during times of inflation. The portion of the NOI which the owner may lose in additional cashflow to the lender, because of negative leverage, he hopes to make up in cashflow due to substantial appreciation.

---

[2] Properties with attractive loans in place *are* worth more.

Risk of Leverage

The same high leverage which can be a wealth generator during inflationary periods can turn into a howling beast during times of deflation. These are times when property rents, and therefore NOI, are declining. The owner who is highly leveraged sends a greater and greater share of the NOI to his creditor, until – in terminal cases – the entire property, equity and all, is delivered to the lender by way of foreclosure.

In the case of a stock, a declining market price prompts a "margin call" since the value of the stock is no longer adequate security for the broker's loan. Therefore the investor may be forced to sell the stock when prices are declining. These margin sales can further depress stock values.

Leverage is the original two-edged sword.

A particularly dangerous position is high leverage using loans that have short call (due) dates. If interest rates have risen substantially, the NOI of the property may not be able to support a replacement loan with a higher interest rate in an amount necessary to retire the existing loan.

Effect on ROI

The effect of high leverage is easy to see.

Suppose that a property worth $100 is controlled by a small amount of equity, say $5. During the year, the property's value increases 5% to $105. The gain due to appreciation, $5, belong entirely to the equity owner. Therefore the equity owner realizes a 100% return on invested capital ($5 return on $5 invested).

On the other hand, suppose that the equity owner invests $95 in the property and borrows only $5 (5%). The property, ignorant of its capital structure, responds to market forces in the same way and rises the same $5 in value to $105. In this case, the equity owner realizes a 5.26% return on invested capital ($5 return on $95 invested).

On the other hand, if a 95% leveraged property declines 5% in value, the owner's equity is expunged.

This is the lure and risk of leverage.

Maximum Leverage

In Chapter 5, which reviews Debt Service Ratios, we discussed how lenders insulate themselves from undue risk due to excessive leverage. Their main tool is, in the case of residential property, the loan-to-value ratio; in the case of commercial property they utilize the debt coverage (or service) ratio *and* the loan-to-value ratio.[3]

The maximum leverage a property can support depends on the cost of money. In terms of property operations, we can say that the maximum supportable debt occurs when:

or,

$$\text{Net Operating Income} = \text{Cost of Debt Service}$$

or,

$$\text{Value * Capitalization rate} = \text{Loan * Loan constant}$$

therefore,

$$\frac{\text{Loan}}{\text{Value}} = \frac{\text{Capitalization Rate}}{\text{Loan constant}}$$

$$\text{Leverage} = \frac{\text{Capitalization Rate}}{\text{Loan constant}}$$

Lenders, however, are quite sensitive to the advantages and disadvantages of leverage and will not permit 100% of the NOI to be devoted to debt service. They require a cushion in the form of the Debt Coverage Ratio. Therefore:

$$\textbf{Maximum Leverage} = \frac{\textbf{Capitalization Rate}}{\textbf{Loan Constant x DCR}}$$

For example, a property with a capitalization rate of 10%, employing a loan whose annual constant is .1053, with a DCR of 1.25, could be leveraged:

$$= \frac{.10}{0.1053 * 1.25}$$

$$= 0.76$$

$$= 76\%$$

As you can see, both the loan constant and the debt coverage ratio vary inversely to the capitalization rate. Therefore during time of high interest rates, or when the lender perceives a property to be risky (and raises the DCR), the amount of available loan decreases.

---

[3] Generally lending according to the mechanism which gives them the least risk exposure.

Effect of Leverage on IRR

The IRR depends on the amount of cash flowing from the operation of the investment, and on the amount of cashflow at final disposition. But the IRR is extremely sensitive to a low initial investment by the investor. Since the IRR is a discount rate which is needed to equate the sum of the Present Value of all future cash receipts to the initial amount invested, the lower the initial amount, the higher must be the discount rate. Therefore, lower initial cash investments result in higher IRRs.

Since a higher leverage position results in more cash going to service high debt levels, the component of the IRR[4] attributable to cashflow from operations declines steeply and the part attributable to reversionary value rises steeply. This is simply another way of saying that if a property is highly leveraged, most of the return will derive from the net sales proceeds at the end of the holding period and little from cash returns during the holding period.

This "wait to see" effect of high leverage is the essence of the risk which frequently accompanies high IRRs.

Spreadsheet SS-2 in the preceding chapter is an example of a property which is positively leveraged: its capitalization rate is slightly in excess of the interest rate charged on the loan.

Chapter Summary

1. Leverage involves the use of borrowed funds in the acquisition or refinance of an investment.

2. Low interest rates encourage the use of leverage since the capitalization rate on the property often exceeds the cost of borrowed funds.

3. Highly leveraged positions carry substantial risk from declining income, and, in the case of adjustable rate mortgages, rising interest rates.

4. Negatively leveraged properties have a negative impact on both ROI and IRR returns, which may be offset by the appreciation.

---

[4] The IRR can be "partitioned" to reveal the value of each of its component parts: Return from operations, Return from tax benefits, Return from reversion.

Chapter 9
Personal Applications for Cashflow Analysis

In this chapter we will cover three additional applications of cashflow analysis of very practical significance to Everyman.

- **Auto and Equipment Leasing**
- **Buy vs. Rent Decisions**
- **When to Refinance Property**

Each of these uses the same principles of cashflow analysis we have covered in previous examples.

1. Auto Leases

A good workable definition of "investment" is the *present expenditure of money in the reasonable expectation of a return of the invested capital together with a profit.*

Personal automobiles are not investments because a reasonable owner or lessee of an automobile does not expect (except in rare situations) a profit at the end of the holding period. He expects a loss. Auto leases are investments only to the lessor-dealer, since he enters into the lease with the reasonable expectation of a profit.

So the question posed by the lessee regarding automobile leasing is "How can I obtain the greatest benefits at the least cost?"

Elements of the Auto Lease

The automobile lease (or any other type equipment lease) has all the elements of the T-Bar that we have used in other matters involving cashflows.

- The **PV** is the cost of the automobile, plus the amount the lessee must pay in "drive-off" fees (excluding tax and license).
- The **PMT** is the monthly payment required under the lease.
- **n** is the number of months of the lease.
- **i** is the lease (interest) rate per period
- **FV** is the "residual value" of the automobile at the end of the lease term.

Some automobile dealers make it quite difficult to determine the true cost of leasing because they put a promotional "spin" on many of the important variables. You must have at least four of five variables to evaluate a lease proposal:

1. The agreed-upon fair market value of the automobile
2. The lease rate
3. The agreed-upon upon residual value
4. The time (period of the lease)
5. The monthly payment required.

For example, the fair market value (**PV**) of the automobile is usually not the Manufacturer's Suggested Retail Price (MSRP). Advertising a lease which is based on the MSRP, however, results in a lease rate which is very low, because a smaller interest rate applied to an inflated price is required to produce an acceptable monthly payment for the dealer. We can restate this to say that a small discount rate is required to discount the future PMTs and reversionary value (FV) to a high PV.

Some manufacturers of luxury cars exaggerate both the residual (Future Value) of the automobile and its fair market value (MSRP) in order to demonstrate a low lease rate. At the termination of the lease, many of these automobiles are purchased from the lessor at prices far below the estimated residual price in the lease contract. The lessee then realizes that both the lease rate and the contract price are artificial numbers.

Buyer's Cost is Dealer's Yield

As was true for mortgages, the lessee's cost and the dealer's yield on a lease are opposite sides of the same coin. Therefore, let's consider the following (actual) advertisement for a lease on a popular make of car:

Advertised Lease Terms

<u>24-Month Lease</u>

Monthly Payment	$399.
"Down Payment"	2,550
Refundable Security Deposit	400
Cash Due at Signing	3,349 (no tax, no license fee)

Reading from the fine print.....

MSRP = 90.22% of MSRP of $38,675 = $34,893

This particular offer to lease does not quote a lease rate, but simply advertises the monthly lease PMT; nor does this advertisement quote the residual value in the lease, only that ...

"Lessee may have the option to buy the vehicle at lease end at a price negotiated with the dealer *at signing*." (Emphasis added)

The dealer has omitted both the lease rate and the residual value of the car in order to leave himself negotiating room. He has also inflated the value of the car over the price at which it can be purchased. This is why it is advantageous to negotiate a lease knowing the price at which the dealer can sell the car.

Automobiles in this price category typically wholesale to the dealer at prices which are 15-20% below the MSRP (say, $30,940). The cash purchase price of any automobile can be, and should be, confirmed through a reputable buying service.[1]

In the same way, the residual value of a 2-year old model of this make can be determined by consulting Kelly's Blue Book,™ or other comparable trade publication which lists the high–low–median used car prices for that model. For the purposes of our example, we will assume that the automobile will lose 15% of its purchase value in the first year and 13% of its value in the second year. Therefore the residual value of this automobile at the end of 24 months will be in the order of $23,880

---

[1]   Many lessees will pay lease rates based on inflated values which they would never agree to in a sale.

Having verified this information, you can re-construct the cashflow which the dealer will receive. His initial cashflow (**PV**) will be the cost of the car (a negative cashflow for him) **plus** the drive-off amount he receives at the inception of the lease (a positive cashflow for him). The drive-off amount consists of the first month's lease payment (in advance), a profit on costs, and charges that are passed to the lessee. Of this amount, $400 is treated, in this case, as a security deposit[2] refundable at termination.

The payments to be received equal $399 per month for (**n**) 2<u>3</u> months, since the first lease payment is collected in the "drive-off" fee. The residual value of the auto, $23,880, is the wholesale value of the vehicle at the end of the 2<u>4</u>th month of the lease (**FV**).

The T-Bar for the 24-month lease looks like:

Dealer invests	−30,940 + 399 + 400 + 2,500 = −27.591
Receives EOP 1	399
2	399
$\boxed{i = ?}$:	:
:	:
23	399
24	23,880 - 400 (residual value less deposit)

The dealer's yield[3] on this lease is .82764% per month, or 9.93% per year. Therefore the lessee's cost is the same: 9.93% per year.

Dealer Variables

There are a number of ways in which a dealer-lessor improves the yield on this lease. The most common method is the use of a contract price higher than the current sales (not lease) value of the car. This raises the PV in the T-Bar and results in a lower lease (discount) rate. If the lease **PMT**s are based on a contract price (**PV**) which reflects the price at which he would be willing to sell the car, the lease rate becomes much higher.

---

2   Part of his profit – since he will have the use of the security deposit interest-free for two years.

3   Internal Rate of Return on his investment

The Lease Contract Price

In the present marketing arena, some dealers train salespeople not to discuss the contract price of the car (PV), but rather to determine the maximum monthly **PMT** the lessee can afford. The lease contract price then becomes equal to the **PMT** divided by the "monthly factor." Many lessees who would not contemplate the purchase of a car without extensive shopping, often accept this contract price without question.

The "monthly factor" is the PMT divided by the contract price.[4] Therefore if the dealer quotes a monthly payment and a monthly factor , it is easy to determine the contract price he is using:

$$\text{Contract Price} = \frac{\$399}{.0116364} = \$34{,}289$$

This contract price can be broken up into a lease value (FMR) of $30,940, plus drive off fees (exclusive of tax and license) of $3,349

Residual Value is Needed

While the residual value of the car may also be negotiated, the dealer structures the lease and monthly payment on his own estimate of the true residual value and not on the residual value published in the lease, since the lessee is not obligated to buy the car at the residual price (**FV**) agreed upon "on signing." Although the residual value (**FV**) is important to the lessee in order to determine the true lease rate (**i**), the agreed-upon sales value (**PV**) and the lease rate (**i**) are the most important negotiable factors for the lessee who does not contemplate buying the vehicle at the end of the lease.

Alternately (or additionally) the dealer can encourage options to be added to the car, which will increase both the drive-off fee and/or the monthly payment. Options increase dealer profit up-front since dealer-installed options generally carry a 40+% mark-up. They also make the auto more readily saleable at term.

A third method is to exaggerate the residual value under the contract. This is a stratagem frequently used by luxury car dealers in order to advertise a low lease rate and in order not to excessively discount the MSRP. This extra amount assures the dealer of a profit over market value should you wish to buy the car for the value agreed upon "at signing." But his yield on the lease will not be calculated on this over-the-market residual value.

If there are charges to be paid for excessive mileage, these charges should be added to the **FV**, since they will be received by the dealer at the time of lease termination.

---

4 Analogous to a monthly loan konstant.

2. Buy vs. Rent Decisions for Housing

The overwhelming majority of residences are purchased for subjective reasons, and not primarily for economic gain. A fortunate few even feel that price is a secondary consideration in the purchase of a home. But the past few years have amply demonstrated that home prices don't always keep rising; they also fall, often with tragic financial consequences. If this is so, are there times when it is more financial prudent to rent than to buy? How much can be expected in savings from home ownership, especially in view of the fact that owning a home costs more than renting one?

The financial question posed by the Rent or Buy decision is simply this: At the end of a reasonable number of years, which option, buying or renting, will result in greater wealth accumulation?

Nothing But Rent Receipts?

It is almost true that renting yields nothing but rent receipts. Renting yields not only living accommodations (or business space), but also makes cash available, which would otherwise be invested as a downpayment, for other forms of investment. Therefore the key to this decision is the alternate opportunities available for the use of the downpayment monies and the return which can be expected from these alternate investments in comparison to equity accumulation through home ownership. Businesses often have uses for this cash which will result in a greater financial return than cash paid to buy a building. Home buyers have less access to such opportunities and therefore make their home their "investment."

Tax Benefits of Home Ownership

The strong advantage in buying a home derives from present tax laws which greatly favor home ownership for most families. These include:

    1. Deduction of mortgage interest from otherwise taxable ordinary income.
    2. Deduction of property taxes from otherwise taxable income
    3. "Forced" savings – since part of the mortgage payment goes to equity
    4. Accumulation of up to $125,000 in long-term capital gains on a principal residence, which is delivered tax-free to owners 55 years or older.[5]

Home owners usually benefit from the use of **leverage** since down payments from as little as 5% to the more typical 20% can control an asset valued in the thousands. As we pointed out in the discussion of the Band of Investment Approach to Cap Rates (Chapter 6), it is the equity owner who receives all the benefit of price appreciation. He also bears the

---

[5] And who meet other requirements. This is the "once-in-a-lifetime" deduction.

greatest risk of loss in leveraged investments. This is also true for the highly leveraged homeowner since a modest decline in real estate prices can easily wipe out his entire equity position.

Wealth Analysis is the Objective

The task in comparing these two options is the task of constructing the most likely cashflow scenarios which would result from the alternate decisions. The objective is to determine which alternative, under a given set of circumstances, results in the greatest net wealth accumulation over a reasonable holding period.

Problems such as this demonstrate the great value in converting your knowledge of cashflow analysis to a computer's spreadsheet. Once a satisfactory format is devised, a number of "what if" (sensitivity) analyses can be made in an instant which would ordinarily require 15-20 minutes' calculation on a hand-held machine.

Buy-Rent Spreadsheet Format

The seven cashflow spreadsheets which follow are each arranged in three main segments: the **Variables** (lines 4-13), the **Owning** scenario (lines 16-39), and the **Renting** scenario lines 41-44).

It is a great advantage to list the variables in a separate section of the spreadsheet as opposed to incorporating the variables in line formulas. By separating them, and then referencing them from other locations in the spreadsheet, a variable can be changed quickly and the result of the change reflected immediately throughout every dependent cell.

For example, line 36 (**Market Value**) depends on an estimated inflation rate (B11) to reflect yearly changes in the anticipated market value of the property. Cell D36 = cell C36 * (1+ inflation rate). Rather than enter the inflation rate into the formula as a numerical value, it is entered by referencing the value contained in Cell B11. Thus, Cell D36 = cell C36 * (1 + $B$11). [6]

Spreadsheet Logic, Owner's Position

The "housing cost" which the owner of his/her residence incurs is the total annual cost of ownership after taxes. As owner of the property, all increases in market value are credited to the owner's equity position. Similarly, all losses in value are borne by the equity owner.

---

[6] The dollar signs hold B11 as an "absolute reference" in fill-right operations.

The owner's net **wealth position** will be the gross equity, measured at the end of the holding period (in this case, 5 years), **less** the net cost of housing expenses in year 5. These expenses are costs of maintenance, and the *after-tax* cost of the mortgage and tax payments.

Spreadsheet Logic, Renter's Position

The "housing cost" which the renter of his/her residence incurs is the total annual after-tax cost of renting. Since there is no federal tax relief to renters, the rent paid *is* the after-tax cost of renting. The renter's net **wealth position** will be the results achieved by investing the downpayment at the projected reinvestment rate, less the net cost of housing expenses at the end of year 5.

The renter has available for investment an amount of money equal to what would have been used as a downpayment (plus closing costs) had he/she purchased a residence. To this amount, we have added the difference between the total cashflow required to support a residence and an estimate of rent for comparable space.[7] Since residences can generally be rented for an amount less than that required to own them, renting initially frees additional (surplus) cash for investment. We have estimated that a renter can invest his downpayment money – plus surplus cash – for an after-tax yield of 200% of the inflation rate. When the annual inflation rate drops below 2.5%, we assume that the renter can still find a 5.0% return in the marketplace.

Results of Various Scenarios

The 7 spreadsheets (Rent-Buy, 1-7) which follow demonstrate the result of purchasing a residence as opposed to renting over a span of 5 years using different variables. The important variables are:

       1. Rate of inflation/deflation (Line 11)
       2. Interest Rate (Line 7)
       3. Percent downpayment (Line 5)
       4. Marginal Tax Rate (Line 13)

These variables do not carry the same weight for all taxpayers, however.

For the most part, buying is very advantageous for *all* homeowners whenever the inflation rate is significant. This is particularly so for buyers in low incremental tax brackets who cannot convert interest and property tax deductions into cash (saved taxes) at a high rate. These homeowners cannot tolerate low inflation rates and still show an ownership advantage.

---

[7] Within reasonable limits, properties tend to rent monthly for .6% -.7% of their current market value.

	A	B	C	D	E	F	G
1	Rent vs. Buy - 1						
2	Introduction to Cashflow Analysis®						
3							
4	Acquisition Value	225,000					
5	Downpayment	20.00%					
6	Mortgage Amount	180,000					
7	Interest Rate	8.50%					
8	Scheduled Term in Years	30					
9	Tax Rate (% of Acq. Cost)	1.25%					
10	Association Fee/Month	0					
11	Estimated Inflation Rate/Yr.	3.50%					
12	After-tax Reinvestment Rate	7.00%					
13	Taxpayer's Fed. Tax Bracket	31.0%					
14							
15		YEAR	1	2	3	4	5
16		Mortgage Payment/Mo.	1,384	1,384	1,384	1,384	1,384
17		Principal Paid/ Yr.	1,361	1,481	1,612	1,754	1,909
18		Interest/ Yr.	15,248	15,128	14,997	14,854	14,699
19		Remaining Bal. EOY	178,639	177,158	175,546	173,792	171,882
20	Owning						
21		Pvt. Mortg. Insurance/Yr.	0	0	0	0	0
22		Association Fee /Yr.	0	0	0	0	0
23	Increase at Inflation rate	Maintenance/Yr.	1,125	1,164	1,205	1,247	1,291
24		Principal Paydown	1,361	1,481	1,612	1,754	1,909
25		Interest/ Yr.	15,248	15,128	14,997	14,854	14,699
26		R.E. Taxes/ Yr.	2,813	2,869	2,926	2,985	3,044
27		Total Cashflow/Yr.	20,546	20,642	20,740	20,840	20,944
28	Housing Cost < Taxes	Pre-Tax Cost/Mo.	1,712	1,720	1,728	1,737	1,745
29		Deductible Interest	15,248	15,128	14,997	14,854	14,699
30		Deductible Taxes	2,813	2,869	2,926	2,985	3,044
31		Total Annual Deductibles	18,060	17,996	17,923	17,839	17,743
32		Taxes Saved	5,599	5,579	5,556	5,530	5,500
33	Federal Tax Saving Only	Tax Savings/Month	467	465	463	461	458
34	Housing Cost > Taxes	Net Housing Cost/Mo.	1,246	1,255	1,265	1,276	1,287
35							
36	Increased at Inflation Rate	Market Value	232,875	241,026	249,462	258,193	267,229
37		-Mortg. Bal.	178,639	177,158	175,546	173,792	171,882
38	Gross Equity End of Year	Gross Equity	54,236	63,867	73,915	84,401	95,347
39		Net After Housing Cost	39,288	48,805	58,731	69,090	79,904
40	Renting						
41	Rent Increase @ Inflation Rate	Rent/Mo.	1,350	1,397	1,446	1,497	1,549
42		Annual Rent	16,200	16,767	17,354	17,961	18,590
43	Uses Reinvestment Rate > Tax	Invested D.P. + Surplus	52,800	60,642	68,510	76,387	84,252
44		Net After Renting	36,600	43,875	51,156	58,425	65,662
45							
46	Wealth	End of 5 yrs. Owning	$79,904				
47	Comparison	End of 5 yrs. Renting	$65,662				
48							
49							
50							
51							
52							
53							
54							
55							
56							
57							
58							

	A	B	C	D	E	F	G
1	Rent vs. Buy -2						
2	Introduction to Cashflow Analysis®						
3							
4	Acquisition Value	225,000					
5	Downpayment	20.00%					
6	Mortgage Amount	180,000					
7	Interest Rate	8.50%					
8	Scheduled Term in Years	30					
9	Tax Rate (% of Acq. Cost)	1.25%					
10	Association Fee/Month	0					
11	Estimated Inflation Rate/Yr.	2.50%					
12	After-tax Reinvestment Rate	5.00%					
13	Taxpayer's Fed. Tax Bracket	31.0%					
14							
15		YEAR	1	2	3	4	5
16		Mortgage Payment/Mo.	1,384	1,384	1,384	1,384	1,384
17		Principal Paid/ Yr.	1,361	1,481	1,612	1,754	1,909
18		Interest/ Yr.	15,248	15,128	14,997	14,854	14,699
19		Remaining Bal. EOY	178,639	177,158	175,546	173,792	171,882
20	Owning						
21		Pvt. Mortg. Insurance/Yr.	0	0	0	0	0
22		Association Fee /Yr.	0	0	0	0	0
23	Increase at Inflation rate	Maintenance/Yr.	1,125	1,153	1,182	1,212	1,242
24		Principal Paydown	1,361	1,481	1,612	1,754	1,909
25		Interest/ Yr.	15,248	15,128	14,997	14,854	14,699
26		R.E. Taxes/ Yr.	2,813	2,869	2,926	2,985	3,044
27		Total Cashflow/Yr.	20,546	20,630	20,717	20,805	20,895
28	Housing Cost < Taxes	Pre-Tax Cost/Mo.	1,712	1,719	1,726	1,734	1,741
29		Deductible Interest	15,248	15,128	14,997	14,854	14,699
30		Deductible Taxes	2,813	2,869	2,926	2,985	3,044
31		Total Annual Deductibles	18,060	17,996	17,923	17,839	17,743
32		Taxes Saved	5,599	5,579	5,556	5,530	5,500
33	Federal Tax Saving Only	Tax Savings/Month	467	465	463	461	458
34	Housing Cost > Taxes	Net Housing Cost/Mo.	1,246	1,254	1,263	1,273	1,283
35							
36	Increased at Inflation Rate	Market Value	230,625	236,391	242,300	248,358	254,567
37		-Mortg. Bal.	178,639	177,158	175,546	173,792	171,882
38	Gross Equity End of Year	Gross Equity	51,986	59,232	66,754	74,566	82,684
39		Net After Housing Cost	37,038	44,181	51,593	59,291	67,290
40	Renting						
41	Rent Increase @ Inflation Rate	Rent/Mo.	1,350	1,384	1,418	1,454	1,490
42		Annual Rent	16,200	16,605	17,020	17,446	17,882
43	Uses Reinvestment Rate > Tax	Invested D.P. + Surplus	51,813	58,631	65,444	72,243	79,018
44		Net After Renting	35,613	42,026	48,423	54,797	61,137
45							
46	Wealth	End of 5 yrs. Owning	$67,290				
47	Comparison	End of 5 yrs. Renting	$61,137				
48							
49							
50							
51							
52							
53							
54							
55							
56							
57							
58							

	A	B	C	D	E	F	G
1	Rent vs. Buy- 3						
2	Introduction to Cashflow Analysis®						
3							
4	Acquisition Value	225,000					
5	Downpayment	20.00%					
6	Mortgage Amount	180,000					
7	Interest Rate	9.50%					
8	Scheduled Term in Years	30					
9	Tax Rate (% of Acq. Cost)	1.25%					
10	Association Fee/Month	0					
11	Estimated Inflation Rate/Yr.	3.50%					
12	After-tax Reinvestment Rate	7.00%					
13	Taxpayer's Fed. Tax Bracket	31.0%					
14							
15		YEAR	1	2	3	4	5
16		Mortgage Payment/Mo.	1,514	1,514	1,514	1,514	1,514
17		Principal Paid/ Yr.	1,110	1,220	1,341	1,474	1,621
18		Interest/ Yr.	17,052	16,942	16,821	16,688	16,542
19		Remaining Bal. EOY	178,890	177,670	176,329	174,854	173,234
20	Owning						
21		Pvt. Mortg. Insurance/Yr.	0	0	0	0	0
22		Association Fee /Yr.	0	0	0	0	0
23	Increase at Inflation rate	Maintenance/Yr.	1,125	1,164	1,205	1,247	1,291
24		Principal Paydown	1,110	1,220	1,341	1,474	1,621
25		Interest/ Yr.	17,052	16,942	16,821	16,688	16,542
26		R.E. Taxes/ Yr.	2,813	2,869	2,926	2,985	3,044
27		Total Cashflow/Yr.	22,100	22,196	22,294	22,394	22,498
28	Housing Cost < Taxes	Pre-Tax Cost/Mo.	1,842	1,850	1,858	1,866	1,875
29		Deductible Interest	17,052	16,942	16,821	16,688	16,542
30		Deductible Taxes	2,813	2,869	2,926	2,985	3,044
31		Total Annual Deductibles	19,865	19,811	19,747	19,673	19,586
32		Taxes Saved	6,158	6,141	6,122	6,099	6,072
33	Federal Tax Saving Only	Tax Savings/Month	513	512	510	508	506
34	Housing Cost > Taxes	Net Housing Cost/Mo.	1,328	1,338	1,348	1,358	1,369
35							
36	Increased at Inflation Rate	Market Value	232,875	241,026	249,462	258,193	267,229
37		-Mortg. Bal.	178,890	177,670	176,329	174,854	173,234
38	Gross Equity End of Year	Gross Equity	53,985	63,356	73,133	83,338	93,996
39		Net After Housing Cost	38,043	47,302	56,961	67,042	77,570
40	Renting						
41	Rent Increase @ Inflation Rate	Rent/Mo.	1,350	1,397	1,446	1,497	1,549
42		Annual Rent	16,200	16,767	17,354	17,961	18,590
43	Uses Reinvestment Rate > Tax	Invested D.P. + Surplus	54,463	64,084	73,855	83,769	93,814
44		Net After Renting	38,263	47,317	56,502	65,808	75,224
45							
46	Wealth	End of 5 yrs. Owning	$77,570				
47	Comparison	End of 5 yrs. Renting	$75,224				
48							
49							
50							
51							
52							
53							
54							
55							
56							
57							
58							

	A	B	C	D	E	F	G
1	Rent vs. Buy - 4						
2	**Introduction to Cashflow Analysis®**						
3							
4	Acquisition Value	225,000					
5	Downpayment	20.00%					
6	Mortgage Amount	180,000					
7	Interest Rate	8.50%					
8	Scheduled Term in Years	30					
9	Tax Rate (% of Acq. Cost)	1.25%					
10	Association Fee/Month	0					
11	Estimated Inflation Rate/Yr.	3.50%					
12	After-tax Reinvestment Rate	7.00%					
13	Taxpayer's Fed. Tax Bracket	20.0%					
14							
15		YEAR	1	2	3	4	5
16		Mortgage Payment/Mo.	1,384	1,384	1,384	1,384	1,384
17		Principal Paid/ Yr.	1,361	1,481	1,612	1,754	1,909
18		Interest/ Yr.	15,248	15,128	14,997	14,854	14,699
19		Remaining Bal. EOY	178,639	177,158	175,546	173,792	171,882
20	Owning						
21		Pvt. Mortg. Insurance/Yr.	0	0	0	0	0
22		Association Fee /Yr.	0	0	0	0	0
23	Increase at Inflation rate	Maintenance/Yr.	1,125	1,164	1,205	1,247	1,291
24		Principal Paydown	1,361	1,481	1,612	1,754	1,909
25		Interest/ Yr.	15,248	15,128	14,997	14,854	14,699
26		R.E. Taxes/ Yr.	2,813	2,869	2,926	2,985	3,044
27		Total Cashflow/Yr.	20,546	20,642	20,740	20,840	20,944
28	Housing Cost < Taxes	Pre-Tax Cost/Mo.	1,712	1,720	1,728	1,737	1,745
29		Deductible Interest	15,248	15,128	14,997	14,854	14,699
30		Deductible Taxes	2,813	2,869	2,926	2,985	3,044
31		Total Annual Deductibles	18,060	17,996	17,923	17,839	17,743
32		Taxes Saved	3,612	3,599	3,585	3,568	3,549
33	Federal Tax Saving Only	Tax Savings/Month	301	300	299	297	296
34	Housing Cost > Taxes	Net Housing Cost/Mo.	1,411	1,420	1,430	1,439	1,450
35							
36	Increased at Inflation Rate	Market Value	232,875	241,026	249,462	258,193	267,229
37		-Mortg. Bal.	178,639	177,158	175,546	173,792	171,882
38	Gross Equity End of Year	Gross Equity	54,236	63,867	73,915	84,401	95,347
39		Net After Housing Cost	37,302	46,825	56,760	67,128	77,952
40	Renting						
41	Rent Increase @ Inflation Rate	Rent/Mo.	1,350	1,397	1,446	1,497	1,549
42		Annual Rent	16,200	16,767	17,354	17,961	18,590
43	Uses Reinvestment Rate > Tax	Invested D.P. + Surplus	52,800	60,642	68,510	76,387	84,252
44		Net After Renting	36,600	43,875	51,156	58,425	65,662
45							
46	Wealth	End of 5 yrs. Owning	$77,952				
47	Comparison	End of 5 yrs. Renting	$65,662				
48							
49							
50							
51							
52							
53							
54							
55							
56							
57							
58							

	A	B	C	D	E	F	G
1	Rent vs. Buy - 5						
2	**Introduction to Cashflow Analysis®**						
3							
4	Acquisition Value	225,000					
5	Downpayment	20.00%					
6	Mortgage Amount	180,000					
7	Interest Rate	8.50%					
8	Scheduled Term in Years	30					
9	Tax Rate (% of Acq. Cost)	1.25%					
10	Association Fee/Month	0					
11	Estimated Inflation Rate/Yr.	5.00%					
12	After-tax Reinvestment Rate	10.00%					
13	Taxpayer's Fed. Tax Bracket	31.0%					
14							
15		YEAR	1	2	3	4	5
16		Mortgage Payment/Mo.	1,384	1,384	1,384	1,384	1,384
17		Principal Paid/ Yr.	1,361	1,481	1,612	1,754	1,909
18		Interest/ Yr.	15,248	15,128	14,997	14,854	14,699
19		Remaining Bal. EOY	178,639	177,158	175,546	173,792	171,882
20	Owning						
21		Pvt. Mortg. Insurance/Yr.	0	0	0	0	0
22		Association Fee /Yr.	0	0	0	0	0
23	Increase at Inflation rate	Maintenance/Yr.	1,125	1,181	1,240	1,302	1,367
24		Principal Paydown	1,361	1,481	1,612	1,754	1,909
25		Interest/ Yr.	15,248	15,128	14,997	14,854	14,699
26		R.E. Taxes/ Yr.	2,813	2,869	2,926	2,985	3,044
27		Total Cashflow/Yr.	20,546	20,659	20,775	20,896	21,020
28	Housing Cost < Taxes	Pre-Tax Cost/Mo.	1,712	1,722	1,731	1,741	1,752
29		Deductible Interest	15,248	15,128	14,997	14,854	14,699
30		Deductible Taxes	2,813	2,869	2,926	2,985	3,044
31		Total Annual Deductibles	18,060	17,996	17,923	17,839	17,743
32		Taxes Saved	5,599	5,579	5,556	5,530	5,500
33	Federal Tax Saving Only	Tax Savings/Month	467	465	463	461	458
34	Housing Cost > Taxes	Net Housing Cost/Mo.	1,246	1,257	1,268	1,280	1,293
35							
36	Increased at Inflation Rate	Market Value	236,250	248,063	260,466	273,489	287,163
37		-Mortg. Bal.	178,639	177,158	175,546	173,792	171,882
38	Gross Equity End of Year	Gross Equity	57,611	70,904	84,919	99,697	115,281
39		Net After Housing Cost	42,663	55,825	69,700	84,331	99,761
40	Renting						
41	Rent Increase @ Inflation Rate	Rent/Mo.	1,350	1,418	1,488	1,563	1,641
42		Annual Rent	16,200	17,010	17,861	18,754	19,691
43	Uses Reinvestment Rate > Tax	Invested D.P. + Surplus	54,281	63,722	73,300	82,986	92,747
44		Net After Renting	38,081	46,712	55,440	64,233	73,056
45							
46	Wealth	End of 5 yrs. Owning	$99,761				
47	Comparison	End of 5 yrs. Renting	$73,056				
48							
49							
50							
51							
52							
53							
54							
55							
56							
57							
58							

	A	B	C	D	E	F	G
1	**Rent vs. Buy - 6**						
2	**Introduction to Cashflow Analysis®**						
3							
4	Acquisition Value	150,000					
5	Downpayment	5.00%					
6	Mortgage Amount	142,500					
7	Interest Rate	8.50%					
8	Scheduled Term in Years	30					
9	Tax Rate (% of Acq. Cost)	1.25%					
10	Association Fee/Month	0					
11	Estimated Inflation Rate/Yr.	3.50%					
12	After-tax Reinvestment Rate	7.00%					
13	Taxpayer's Fed. Tax Bracket	20.0%					
14							
15		YEAR	1	2	3	4	5
16		Mortgage Payment/Mo.	1,096	1,096	1,096	1,096	1,096
17		Principal Paid/ Yr.	1,077	1,172	1,276	1,389	1,512
18		Interest/ Yr.	12,071	11,976	11,872	11,760	11,637
19		Remaining Bal. EOY	141,423	140,250	138,974	137,585	136,074
20	Owning						
21		Pvt. Mortg. Insurance/Yr.	527	527	527	527	527
22		Association Fee /Yr.	0	0	0	0	0
23	Increase at Inflation rate	Maintenance/Yr.	750	776	803	832	861
24		Principal Paydown	1,077	1,172	1,276	1,389	1,512
25		Interest/ Yr.	12,071	11,976	11,872	11,760	11,637
26		R.E. Taxes/ Yr.	1,875	1,913	1,951	1,990	2,030
27		Total Cashflow/Yr.	16,301	16,364	16,430	16,497	16,566
28	Housing Cost < Taxes	Pre-Tax Cost/Mo.	1,358	1,364	1,369	1,375	1,380
29		Deductible Interest	12,071	11,976	11,872	11,760	11,637
30		Deductible Taxes	1,875	1,913	1,951	1,990	2,030
31		Total Annual Deductibles	13,946	13,888	13,823	13,749	13,666
32		Taxes Saved	2,789	2,778	2,765	2,750	2,733
33	Federal Tax Saving Only	Tax Savings/Month	232	231	230	229	228
34	Housing Cost > Taxes	Net Housing Cost/Mo.	1,126	1,132	1,139	1,146	1,153
35							
36	Increased at Inflation Rate	Market Value	155,250	160,684	166,308	172,128	178,153
37		-Mortg. Bal.	141,423	140,250	138,974	137,585	136,074
38	Gross Equity End of Year	Gross Equity	13,827	20,433	27,333	34,543	42,079
39		Net After Housing Cost	316	6,847	13,668	20,796	28,247
40	Renting						
41	Rent Increase @ Inflation Rate	Rent/Mo.	900	932	964	998	1,033
42		Annual Rent	10,800	11,178	11,569	11,974	12,393
43	Uses Reinvestment Rate > Tax	Invested D.P. + Surplus	13,911	20,434	27,065	33,799	40,630
44		Net After Renting	3,111	9,256	15,496	21,825	28,237
45							
46	Wealth	End of 5 yrs. Owning	$28,247				
47	Comparison	End of 5 yrs. Renting	$28,237				
48							
49							
50							
51							
52							
53							
54							
55							
56							
57							
58							

	A	B	C	D	E	F	G
1	Rent vs. Buy - 7						
2	Introduction to Cashflow Analysis®						
3							
4	Acquisition Value	150,000					
5	Downpayment	5.00%					
6	Mortgage Amount	142,500					
7	Interest Rate	8.50%					
8	Scheduled Term in Years	30					
9	Tax Rate (% of Acq. Cost)	1.25%					
10	Association Fee/Month	0					
11	Estimated Inflation Rate/Yr.	2.50%					
12	After-tax Reinvestment Rate	5.00%					
13	Taxpayer's Fed. Tax Bracket	20.0%					
14							
15		YEAR	1	2	3	4	5
16		Mortgage Payment/Mo.	1,096	1,096	1,096	1,096	1,096
17		Principal Paid/ Yr.	1,077	1,172	1,276	1,389	1,512
18		Interest/ Yr.	12,071	11,976	11,872	11,760	11,637
19		Remaining Bal. EOY	141,423	140,250	138,974	137,585	136,074
20	Owning						
21		Pvt. Mortg. Insurance/Yr.	527	527	527	527	527
22		Association Fee /Yr.	0	0	0	0	0
23	Increase at Inflation rate	Maintenance/Yr.	750	769	788	808	828
24		Principal Paydown	1,077	1,172	1,276	1,389	1,512
25		Interest/ Yr.	12,071	11,976	11,872	11,760	11,637
26		R.E. Taxes/ Yr.	1,875	1,913	1,951	1,990	2,030
27		Total Cashflow/Yr.	16,301	16,357	16,414	16,473	16,533
28	Housing Cost < Taxes	Pre-Tax Cost/Mo.	1,358	1,363	1,368	1,373	1,378
29		Deductible Interest	12,071	11,976	11,872	11,760	11,637
30		Deductible Taxes	1,875	1,913	1,951	1,990	2,030
31		Total Annual Deductibles	13,946	13,888	13,823	13,749	13,666
32		Taxes Saved	2,789	2,778	2,765	2,750	2,733
33	Federal Tax Saving Only	Tax Savings/Month	232	231	230	229	228
34	Housing Cost > Taxes	Net Housing Cost/Mo.	1,126	1,132	1,137	1,144	1,150
35							
36	Increased at Inflation Rate	Market Value	153,750	157,594	161,534	165,572	169,711
37		-Mortg. Bal.	141,423	140,250	138,974	137,585	136,074
38	Gross Equity End of Year	Gross Equity	12,327	17,343	22,559	27,987	33,638
39		Net After Housing Cost	-1,184	3,764	8,910	14,263	19,838
40	Renting						
41	Rent Increase @ Inflation Rate	Rent/Mo.	900	923	946	969	993
42		Annual Rent	10,800	11,070	11,347	11,630	11,921
43	Uses Reinvestment Rate > Tax	Invested D.P. + Surplus	13,651	19,885	26,200	32,595	39,067
44		Net After Renting	2,851	8,815	14,853	20,964	27,146
45							
46	Wealth	End of 5 yrs. Owning	$19,838				
47	Comparison	End of 5 yrs. Renting	$27,146				
48							
49							
50							
51							
52							
53							
54							
55							
56							
57							
58							

Under the circumstances of Rent-Buy–7, which depicts a 2.5% inflation rate per year,[8] a low marginal taxpayer would be much better off by renting. For low income homeowners the relatively higher initial cost of ownership is generally offset by appreciation and by the fact that they are reasonably insulated from large rent increases.[9] While zero inflation rates have never occurred for five consecutive years, losses of 5% and greater in just a few years are not uncommon. Since low marginal tax rate owners are usually very highly leveraged, even small percentage declines in property values can be financially ruinous.[10]

But taxpayers in high marginal rates (Buy-Rent -2) can tolerate low inflation rates very well since they convert tax advantages into cash at a rate high enough to offset the higher pre-tax cost of home ownership and low inflation rates.

Summary of Variables in Seven Spreadsheets

In the table below, the "Buy Advantage" is the net, 5-year financial advantage in buying a residence over renting. All "runs" of these variables testify as to how very sensitive real estate returns are to inflation.[11] The last spreadsheet (R-B-7) has demonstrated that in the absence of an inflation rate in excess of 3.5% annually, low marginal tax rate homeowners who cannot convert tax benefits to cash do not do very well, and should probably not be encouraged to buy during deflationary periods.

B-R No.	Acquisition. Price	Down Payment	Interest Rate	Tax Rate	Inflation Rate	Buying Advantage
#1	$225,000	20%	8.5%	31%	3.5%	$14,242
#2	225,000	20%	8.5%	31%	2.5%	6,153
#3	225,000	20%	9.5%	31%	3.5%	2,526
#4	225,000	20%	8.5%	20%	3.5%	12,290
#5	225,000	20%	8.5%	31%	5.0%	26.705
#6	150,000	5%	8.5%	20%	3.5%	10
#7	150,000	5%	8.5%	20%	2.5%	-7,308

These example cashflow spreadsheets can easily be modified to suit any set of variables and market conditions. The results can be very helpful to individuals seeking to know whether to Buy or Rent, and to anticipate the added cost or savings resulting from ownership.

---

8   Inflation rates have been negative in only two years since 1970. But real property values have declined more than 5% in one year a number of times.

9   Adjustable Rate Mortgages in recent years have transferred the bulk of this risk to the borrower.

10 The overwhelming majority of foreclosures occurs to owners with less than 10% equity in their homes.

11 Real estate has long been characterized as the preferred investment for inflationary times.

3. Whether To Refinance a Property

Many property owners in recent years have faced the decision to refinance or not. A general rule given in these circumstances is to refinance whenever the difference between the existing interest rate and the new interest rate is 2% or more.

The financial objective is a course of action which will result in the greatest wealth accumulation over the remaining holding period. The "remaining holding period" is an important variable in the problem, but the second key variable is the number of points and closing costs to be charged on the new loan. Since refinancing can be expensive, an owner who plans to dispose of the property in the near future may not have sufficient time over which to recapture (amortize) these additional costs. Any un-amortized costs of refinancing act as deductions from the savings realized through lower monthly payments.

Let's take an example:

The Bernsteins purchased their $275,000 home at a time when interest rates were 10.5%. They obtained an 80% loan-to-value mortgage, fully amortized over 30 years.

Now, exactly five years later, interest rates have declined 1.5% to 9.0%. A lender will extend a new 30-year loan in the amount of the balance of the existing mortgage and will also include the points and closing costs in the new loan. The costs of a new loan will be 2 points plus $750. The Bernsteins anticipate moving to another state in three years. Is it profitable for them to refinance their present home, and if so, how much will they save?

Calculating the Remaining Balance of Existing Loan

First, we need to determine the monthly payments and remaining balance on the existing mortgage:

	n	i	PV	PMT	FV
	360	$\frac{10.5}{12}$	-220,000	?	0
solving				2,012.43	

Since **60 PMT**s have been made, the Remaining Balance (**FV**) of the present mortgage is:

n	i	PV	PMT	FV
60	$\frac{10.5}{12}$	-220,000	2,012.43	?

Solving

213,139.74

In an additional 36 months, when they move, the balance of this loan will be:

n	i	PV	PMT	FV
96	$\frac{10.5}{12}$	-220,000	2,012.43	?

Solving

206,931.80

The amount of the new loan necessary to cover miscellaneous costs will be:

Balance of old loan................... $213,139.74
Plus Misc. Costs of new loan............. 750.00
New Loan Before Points $213,889.74

This amount, $213,889.74, will be the net amount available *after* payment of 2 points (2.0%). Therefore this amount is 98% of the new loan amount. The amount of the new loan will be:

$$\frac{213889.74}{.98} = \$218,254.84$$

Payments required under the new loan will be:

n	i	PV	PMT	FV
360	$\frac{9}{12}$	-218,254.84	?	0

Solving

1,756.13

The remaining balance of this loan after **36 PMT**s will be:

n	i	PV	PMT	FV
36	$\frac{9}{12}$	-218,254.84	1,756.13	?

Solving

213,348.75

As you can see, the remaining balance of the new loan in three years will be $6,418 higher than would be the balance of the original loan ($213,348 vs. $206,932). But the **PMT**s on the new loan will have been substantially less for 36 **PMT**s.

How can these cashflow trade-offs be measured and evaluated?

Calculating the APR for Refinance

You will recall, from Chapter 4, that the **APR** (Annual Percentage Rate) reflects the true cost of borrowing and includes all the elements of this refinance problem: beginning balances (**PV**s), payments under the schedule (**PMT**s), remaining balances (**FV**s) and finance charges (points + loan closing costs). Although the APR is restricted to costs involving the loan only (e.g. no escrow costs), the Bernsteins should include all costs associated with the refinance, since their goal is not to determine the bank's true interest rate, but rather their true *total* cost.

The solution to a question involving the advisability of refinancing an existing loan is to calculate the (modified) **APR** on the proposed loan. By including **all costs**, the entire cost of the refinancing can be determined. It is not necessary to calculate the APR for the existing loan since it may continue at an interest rate of 10.5% with no points or added charges. Therefore its APR is now equal to its interest rate.

We have already determined the monthly PMT for the Bernstein's under a new loan: $1,756.13

Remember that while the Bernsteins will make new loan **PMT**s based on the total of their new loan, $218,254.80, which includes the points and all closing costs, they will receive only $213,139.74 with which to pay off their original loan. The difference will pay the costs and points. With this in mind, we can determine the **APR** viewed from the vantage point of the new lender.

Solving for $\boxed{i}$:

n	$\boxed{i}$	PV	PMT	FV
$\boxed{36}$	?	-213,139.74	1,756.13	213,348.75

Yields :
$$0.8263 \quad x \quad 12 = 9.916\%$$

Since this **APR** is less than the 10.5% the Bernsteins are currently paying, it is profitable to refinance this loan, even though the spread between the old loan and the new loan is less than 2 points.

How Much Will The Bernsteins Save ?

In order to find the Present Value of the cashflow which will result from a new loan over a three-year period, we need only discount the cashflow of the new loan <u>by the rate which the Bernsteins are currently paying for their present money:</u>[12]

n	i	PV	PMT	FV
$\boxed{36}$	$\frac{10.5}{12}$-	?	1,756.13	213,348.75

Solving :
$$-209,943.66$$

The Bernsteins will reduce the Present Value of the loan encumbering their property from $213,139.74 to $209,943.66, a loss of $3,196.08 to the lender and a saving to them.

Refi Spreadsheet

Those interested can mount the following Spreadsheet, **"Whether to Refinance ?"** on their own computers. This simple program makes use of many of the cashflow principles that have been covered. It permits manipulation of all the variables in the problem and enables one to discover the impact of each variable on the profitability of the refinance alternative. (Although columns E and F are provided for purposes of easy comparison, only column D is essential since the changing variables in column C (lines 13-19) will yield the desired information in column D.)

The formulas necessary to mount the program are also included (Excel®).

---

[12] We know that if we discount the cashflows attendant to the original loan, the result will be the present balance of the original loan (try it). Here, we want to know the PV, or dollar value, of the new cashflow discounted *at the same rate*.

	A	B	C	D	E	F
1	**Whether to Refinance?**					
2	**Introduction to Cashflow Analysis**					
3			Original Loan			
4						
5		Beginning Balance	$220,000			
6		Interest Rate	10.50%			
7		Scheduled Term/Mos.	360			
8		No. Months Paid	60			
9		Remaining Balance	$213,139.74			
10		Payment	$2,012.43			
11				New Loan Holding Period, Months		
12			New Loan			
13		Beginning Balance	$218,254.84	218254.84	218254.84	218254.84
14		Interest Rate	9.00%	9.00%	9.00%	9.00%
15		Scheduled Term/Mos.	360	360	360	360
16		No. Months To Be Held	–	12	24	36
17		Payment	$1,756.13	$1,756.13	$1,756.13	$1,756.13
18	Estimated Closing Costs, New Loan		$750.00			
19		Point fee, New loan	2.00%			
20						
21		Remaining Balances	Original Loan		New Loan	
22		60	$213,139.74			
23		72	$211,282.61	$216,763.73		
24		84	$209,220.81		$215,132.74	
25		96	$206,931.80			$213,348.76
26						
27		APR Calculation	Original Loan		New Loan	
28		12	10.5000%	11.50%		
29		24	10.5000%		10.31%	
30		36	10.5000%			9.92%
31						
32			Potential Savings	($2,029.46)	$730.04	$3,196.08
33						
34						
35						
36						
37						
38						
39						
40						
41						
42						
43						
44						
45						
46						
47						
48						
49						

	A	B	C
1	Refinance Formulas		
2			
3		Original Loan	
4			
5	Beginning Balance	220000	
6	Interest Rate	0.105	
7	Scheduled Term/Mos.	360	
8	No. Months Paid	60	(Only One Column Needed –
9	Remaining Balance	=FV(B6/12,B8,-B10,B5,0)*-1	Simply change variables)
10	Payment	=PMT(B6/12,B7,B5,0,0)*-1	
11			
12		New Loan	
13	Beginning Balance	=(B9+B18)/(1-B19)	=B13
14	Interest Rate	0.09	0.09
15	Scheduled Term/Mos.	360	360
16	No. Months To Be Held		12
17	Payment	=PMT(B14/12,B15,-B13,0,)	=PMT(C14/12,C15,-C13,0,)
18	Est Closing Costs, New Loan	750	
19	Point fee, New loan	0.02	
20			
21	Remaining Balances	Original Loan	New Loan
22	60	=FV($B$6/12,A22,$B$10,-$B$5,0)	
23	72	=FV($B$6/12,A23,$B$10,-$B$5,0)	=FV(C14/12,C16,C17,-C13,0)
24	84	=FV($B$6/12,A24,$B$10,-$B$5,0)	
25	96	=FV($B$6/12,A25,$B$10,-$B$5,0)	
26			
27	APR Calculation	Original Loan	
28	12	=RATE(A28,$B$10,-$B$22,B23,0,0.1)*12	=RATE(C16,C17,-B9,C23,0,0.1)*12
29	24	=RATE(A29,$B$10,-$B$22,B24,0,0.1)*12	
30	36	=RATE(A30,$B$10,-$B$22,B25,0,0.1)*12	
31			
32		Potential Savings (Loss)	=PV($B$28/12,C16,C17,C23)+$B$22
33			
34			
35			
36			
37			
38			
39			
40			
41			
42			
43			
44			
45			
46			
47			
48			
49			

Chapter Summary

1. Cashflow analysis can be put to good use in everyday financial decisions involving the flow of money from one party another. Common problems which yield to simple solutions include determining the true cost of a equipment (car) lease, whether to buy or rent (anything), and whether or not to refinance a property with a new loan.

2. In each case, the objective is wealth enhancement, either by accruing cash or reducing expense.

3. The use of a financial spreadsheet has been illustrated and recommended, especially for those financial problems involving many variables.

4. The ability to determine Annual Percentage Rates is an important skill in these everyday financial determinations since it is the best measure of true cost to the consumer when financial arrangements are extended over time.

Solving problems is the key to mastery of the mathematics of cashflow analysis. So here are some problems which you are invited to solve. Answers appear at the end of the chapter.

Chapter 10
Problems...
Problems...
Problems...

Consider all PMTs to be EOP unless specified otherwise.

Group I

1. What is the equivalent present value of a note which promises to pay you $1,000 in one year, if you could otherwise invest the cash at 12% p.a.(per annum)?

2. What would be the value of $2,000 deposited in a bank paying interest at the annual rate of 4.5% for two years if savings are compounded:
quarterly? _____
monthly? _____
daily (360 days/per year)? _____
continuously? _____

3. How long would it take for an investment of $5,000 to double if the investment earns a return of 10% p.a., compounded quarterly, and the returns are similarly invested?

4. You plan to buy a new car costing $16,000. What annual interest must your savings earn if you invest $5,000 initially and then $250 at the end of every month for three years? Assume earned interest to be credited to principal

monthly. How much would you be required to invest monthly if you desired to to buy the car at the end of the second year?

5. You decide to buy a new large-screen TV costing $2,000. Dealer A offers to sell the TV for $500 down and 36 monthly payments of $54.23. Dealer B offers exactly the same machine with $750 down and 36 monthly payments of $49.04 over the same time period. What interest rate is charged by each dealer?

6. How much cash must you deposit in an account bearing 8.5% interest p.a., compounded monthly, if you wish to withdraw end-of-the-month payments of $250 over the next 15 years?

7. Jones desires to establish a trust account which will provide $1,500 per month in living expenses for 10 years, to commence 5 years from today. The payment will be made at the beginning of the month. He anticipates no contributions to the trust once payments begin. What sum must Jones deposit at the end of each month over the next 5 years if the trust invests the funds at 7% interest p.a., compounded monthly?

8. Mary Dee seeks to add to her assets by purchasing shares in a mutual fund which sells for $52 per share, and which pays annual dividends of $3.50 per share. Disregarding share appreciation and a change in dividend policy, how many shares must she purchase at the beginning of each year if her goal is to accumulate $10,000 at the end of 5 years? Assume that all dividends are reinvested.

9. Joseph Grange purchased a farm for $275,000 with a down payment of $100,000. The seller agreed to carry back a note for the remainder of the price for 5 years with monthly payments of $1,500, including interest at the annual rate of 8%. What amount will farmer Grange need to finance at the end of 5 years?

10. What end-of-month investment would be required in order to accumulate $1 million at the end of 40 years if the cash could be invested at the rate of 10% p.a., compounded monthly?

11. What would be the future purchasing power in *today's dollars* of $10,000 invested at the end of each year for 20 years at 8% interest, if the inflation rate over that time averaged 5% per year?

12. What sum today (in constant dollars) is financially equivalent to investing $10,000 at the end of each year for 20 years if the investment earns 8% p.a. and inflation averages 5%?

13. If you desire to realize a 20% annual return on your investment, what price would you offer for a 3-year trust deed note in the amount of $25,000 if the note provided interest-only, monthly payments of $250.00 ?

Group II

1. What is the value today of a series of annual payments over three years which begins at $1000, payable at the end of the first year, and then increases 10% per year, if the opportunity cost of money is 15%?

2. You are scheduled to receive a guaranteed annuity of $2,000 per year for 5 years. The annuity will then increase to $3,000 for the next five years. How much could be borrowed from a banker who will lend 50% of the present value of the annuity and who discounts future cash receipts from this annuity at 12% per year?

3. What price would you pay for a lease which has a term of 15 years if the first 5 years of the lease requires rent of $3,000 per month in advance, and the remaining term requires rent at the rate of $3,750 per month in advance, if you require a 12% return on invested capital?

4. If you were able to acquire the lease described in #3 for $275,000, what would the Net Present Value of this investment be?

5. You have been asked to invest $20,000 in new venture which will not provide any returns for three years. Thereafter, the investment is expected to return $10,000 per year for 8 years? What is the Net Present Value of this investment if you require a 20% return on this type risk?

6. If the investment in problem #5 met forecasts, would would be your yield on this investment?

7. If the start of the returns in problem #5 were delayed one year, what would the Net Present Value of the 8 annual payments be? Would you make this investment? Why?

8. The owner of an office building has secured a tenant for 10,000 s.f. The tenant has agreed to lease the property for 5 years, but requires very specialized space improvements that will cost an extra $120,000. The tenant can pay for half the estimated $12 / s.f. cost but requests the owner to finance the balance and to add the amount to the agreed upon base monthly rent of $1.20/s.f. payable monthly, in advance over the term of the lease. The owner requires a 15% return on invested capital. What will be the total monthly rent if the owner agrees to this proposal?

9. A fast food restaurant presently nets $180,000 per year, representing a growth in annual earnings of 20% per year over the past 5 years. If this growth rate slowed to 15% per year over the next 5 years, what would be the present value of the business to a new owner who requires an 18% p.a. return on capital?

10. You have created a vacation fund by opening a savings account with $5,000 in a bank which compounds the interest rate of 5.5% on a monthly basis. At the end of each month, except the 12th month, you deposit an additional $75.00. At the beginning of the 12th month, you withdraw $2,000 for your annual vacation, which lasts one month. On your return you resume your EOM PMTs of $75. What will your account balance be at the start of your next annual vacation?

Group III

1. A block of stock purchased on January 1 of a certain year for $100,000, and held for exactly 5 years, increased in value 8% each year. During this time, the stock returned a 5% dividend rate on its value at the end of the year. If all proceeds were reinvested in the stock, what is the investor's yield on this investment if he liquidates the investment at the end of the 5th year.?

2. A small business owner acquired a business by discounting the anticipated income of $50,000 the first year at a 20% rate, $65,000 the second year by a 25% rate, and the third year's income of $85,000 by a 30% rate. If these incomes are realized at the end of each year, what will be his Internal Rate of Return on the price he paid? Disregard residual value.

3. An investor purchased a small residential investment property needing extensive rehabilitation. The property produced the following year-end net operating incomes over a five-year holding period: Year 1, (5,000); Year 2, $22,000; Year 3, $24,500; Year 4, $27,000; Year 5, $30,000. It was sold at the end of the 5th year and delivered $325,000 net after selling expenses. The owner paid $170,000 for the property, requires a return of 25% p.a., and has an opportunity cost of money equal to 10% per year. What is the Net Present Value of his investment? What was his yield on capital invested?

4. A utility stock purchased for $100 has produced consistent dividends of 6% of the original price each year for 7 years. To what value must the stock have appreciated for the owner to realize a 12% yield on invested capital if he chooses to sell at the end of the seventh year?

5. An investor with $20,000 cash is offered an attractive limited partner interest in a motion picture enterprise which will require $20,000 on signing. Each partner will also be responsible for additional payments of $5,000 the first year and $3,000 the second year. Thereafter, the investment is forecast to return $15,000 at the end of the third year, $18,000 at the end of the fourth year, and $25,000 at

the end of the last year. The general partner will accept a note in lieu of the first and second year's payment, which note will earn interest at the rate of 12% p.a., payable monthly. If the investor buys this interest, and makes the monthly payments, what will be his IRR if this investment meets forecast?

6. An automobile dealer is willing to lease a car which costs him $23,000 for $399 per month for 36 months. The wholesale value of the car is estimated to be $14,000 at the end of the lease. What will be his yield on investment in this lease?
If the lessee pays an additional $2,500 in drive-off fees, what will be the dealer's yield?
What would be the dealer's yield, including drive-off fees of $2,500, if he can sell the car at a $4,000 margin over wholesale value at the end of the lease?

7. A beginning property investor purchased a condominium for $115,000 utilizing an 85% loan. Over a holding period of 7 years, she realized the following annual amounts after taxes: $2,000, $2,400, $2,700, $3,000, $3,300, $3,450, $3,350. What must be her net sales proceeds at the end of the 7th year if she is to achieve a yield of 12% on her original investment?

Group IV

1. What amount will retire a level-payment mortgage of $200,000 over a 15-year term if the monthly payments include interest at the rate of 8-7/8% per year?

2. How much total interest will be paid on the loan in problem #1?

3. What will the monthly payment be for the loan described in #1 above if the amortization schedule were 25 years? 30 years? 40 years?

4. What is the total interest to be paid for each option cited in problem #3?

5. At the end of which payment, for the loan described in problem #1 above, will the remaining balance of the loan be reduced below one-half the original amount borrowed?

6. Jones has completed 5 years of fixed, monthly payments of $1,345.60 on a 30-year, fully amortizing loan in the original amount of $175,000. How much interest will he pay in the coming year?

7. A home buyer originated an Adjustable Rate Mortgage (ARM) in the amount of $125,000 at a beginning interest rate of 5.5%, payable monthly over a 30-year term. At the end of the first 6 months, the interest rate is expected to adjust to 7.75%. What payment will be required to retire the loan over the time remaining?

8. If the ARM described in problem #7 contains a clause barring any changes in monthly payment until the end of the first year of the mortgage, what payment will be required to retire the loan over the time then remaining? Assume a constant 7.75% interest rate.

9.The interest rate of an adjustable rate mortgage, payable monthly, is programmed to be equal to the 1-year Treasury bill plus 250 basis points. The maximum rate of interest, however is 5 points over the starting rate of 6% p.a. What is the maximum payment for which a borrower could be liable on a $200,000 loan which was scheduled to be amortized over 30 years?

10. During a period of high interest rates, a builder suffers from slow sales on a new mid-price-range project. As his marketing consultant, you recommend the use of a 5-3-1 *buydown* to stimulate sales. Current interest rates for a fully amortized, fixed-rate loan, payable monthly over a 30-year term, are 11%. The average model retails for $450,000, and requires a 20% down payment. The builder's lender requires a lump sum payment from the builder in an amount equal to the builder's total 36-payment obligation. What would be the effective selling price to the builder if he accepts your recommendation and agrees to the lender's terms? What percent of the selling price does the cost of the buydown represent to the builder?

11. A mobile-home park investor purchased a 300-space property in 1978 utilizing a 25-year fully amortizing mortgage of $3,000,000 payable at the rate of $21,203.38 per month. The promissory note he signed had no due-on-sale clause. Exactly 15 years later, he closed an agreement for the sale of the property for $5,750,000. The buyer will make a 15% down payment and the seller will carry the balance of the purchase price in the form of an amortizing AITD, scheduled over 30 years, payable monthly, bearing interest at the rate of 10.5% annually. The AITD is all due and payable in 10 years.
What will be the seller's yield on his note?
What will be the balance of the AITD at the end of 10 years?
What will be the balance of the original loan at the end of the same ten years?

12. A self-storage property collects $225,000 after allowances for vacancy and bad debts. Its operating expenses are $62,000 per year. A lender for this type property requires a Debt Coverage Ratio of 1.4. What is the maximum loan which this lender will furnish if the current interest rate for a fixed-rate, 20-year mortgage, payable monthly, is 10.5%?
How much greater a mortgage would be available from a lender who requires a 1.3 DCR but charges the same interest rate for a loan amortized over 25 years?

13. If a mortgage in the amount of $125,000 requires a monthly payment of $1,096.95, what is its *annual* loan constant per $100 of loan?

14. A new home buyer is presented with two alternate loan offerings. The first loan, in the amount of $130,000 is offered at a fixed-interest rate of 8.875% per year, payable monthly over 30 years. Loan fees are 2 points plus estimated loan costs of an additional $1,750.

    The second offering, in the same amount, proposes a fixed-rate, 25-year amortizing loan bearing interest at the rate of 9.375%, no points and no other fees.

    Which loan is less expensive if the borrower intends to move in **ten** years?

    Which loan is less expensive if the borrower intends to move in **five** years?

    Which loan is less expensive if the borrower intends to move in **three** years?

15. A homeowner who originated a loan in the amount of $145,000, payable monthly over 29 years, including interest at the rate of 7.5% p.a., obtains the lender's agreement to recast the loan payments over the remaining schedule if the borrower reduces the loan balance by any one payment by at least $2,000. At the end of the second year of the loan, the borrower pays the remaining principal down by $3,000. What will his new payments be?

Group V

1. Calculate the overall capitalization rate of a property which collects $42,000 per month before expenses of $11,250 per month, and which recently sold for $4,100,000.

2. What would be the expected selling price for a property earning $126,000 net per year before taxes if comparable properties command a capitalization rate of 8.5%?

3. An office building recently sold for $3,750,000. Its next-door twin nets $350,000 before debt service. What is a likely capitalization rate for the property recently sold?

4. An investor is interested in acquiring a retail center. The negotiated sales price is expected not to exceed $6,000,000. A lender requiring a 10.5% interest rate loan will make a 65% loan on the property, amortized over 20 years. The seller has agreed to carry back 10% of the purchase price in an interest-only note 1 point higher than the interest rate on the first trust deed loan. What must the property earn in the first year of operation in order to return 14% cash-on-cash (pre-tax) to the buyer? What must be its minimum capitalization rate?

5. An investor purchases a small strip-retail center for $650,000 with a down payment of 25%. The loan provides for monthly payments on a 25-year, fully amortizing schedule of payments, including interest at the rate of 9.75% p.a. If

the center performs at a 10% capitalization rate in the first year of ownership, what will be the first year pre-tax Cash-on-Cash return to the owner?

6. A commercial loan of $2,000,000 with a ten-year due date was obtained at a cost of 1.5 points. What is the amount of the annual deduction from income attributable to the amortization of the points?

7. Given the mid-month convention used in calculating the depreciation allowance for non-residential property, what would be the first year's total depreciation deduction for the retail center in problem #5 if the value of the improvements is 75% of the acquisition cost?

8. If the owner of the property in problem #5 pays taxes at the marginal rate of 36%, what would be the after-tax value of the both his depreciation deduction and interest payments at the end of the first year of ownership?
What, then, will be his first-year After-tax Cash-on Cash return?

9. A 6-unit residential income property was acquired for $450,000, all cash, plus closing costs of $4,500. The property was held for exactly 6 years when it was sold for $454,500 after deductions for all costs of sale. No capital improvements were made during the holding period and no part of the property was sold. What is the amount of the indicated gain if the improvements are 80% of total property value?

10. An industrial building was purchased for $1,750,000 utilizing a 75% loan-to-value, 20-year loan which cost 2 points. If the property were held for 5 years, what amount would be added at the time of sale to the Adjusted Basis to reflect un-amortized loan points?

Group VI

1. Your best client has approached you with a difficult problem. She anticipates that her daughter will matriculate at Stanford 15 years from today. Current annual expenses at Stanford are $26,500 and are forecasted to increase at an annual rate of 7.0% per year.
If your client can invest her monthly savings at a guaranteed net annual rate of 9%, compounded monthly, what beginning-of-the-month amount must she set aside, starting today, to finance her daughter's education if inflation is expected to average 3.5% per year? (No contributions to the plan once school has started.)

2. The owner of a property subject to a groundlease has come to you for advice. The lease on his property has only three more years to run, but he has an excellent investment opportunity which requires $400,000 in up-front capital. His leasehold tenant is scheduled to pay $12,500 per month, in advance, for the

remaining three years of the groundlease. What yield could be achieved by an investor willing to advance the required $400,000 with a personal guarantee of the rents?

What would be the return to the investor if your client were willing to accept $350,000 for the remaining lease payments?

3. A Treasury bond carrying a coupon of 4.6% and maturing Aug. 15, 2006 is presently quoted at 89:18 (Ask). What would be the Yield-to-Maturity if the purchaser paid the Ask price on Dec. 10, 1997?

4. A corporate bond carries a coupon of 6.5% and provides for a call date of Jan. 2, 2000 at 105. The current rate for comparable issues is 7.2%. The bond matures on April 20, 2010. What is the most likely Ask price for this bond if purchased on Feb. 1, 1998?

5. A stock analyst projects that shares of USX (US Steel) will earn $4.40 in the coming year and that the price will rise to $35.20. USX pays out 25% in dividends and currently sells sells for $32.00. What is the expected market capitalization for this stock?

Answers to Problems

Group I

1. This problem asks for the PV of the future amount:

n	i	PV	PMT	FV
1	12	?	0	1,000

Ans. -$892.86 (Note the sign convention at work)

2. These four problems require you to correlate the times of n and i:

n	i	PV	PMT	FV
8	4.5÷4	-2,000	0	?
24	4.5÷12	-2,000	0	?
720	4.5÷360	-2,000	0	?

Ans.   2,187.25

2,187.98

2,188.34

2,188.35 $FV = PV(e)^{.045*2}$

3. The point will be reached when the FV = $10,000

n	i	PV	PMT	FV
?	10÷4	-5,000	0	10,000

Ans. = 29 quarters = 87 months . Resolve for FV. What does this tell you?

4. This problem emphasizes the importance of a single vantage point, The $250 monthly payment is also a negative cashflow for the saver.

n	i	PV	PMT	FV
36	?	-5,000	-250	16,000

Ans. 0.546 per month, or 6.56% per year.
Ans. $402.87

5. Take the viewpoint of the dealer. Then construct your T-Bar.
   Ans. Dealer A earns 18% per year; Dealer B earns 24% per year.

6. This problem depicts an initial negative cashflow of an unknown amount and a later positive cashflow of $250. The FV at the end of 15 years will be zero.

n	i	PV	PMT	FV
180	8.5÷12	?	250	0

   Ans. $25,387.42 (Presented as a negative)

7. First, determine how much the trust must have on hand when it begins its 10 year payout. Set calculator to BEGIN (1,6). Then determine how much Jones must deposit each year to reach this figure with end-of-the-month payments.

n	i	PV	PMT	FV
120	7÷12	?	-1,500	0

The trust must have accumulated $129,943.13.
 In order to accumulate this FV amount requires monthly PMTs (set calculator to END) over 5 years of:

n	i	PV	PMT	FV
60	7÷12	0	?	129,943.13

   Ans. $1,815.03

8. If Mary invests $52 and has $55.5 0 at the end of one year, her investment is growing at a rate $=\frac{\$3.50}{\$52}= 6.73077\%$. Set calculator to BEG.

n	i	PV	PMT	FV
5	6.73	0	?	10,000

Ans. $1,638.02/year ÷ $52/ share = 31.50 shares per year.

To verify this, invest the single sum of $1,638.02 at 6.73077% for 5 years, then for 4 years, then for 3 years etc.etc... Then add all the future values together.

9. This is a problem in determining the remaining balance of a note.

$\boxed{n}$	$\boxed{i}$	$\boxed{PV}$	$\boxed{PMT}$	$\boxed{FV}$
60	8÷12	-175,000	1,500	?

Ans. $150,507.71

10. This is a simple PMT problem

$\boxed{n}$	$\boxed{i}$	$\boxed{PV}$	$\boxed{PMT}$	$\boxed{FV}$
480	10÷12	0	?	1,000,000

Ans. $158.13

11. Since you are seeking a **FV**, the Inflation-Adjusted Rate can be used:

$$\text{Effective Rate} = \frac{1.08}{1.05} - 1 = .028571 = 2.8571\%$$

$\boxed{n}$	$\boxed{i}$	$\boxed{PV}$	$\boxed{PMT}$	$\boxed{FV}$
20	2.8571	0	-10000	?

Ans. $264,833 (in constant dollars)

12. Since you are seeking a **Present Value** *with PMTs made at the EOP*, the inflation-adjusted rate is not appropriate. Use formula #8 from Appendix. See matrix on page 33.

$$PV = \frac{\$10000}{.08-.05} * \left(1 - \left(\frac{1.05}{1.08}\right)^{20}\right)$$

$$PV = \frac{\$10000 * 0.43074}{0.03}$$

$$PV = \$143,579.91$$

13. If the note provides for interest-only PMTs, the FV will be equal to $25,000.

n	i	PV	PMT		FV
36	20÷12	?	250		25,000

Ans. $20,515.32

Group II

1. Ans. $2,496.92 (Uses Formula #6 in Appendix, q.v.)

2. Use the banker's 12% discount rate to calculate the PV of this uneven cashflow series. The loan value will be half this amount.
Ans. $6,672.95

3. This is a problem in uneven cashflows with PMTs in advance. The BEG/END buttons have no effect. Store the first PMT in CFo as a positive number. Then solve as though the remaining PMTs occur at the end of the periods. Remember that Njs cannot exceed 99 per storage cell.
Ans. $281,527.36

4. This complicates the solution to #3 because you have already stored $3,000 in CFo. But if you pay $275,000 out and receive $3,000 back at the beginning of the lease, your net initial investment is -$272,000. Store this in memory cell 0 and resolve.
Ans. NPV = $6,527.36

5. This problem emphasizes the necessity of inserting zeros in a cashflow series to maintain the time relationship of all the cashflows. The first cash entry, CFj, will be 0, occurring 3 times (Nj). Then enter the remaining cashflows.
Ans. $2,205.79

6. Without disturbing any entries, simply solve for the IRR.
Ans. 21.94%

7. Correct the Njs for the first cashflow from 3 times to 4 times.
Ans. -$1,495.18. No, because it furnishes a negative Net Present Value.

8. The owner is being asked to amortize (finance) $60,000 in improvements over 60 months at a 15% interest rate. **Set = BEG Lease PMTs are in advance**

n	i	PV	PMT	FV
60	15÷12	-60,000	?	0

Ans. $1,409.77 per month over 10,000 s.f. = $0.14098 added to $1.20 = $1.341/s.f. per month.

9. Use the formula for the PV of a finite cashflow growing at a constant rate. When is first PMT made? How much will it be? How many years will be left?
Ans. $833,638.93

10. This is a problem involving uneven cashflows made on an uneven schedule. Solve the problem in three steps since there is no way for a calculator to carry uneven cashflows forward in time to express a Future Value. First, calculate the remaining balance of the account after the withdrawal of $2,000. Then carry this balance forward in time one month. Then invest that sum as a -PV together with 11 subsequent monthly PMTs of -$75. Solve for FV.

n	i	PV	PMT	FV
11	5.5÷12	-5,000	-75	?

Balance will be $6,102.11 before withdrawal of $2,000. New balance will be $4,102.11 to be invested for one month at 5.5% p.a. Note no PMTs this month.

n	i	PV	PMT	FV
1	5.5÷12	-4,102.11	0	?

FV will be $4,120.91   Then,

n	i	PV	PMT	FV
11	5.5÷12	-4,120.91	-75.00	?

Ans. $5,177.67

Group III

1. This is a problem asking for the IRR of the investment. Since the percent increase each year is the same (1.08 * 1.05) the yield is equal to the annual percent increase. (There are more difficult ways to get the same answer.)

   Ans. 13.4%

2. This problem contrasts variable discount rates which can be applied to a cashflow with thc IRR, which is a single discount rate.
   Ans. IRR = 26.59% (only if the business has no residual value at the end of the 3rd year)

3. This is a problem in the use of the Modified Internal Rate of Return because of the negative cash flow at the EOY 1. How much more does the investor need to invest, in addition to $170,000, to have the $5,000 available to cover the negative?
   Ans. NPV = –$20,535.85.
        MIRR = 21.6%

4. This problem, involving even PMTs, asks for the Future Value of the investment.

n	i	PV	PMT	FV
7	12	-100	6	?

   Ans. $160.53

5. In this case the limited partner would sign a note in the face amount of $8,000, payable $376.59 per month for 24 months, which PMTs will zero out the $5,000 and $3,000 future obligations. The limited partner therefore have a monthly negative cashflow of $376.59 for 24 months. Thereafter he would have 11 monthly periods of no income, one month of $15,000, 11 more months of no income, one month of $18,000, 11 months of no income and one final cashflow of $25,000.
   Ans. 18.27%

6. Since lease PMTs are paid in advance, the dealer makes an investment of –$23,000 but receives the first PMT, $399, at inception of the lease. Following this, the lessor will receive 35 additional PMTs of $399 and the return of the auto, worth $14,000 at the end of the 36th month. This is an uneven cashflow.
   Ans. 0.81% per month, or 9.7% p.a.
   Ans. 1.27% per month, or 15.25% p.a.
   Ans. 1.73% per month, or 20.8% p.a.

7. The investor used $17,250 of her own funds. Calculate the NPV of this cashflow over 7 years, discounted at 12% per year. The result, -$4,586.90 is the NPV. Since this negative PV must be covered by the PV of the reversion amount, the task is to solve for the FV of this PV when invested at 12%.
Ans. $10,140.18
Using your answer, calculate the IRR of the investment.
Why did you obtain 12% ?

Group IV

Questions 1 through 4 deal with an even-payment amortized loan.

1. | n | i | PV | PMT | FV |
    |---|---|----|-----|-----|
    | 180 | 8.875÷12 | -200,000 | ? | 0 |

Ans. $2,013.69

2. The total interest is the total amount of PMTs over the life of the loan *less* the original loan amount.

   Ans. = 180 x 2,013.69 - 200,000 = $162,463.87

3. Ans. $1,661.31
   Ans. $1,591.29
   Ans. $1,523.50

4. Ans. $298,391.92
   Ans. $372,864.32
   Ans. $531,282.02

5. This point will occur when the FV (Remaining Bal.) of the loan ≤ $100,000.

n	i	PV	PMT	FV
?	8.875÷12	-200,000	2,013.69	100,000

   Ans. Before the 118th payment and after the 117th payment. (Resolve for FV)

	n	i	PV	PMT	FV
	118	8.875÷12	-200,000	2,013.69	?

6. You need first to calculate the interest on the loan. Since you know the PMT, this is easy. Then amortize the loan 60 PMTs, and then 12 PMTs to find the answer.
Ans. $14,126.69

7. This is a common ARM problem. First, find the remaining balance at the end of the 6th month. Then amortize this balance over the time remaining at the higher interest rate.
Ans. $893.41

8. First, determine the initial monthly payment and then the balance of the loan at the end of the first 6 months. Then, <u>without changing the payment,</u> change the interest to reflect a 7.75% rate payable monthly, and determine the remaining balance at the end of the next 6 months. Then amortize this balance over the time *remaining* in the original schedule.
Ans. $901.51 per month.

9. Simply determine the highest payment due if the interest rate = (6+5%) = 11%.
Ans. $1,904.65

10. Calculate what monthly PMT the bank must receive at 11% interest rate. Calculate what the buyer must pay as though the interest rate were 5% less in the first year, 3% less in the second year and 1% less in the third year. The differences, per month, per year, are the amounts the builder must pay, which is $27,910.
Ans. $422,089
Ans. 6.2%

11. This is a problem in calculating the yield (IRR) on an AITD (q.v)
Ans. 11.67%
Ans. $4,478,043.24
Ans. $0.00

12. Determine the NOI and calculate the annual amount available for debt service, using the DCRs of 1.4 and 1.3 Then determine how large a loan these amounts will support, on a monthly basis, given the interest rate and amortization schedule.
Ans. 1.4 = $971,813
Ans. 1.3 =$1,106,643. Therefore, $134,830 larger.

13. The annual loan constant for a loan paid monthly is the ratio of one year's total monthly payments to the loan amount. Multiply by 100.
    Ans. $10.5307/$100 of loan

14. This is a problem in calculating the APR of a loan. Deduct loan points and charges from PV. Determine the remaining balance at 10, 5 and 3 years. Using these balances, change **n** to 120, 60 and 36 periods and recalculate **i.**
    Ans. The APR for the loan requiring points and fees is as follows:
    Move in 36 months, APR = 10.1875%
    $\qquad$ 60 $\quad$ " $\qquad$ APR = 9.738%
    $\qquad$ 120 $\quad$ " $\qquad$ APR = 9.413%

    The APR for a loan requiring no points and no fees is always equal to the interest rate, 9.375% in this case, which is superior in all instances.

15. Calculate the balance of the loan after 24 PMTs; deduct $3000 and amortize the balance (as a new loan) over the remaining 27 years.
    Ans. $1,001.67

Group V

1. Calculate the *annual* NOI and divide by the sales price.
   Ans. 9.0%.

2. NOI÷ Capitalization rate = Fair Market Value
   Ans. $1,482,353

3. Net Operating Income ÷ Fair Market Value = Capitalization Rate
   Ans. 9.33%

4. This is a problem in constructing a cap rate using the Band of Investment technique.
   Ans. 12.44%

5. Calculate the NOI. Then calculate the annual debt service. The difference is the spendable income. Compare this (divide by) to the buyer's cash down payment.
   Ans. 7.9%

6. The loan points ($2,000,000 * 1.5%) must be amortized over 10 years.
   Ans. $3,000

7. Ans. $11,979.17 (11.5/12 of ($650,000*75%)) (See Mid-month convention)

8. Ans.

NOI	$65,000	
Interest	-47,320	
Depreciation	-11,979	
Total Taxable	5,701	
Tax	2,052	(Now compute the after-tax income)

Ans. 6.7%

9. The gain would be equal to the depreciation amounts taken, since they reduce Adjusted Basis. The Depreciable Basis is written off over a 27.5 year schedule, but there is a loss of one-half month's depreciation at the beginning and end of the holding period. Therefore only 71 months of depreciation would be taken in 6 years.
Ans. $78,229.09

10. The amount of the un-amortized loan points would be the cost of the loan points ($26,250) less the amount amortized over the holding period – $6,562.50
Ans. $19,687.50

Group VI

1. The best way to handle this kind of problem is to convert all interest and investment rates to inflation-adjusted rates which can be used with constant dollars. First, calculate the effective *monthly* rate at which the tuition will accumulate in constant dollars.

Effective tuition rate $= \dfrac{12+.07}{12+.035} - 1 = 0.29082\%$ per month.

Her investment will accumulate at an effective rate of:

Effective investment rate $= \dfrac{12+.09}{12+.035} - 1 = 0.4570\%$ per month.

Measured in constant dollars, the tuition will for each of the years will be:

$\boxed{n}$	$\boxed{i}$	$\boxed{PV}$	$\boxed{PMT}$	$\boxed{FV}$
:	.29082	-26500	0	?
:				
180			Year 1	44,695
192			Year 2	46,280
204			Year 3	47,921
216			Year 4	49,620

These lump sums must be available at the beginning of each school year. In the interim, funds on deposit will continue to earn interest during the school year at the effective investment rate (in constant dollars).

Therefore, you should discount this uneven cashflow as <u>monthly</u> PMTs to be received at the BOP. The discount rate is the effective investment monthly rate of .4570%

The PV of this cashflow series is $172,626.25, which is also the amount of cash needed to be on hand at the end of the 180th month.

Since this problem seeks the monthly **PMT** (BOP) which will result in a FV of $172,626.25 (in constant dollars), the problem is easily solved:

Set calculator to BOP

n	i	PV	PMT	FV
180	.4570	0	?	172,626.25

Ans. $617.31 per month.

2. The Present Value of the remaining PMTs under the ground lease is an even cashflow situation, with PMTs occuring BOP.
   Ans. 8.28%
   Ans. 18.2%

3. Convert (89+18 ticks) to (89+ percent of 1$).
   Ans. 6.17%

4. Ans. 94.36. Bond will not be called since coupon rate is less than market rate.

5. $1 + r = \dfrac{1.10 + 35.20}{32} = \dfrac{36.30}{32} = 1.134$

   Ans. r = 13.4%

Appendix

Derivations of Cashflow Formulas

(1) Simple Interest

In simple-interest situations, the capital invested earns interest at a constant rate (not compounded). Therefore:

$$FV = PV + n*i*PV, \text{ where n is the number of periods and i the rate.}$$
$$FV = PV(1+ (n*i))$$

(2) Compound Interest

But when interest is compounded, the interest earned per period is added to the principle and the total then earns interest at the stated rate. At the end of the first period

$$FV = PV + PV*i = PV(1+i)$$

At the end of the next period, this total, PV(1+i) earns interest at rate i:

$$FV_2 = PV(1+i)(1+i) = PV(1+i)^2$$

Therefore $\quad\quad FV = PV(1+i)^n \quad\quad$ (basic formula for compounded interest)

And, $\quad\quad PV = \dfrac{FV}{(1+i)^n}$

(3) PV of an infinite series of equal cashflows, payment at end of period.
This formula can be used to determine the amount necessary to fund a perpetual annuity whose payments begin one period following the date of funding. It is also the derivation of the capitalization method used to establish stock values using dividends, and real estate values using net operating income.

$$PV = \frac{C}{(1+i)} + \frac{C}{(1+i)^2} + \frac{C}{(1+i)^3} + \frac{C}{(1+i)^4} \quad \dots\dots\dots\dots\dots\dots\dots\dots\dots\infty$$

Let $a = \dfrac{C}{(1+i)}$ and $x = \dfrac{1}{(1+i)}$ Then,

$$PV = a + ax + a x^2 + ax^3 + ax^4 \ldots \ldots \infty$$

Multiplying both sides by x,

$$PVx = ax + ax^2 + ax^3 + a_x4 \ldots \ldots \infty$$

Subtracting last equation from first,

$$PV - PVx = a$$

$$PV(1-x) = a$$

$$PV = \frac{a}{(1-x)} = \frac{C}{(1+i)} \div 1 - \frac{1}{(1+i)} = \frac{C}{(1+i)} \div \frac{1+i-1}{(1+i)}$$

$$PV = \frac{C}{i}$$

(4) PV of an infinite series of equal cashflows, payment at beginning of period.
It is easy to see that the PV of an infinite series with the first payment made in advance is the same as the PV of an infinite series with payments at the end of the period, plus C.

Therefore, $PV = \dfrac{C}{i} + C$

(5) PV of a finite series of equal cashflows, n long, payment at end of period.

$$PV = \frac{C}{(1+i)^1} + \frac{C}{(1+i)^2} + \frac{C}{(1+i)^3} \ldots \frac{C}{(1+i)^n}$$

Let $a = \dfrac{C}{(1+i)}$ and $x = \dfrac{1}{(1+i)}$

Then

$$PV = a + ax + a x^2 + ax^3 + \ldots ax^{n-1}$$

Multiplying both sides by x,

$$PV_x = ax + a\,x^2 + ax^3 + \cdots\cdots ax^n$$

Subtracting the second equation from the first,

$$PV - PV_x = a - ax^n$$

$$PV(1-x) = a(1-x^n)$$

$$PV = \frac{a(1-x^n)}{(1-x)} = \frac{C}{(1+i)} * \left(1 - \frac{1^n}{(1+i)^n}\right) \div (1-x)$$

$$PV = \frac{C}{i} - \frac{C}{i(1+i)^n}$$

$$PV = \frac{C}{i}\left(1 - \frac{1}{(1+i)^n}\right)$$

(6) PV of a finite series of equal cashflows, n long, payment at beginning of period. Note that the series is foreshortened by one period, and that the first period is not discounted, but rather added at full value to the discounted total of those remaining.

$$PV = C + \frac{C}{(1+i)} + \frac{C}{(1+i)^2} + \frac{C}{(1+i)^3} \cdots \frac{C}{(1+i)^{n-1}}$$

Let $a = C$ and $x = \frac{1}{(1+i)}$ Then,

$$PV = a + ax + a\,x^2 + ax^3 + \cdots\cdots ax^{n-1}$$

Multiplying both sides by x,

$$PV_x = ax + ax^2 + ax^3 + \cdots\cdots ax^n$$

Subtracting the second equation from the first,

$$PV - PV_x = a - ax^n$$

$$PV(1-x) = a(1-x^n)$$

$$PV = \frac{a(1-x^n)}{(1-x)} = C * \left(1 - \frac{1^n}{(1+i)^n}\right) \div (1-x)$$

$$PV = \frac{C(1+i)}{i}\left(1 - \frac{1^n}{(1+i)^n}\right)$$

(7) Present Value of an infinite series growing at constant rate g, payments at end of period. First payment is not adjusted for growth.

$$PV = \frac{C}{(1+i)^1} + \frac{C(1+g)^1}{(1+i)^2} + \frac{C(1+g)^2}{(1+i)^3} + \frac{C(1+g)^3}{(1+i)^4} + \frac{C(1+g)^4}{(1+i)^5}$$
$$\dots\dots\dots\dots\dots\dots\infty$$

Let $a = \frac{C}{(1+i)}$ and $x = \frac{(1+g)}{(1+i)}$ Then,

$$PV = a + ax + a\,x^2 + ax^2 + ax^4 \dots\dots\infty$$

Multiplying both sides by x,

$$PVx = ax + ax^2 + ax^2 + a_x4\dots\dots\infty$$

Subtracting last equation from first,

$$PV - PVx = a$$

$$PV(1-x) = a$$

$$PV = \frac{a}{(1-x)} = \frac{C}{(1+i)} \div 1 - \frac{(1+g)}{(1+i)} = \frac{C}{(1+i)} \div \frac{1+i-1-g}{(1+i)} = \frac{C}{(1+i)} \div \frac{(i-g)}{(1+i)}$$

$$PV = \frac{C}{i-g}$$

(8) PV of a finite series growing at constant rate g, first payment at end of period. This involves a growth rate, g, and a discount rate, i, in a series n long. First payment is <u>not</u> adjusted for inflation.

$$PV = \frac{C}{(1+i)^1} + \frac{C(1+g)^1}{(1+i)^2} + \frac{C(1+g)^2}{(1+i)^3} + \frac{C(1+g)^3}{(1+i)^4} + \frac{C(1+g)^4}{(1+i)^5} \dots + \frac{C(1+g)^{n-1}}{(1+i)^n}$$

Let $a = \frac{C}{(1+i)}$ and $x = \frac{(1+g)}{(1+i)}$ Then,

$$PV = a + ax + ax^2 + ax^3 + ax^4 + ax^5 \dots ax^{n-1}$$

Multiplying both sides by x

$$PVx = ax + ax^2 + ax^3 + ax^4 + ax^5 \ldots ax^n$$

Subtracting the second equation from the first,

$$PV - PVx = a - ax^n$$

$$PV = \frac{a*(1-x^n)}{(1-x)} = \frac{C}{(1+i)}\left(1 - \frac{(1+g)^n}{(1+i)^n}\right) * \frac{(1+i)}{(i-g)}$$

$$PV = \frac{C}{(i-g)}\left(1 - \frac{(1+g)^n}{(1+i)^n}\right)$$

(9) PV of a finite series growing at constant rate g, first payment at end of period. This involves a growth rate, g, and a discount rate, i, in a series n long. First payment <u>is</u> adjusted for inflation.

$$PV = \frac{C(1+g)^1}{(1+i)^1} + \frac{C(1+g)^2}{(1+i)^2} + \frac{C(1+g)^3}{(1+i)^3} + \frac{C(1+g)^4}{(1+i)^4} + \frac{C(1+g)^5}{(1+i)^5} \ldots + \frac{C(1+g)^n}{(1+i)^n}$$

Let $a = \dfrac{C(1+g)}{(1+i)}$ and $x = \dfrac{(1+g)}{(1+i)}$ Then,

$$PV = a + ax + ax^2 + ax^3 + ax^4 + ax^5 \ldots ax^n$$

Multiplying both sides by x

$$PVx = ax + ax^2 + ax^3 + ax^4 + ax^5 \ldots ax^{n+1}$$

Subtracting the second equation from the first,

$$PV - PVx = a - ax^{n+1} = ax(1 - x^n)$$

$$PV = \frac{ax*(1-x^n)}{(1-x)} = \frac{C(1+g)}{(1+i)}\left(1 - \frac{(1+g)^n}{(1+i)^n}\right) * \frac{(1+i)}{(i-g)}$$

$$PV = \frac{C(1+g)}{(i-g)}\left(1 - \frac{(1+g)^n}{(1+i)^n}\right)$$

(10) PV of a finite series growing at constant rate g, first payment at beginning of period. This involves a growth rate, g, and a discount rate, i, in a series n long. First payment is not adjusted for inflation.

$$PV = C + \frac{C(1+g)^1}{(1+i)^1} + \frac{C(1+g)^2}{(1+i)^2} + \frac{C(1+g)^3}{(1+i)^3} + \frac{C(1+g)^4}{(1+i)^4} + \frac{C(1+g)^5}{(1+i)^5} \cdots + \frac{C(1+g)^{n-1}}{(1+i)^{n-1}}$$

Let $a = C$ and $x = \frac{(1+g)}{(1+i)}$ Then,

$$PV = a + ax + ax^2 + ax^3 + ax^4 + ax^5 \ldots ax^{n-1}$$

Multiplying both sides by x

$$PVx = ax + ax^2 + ax^3 + ax^4 + ax^5 \ldots ax^n$$

Subtracting the second equation from the first,

$$PV - PVx = a - ax^n = a(1 - x^n)$$

$$PV = \frac{a*(1-x^n)}{(1-x)} = C\left(1 - \frac{(1+g)^n}{(1+i)^n}\right) * \frac{(1+i)}{(i-g)}$$

$$PV = \frac{C(1+i)}{(i-g)}\left(1 - \frac{(1+g)^n}{(1+i)^n}\right)$$

(11) Future Value of an even cashflow bearing interest for a finite number of periods.

$\boxed{\text{When the PMT is received at the end of the period:}}$

$$FV = C + C(1+i)^1 + C(1+i)^2 + C(1+i)^3 + C(1+i)^4 \cdots + C(1+i)^{n-1}$$

Let $a = C$ and $x = (1+i)$, then:

$$FV = a + ax + ax^2 + ax^3 + ax^4 + \ldots ax^{n-1}$$

Multiplying both sides by x,

$$FV = ax + ax^2 + ax^3 + ax^4 + \ldots ax^n$$

Subtracting equation two from one,

$$FV - FVx = a - ax^n$$

$$FV = \frac{a(1-x^n)}{-i} = C\frac{(1-(1+i)^n)}{-i}$$

$\boxed{\text{When the PMT is received at the beginning of the period:}}$

$$FV = C(1+i)^1 + C(1+i)^2 + C(1+i)^3 + C(1+i)^4 \cdots + C(1+i)^n$$

Let $a = C$ and $x = (1+i)$, then:

$$FV = ax + ax^2 + ax^3 + ax^4 + ...ax^n$$

Multiplying both sides by x,

$$FV = ax^2 + ax^3 + ax^4 + ...ax^{n+1}$$

Subtracting equation two from one,

$$FV - FVx = ax - ax^{n+1} = ax(1-x^n)$$

$$FV = \frac{ax(1-x^n)}{(1-x)} = C\frac{(1+i)(1-(1+i)n)}{1-(1+i)}$$

$$FV = C\frac{(1+i)(1-(1+i)^n)}{-i}$$

(12) Constant Payment Required to Retire Loan (PV) at i rate of interest, over n periods.

$$PV = \frac{C}{i}\left(1 - \frac{1}{(1+i)^n}\right) \quad \text{(the PV of a cashflow bearing i interest for a finite period, n)}$$

Then

$$C = PV*i \div \left(1 - \frac{1}{(1+i)^n}\right)$$

$$C = PV * i * \frac{(1+i)^n}{(1+i)^n - 1}$$

C = payment required per period

INDEX